M000216901

BENJAMIN FRANKLIN'S FAMILY

BENJAMIN FRANKLIN'S FAMILY

Volume One
English Ancestors

Michael J. Leclerc, CG

www.franklinsfam.com

Copyright © 2019 by Michael J. Leclerc

All rights reserved. Published in the United States.

Michael J. Leclerc, CG

All rights reserved. No part of this publication may be reproduced or transmitted in any form or by any means without the express written permission from the copyright holder, except for brief quotations for reviews.

ISBN 978-0-578-60522-7

Front cover:
St. Mary Magdelene Church, Ecton, Northamptonshire, taken by the author.

Back cover:
Portrait of Benjamin Franklin, painted 1767 by David Martin (1737–1797). White House Accession Number 1962.187.1.

The words Certified Genealogist and its acronym, CG, are registered certification marks, and the designations Certified Genealogical Lecturer and its acronym, CGL, are service marks of the Board for Certification of Genealogists, used under license by board certificants after periodic evaluation, and the board name is registered in the U.S. Patent & Trademark Office.

DEDICATION

To Patrica Law Hatcher,
my mentor and very dear friend
with whom I've shared so many adventures.

You have taken more Care to preserve the Memory of our Family, than any other Person that ever belonged to it, tho' the Youngest Son of five Generations. And tho' I believe it never made any great Figure in this County, Yet it did what was much better, it acted that Part well in which Providence had placed it, and for 200 Years all the Descendants of it have lived with Credit, and are to this Day without any Blot in their Escutcheon, which is more than some of the best Families i: e. the Richest and highest in Title can pretend to. I am the last of my Fathers House remaining in this Country, and you must be sensible from my Age and Infirmities, that I cannot hope to continue long in the Land of the Living. However I must degenerate from my Family not to wish it well; and therefore you cannot think but that I was well pleased to see so fair Hopes of its Continuance in the Younger Branches, in any Part of the World

~ Mary (Franklin) Fisher to Benjamin Franklin
14 August 1748

TABLE OF CONTENTS

PREFACE

This volume represents the culmination of decades of research on one of the most interesting and influential families in American history. It seems like only yesterday that I was working on my friend Ruth's ancestry and discovered that she is a descendant of Samuel Franklin, Benjamin Franklin's eldest half-brother. My original intent was only to discover who her ancestors were. But determining what happened to Samuel's wife Elizabeth (Tyng) Franklin led to investigating everyone named Franklin in Boston in the 17th century.

This search quickly led to the discovery of how little is in print about the family. Benjamin Franklin was himself an amateur genealogist and collected information on his family. He wrote some stories about the family in his autobiography, relying a great deal on information from other family members. Some of this information adds a great deal to the family stories.

After Benjamin's autobiography, the first genealogical compilation of any sort was published by his great-grandson, William Bache, in the *New England Historical and Genealogical Register* in 1857. It had little detail and no documentation. It included information not only from Benjamin Franklin the Elder's account, but other stories his great-grandfather Benjamin collected.

Although the foundation is strong, there are errors in the previously published information on the family, starting with Benjamin Franklin's autobiography and continuing with other published material. Franklin said that he learned from his uncle's notes that the Franklin family had been at Ecton for three hundred years.[1] He is likely referring to his Uncle Benjamin's "Short account of the family of Thomas Franklin of Ecton, Northamptonshire" (see Appendix B). Extensive examination of parish registers, wills, and other documents helps clarify problems with the information in this manuscript, as well as other published versions of the family.

---

[1] Carl Van Doren, ed., *Benjamin Franklin's Autobiographical Writings* (New York: Viking Press, 1945) 217 (hereafter Van Doren, *Autobiographical Writings*).

Ecton parish registers contradict the belief that the Franklins had been there for hundreds of years. The registers start in 1559, and are remarkably complete during the Commonwealth period, which is rare. While not limited to Ecton, the family has solid, centuries-long ties to Northamptonshire. It has links to more than two dozen parishes in the county, as well as more than another half dozen in four other counties.

Access to Northamptonshire parish records has been very limited. Only about a third of the parishes were abstracted by the Genealogical Society of Utah into the International Genealogical Index. Wills and admons have been available on microfilm, and sometimes required researching onsite at repositories in England.

The records of a few parishes were published, but not the ones most critical to this family. Commercial groups like Ancestry, FamilySearch, and Find My Past are working to create modern indexes and make images of the originals available online. There is still much work to be done, but when completed they will hopefully help to solve some of the unknown mysteries we still have on the family.

There are many families in England that bear the Franklin surname (and spelling variations thereof). In medieval times, the name was usually used for "the son or descendant of a vilein, who had become rich; but the term was also applied to farmers and country gentlemen of inconsiderable property."[2] Given the large number of people to whom this definition applied, it is unsurprising that not all individuals who took the name Franklin as a surname were related.

Two of Josiah's direct-line ancestors, his father Thomas and his great-great-grandfather Robert, left wills. Several other family members also left wills. Not only were these examined, but every will in Northamptonshire for an individual named Franklin that was entered into probate by 1700 was also examined for clues to other possible family members. This was also quite helpful in ruling people out as family members as well. Those families with no clear connection are spelled out in a separate section of the book.

---

[2] Mark Antony Lower, *A Dictionary of the Family Names of the United Kingdom* (London: John Russell Smith, 1860) 120.

In all, sixteen direct ancestors of Josiah Franklin are examined in this work. The Franklin line goes back four more generations from Josiah[1]: Thomas[A], Henry[B], Thomas[C], and Robert[D]. New information was found in each one. Robert, the earliest known ancestor, was from Earls Barton. Twenty-five decendant families of Robert containing 108 descendants were examined. A number of the families disappear, as the names are too common to identify the descendants.

In addition to the Franklin ancestry, the lineages of the women who married into the family were examined for the first time: Anne Child, Jane White, Agnes Jones, and Margery Meadows. These lineages have not been extensively examined before and introduce new ancestors into the Franklin family.

Thomas[A] and Jane (White) Franklin (Josiah's parents) were responsible for the largest chunk of known desdendants. They had nine children, six of whom married and had children. Of their thirty-eight grandchildren, however, only twelve had children of their own. One of these was Benjamin's son Samuel. Two were from John's children Thomas and Anne. Nine of the twelve, however, were children of Josiah[1] Franklin and his two wives.

This first volume deals with the English ancestry. Future volumes will document the descendants of Benjamin[1] Franklin and Josiah[1] Franklin, the two brothers who emigrated to Boston.

Michael J. Leclerc, CG
Boston, Massachusetts
November 1, 2019

ACKNOWLEDGMENTS

No genealogist works in a vaccuum. Our best work is done in groups, bouncing ideas off each other, discussing problems, developing research avenues, providing advice, etc. And our friends and families keep us going and support us through good times and challenging ones.

I must start with my gratitude for the many friends and colleagues at the New England Historic Genealogical Society, where I worked for so many years. Special thanks to Henry B. Hoff, CG, FASG, editor of the *New England Historical and Genealogical Register*, and my co-editor on *Genealogical Writing in the 21st Century: A Guide to Register Style and More*, Second Edition. And to Brenton Simons, Scott Steward, Penny Stratton, Gary Boyd Roberts, and Lynn Betlock who also taught me much about writing and publishing, and to Chris Child, Alice Kane, and David Lambert, who have so often helped me by retrieving documents and information for me when I couldn't make it to the library.

The staffs at so many repositories have been instrumental in providing resources, as well as friendly and welcoming places to work. I'm especially grateful to the staffs of the American Philosophical Society, Beinecke Library at Yale University, Boston Athenaeum, Boston Public Library, Franklin Papers at the Sterling Memorial Library at Yale Univeristy, Historical Society of Pennsylvania, Massachusetts Historical Society, and the Northamptonshire Archives. My friend Else Churchill and the staff at the Society of Genealogists, London, helped me access the many treasures in their collections.

And the inimitable Audrey Collins from the National Archives at Kew, in addition to sharing her vast store of knowledge and introductions to personal connections, has become one of my dearest friends.

On this side of the pond, my friends and colleagues Patricia Law Hatcher, FASG, FGSP, and Paul Milner helped me tremendously in teaching me about researching and records in the United Kingdom.

My friend and former colleague at Mocavo and Find My Past, Alex Lindsay, has been incredibly helpful. Not only by listening to me when I've made a great discovery (or when I've plowed into a frustrating brick wall), but with business ideas about organizing and marketing that have had a huge impact on my work.

Maureen Taylor gave me my first job as a professional genealogist, and her friendship and guidance have been invaluable as I moved through the process of working on this project over the years.

My eternal gratitude to my parents, Omer and Aline (Morin) Leclerc, who gave me my start at life, and continue to support me through the good times and the challenging ones.

And to the Happiness Patrol, family of choice for so many years. Especially Ruth[12] (Upper) Foley (*Norma*[11] *Kerkhoff, Florence*[10] *Adams, Herbert*[9]*, William*[8]*, Eliza Jane*[7] *Mereweather, William*[6] *Gilmore, Elizabeth*[5] *Gilmore, Ann*[4] *Compton, Elizabeth*[3] *Franklin, Samuel*[2]*, Josiah*[1]*, Thomas*[A]*, Henry*[B]*, Thomas*[C]*, Robert*[D]), the twelfth-generation descendant of Josiah[1] Franklin, who started it all.

This book follows a numbering system for compiled genealogies created by the *New England Historical and Genealogical Register* in the 1870s. Arabic numerals identify specific individuals. Lowercase roman numerals are used to identify the birth order of children in genealogical summaries.

Superscripted numbers and letters used in a name are generational references. In this instance, Josiah Franklin and his brother Benjamin Franklin the Elder immigrated to the United States. They are shown as Josiah^1 Franklin and Benjamin^1 Franklin, indicating that they were the first generation in America. Letters are used to indicate previous generations back in England. Thus, the father of Josiah^1 and Benjamin^1 is referred to as Thomas^A Franklin, his father as Henry^B Franklin, etc.

These letters are used only for the direct-line ancestors, not collateral lines. The same system is used for the women who married into the family. In each case, the numbers and letters refer only to the generations in the direct line.

Church of England parish registers are generally not paginated in early eras. They are usually organized chronologically, with later records grouping baptisms, marriages, and burials. At the time the research was conducted, parish registers were available only in the original at local Record Offices, occasionally in published form, and sometimes on microfiche or microfilm at the Family History Library in Salt Lake City. Citations are to the version available on Family Search for free when possible. A single citation is generally provided for groups of extracted records.

The reader should be aware that as of the time of publication of this work in late 2019, genealogy websites are creating greater access to original records from England. Find My Past now has indexes for relevant Northamptonshire records available online. Ancestry.com is starting to put indexed images of Northamptonshire parish registers online. And FamilySearch is now providing access to images of parish registers as well as wills and probates through their Family History Center network. As more of these database images are indexed, additional information may come to light and it may be possible to trace some lines further.

ABBREVIATIONS

Those unfamiliar with compiled genealogies may be unfamiliary with standard abbreviations used in the field. Below is a list of abbrevations used in this volume.

b.	born
bp.	baptised
bur.	buried
ca.	circa, about
CG	Certified Genealogist
d.	died
FASG	Fellow of the American Society of Genealogists
FGSP	Fellow of the Genealogical Society of Pennsylvania
liv.	living
m.	married
m. (1)	married first, etc.
poss.	possibly
res.	resides/resided

An ahnentafel (German for ancestor table) is a system that allows you to look at an individual's direct ancestors in a clear sequence. The base individual is number one. Each generation is grouped separately, as couples. The ahnentafel is numbered consecutively, starting with the first individual in the table. Thus, the first person's father is number two and mother is number three, paternal grandfather is four, and paternal grandmothr is five, etc.

GENERATION ONE

1. **JOSIAH FRANKLIN** was born at Ecton, Northamptonshire, 24 December 1657.[3] He was baptised there 28 December.[4] He died at Boston, Suffolk County, Massachusetts, 16 January 1644/45.[5] He married first at Ecton ca. 1676, Anne Child. She was baptised there 21 January 1654, daughterof Robert and Deborah (—?—) Child. She died at Boston 9 July 1689.[6] He married second at Boston 25 November 1689

---

[3] Benjamin Franklin [the Elder], "A short account of the Family of Thomas Franklin of Ecto in Northamptonshire." 2 (hereafter Franklin, "Short Account") [see Appendix B].

[4] All references to baptisms, marriages, and burials at Ecton from Church of England Parish Register, Ecton St. Mary Magdelene, Northamptonshire, 1559 to 1584, 1592 to 1598, Northamptonshire Record Office 114P/201 [FHL Fiche #6,127,380; DGS #101,392,523]; 1559–1637. Northamptonshire Record Office 114P/202 [FHL Fiche #6,127,381]. Baptisms and Burials 1638–1754, Marriages 1638–1753, Northamptonshire Record Office 114P/203 [FHL Fiche #6,127,382; DGS #100,430,949]; 1653–1658. Northamptonshire Record Office 114P/ 204 [FHL Fiche #6,127,383; DGS #100,430,966]. Books are unpaginated; records are in chronological order, grouped by record type.

[5] *The Boston Weekly News-Letter* (Boston, Massachusetts), January 17, 1745, p. 2.

[6] "Ann wife of Josiah Francklin | Aged abo^t 34 Years Died July | y 9 1689" Gravestone of Anne (Child) Franklin, Granary Burying Ground, Boston, Massachusetts.

Abiah Folger.[7] She was born at Nantucket, Nantucket Co., Massachusetts, 15 August 1667, daughter Peter and Mary (Morrell) Folger.[8] She died at Boston 8 May 1752. The three are buried together at Boston in the Granary Burying Ground.[9]

GENERATION TWO

2. **THOMAS FRANKLIN** was baptised at Ecton, 8 October 1598. He died at Banbury, Oxfordshire, 21 March 1682, and was buried there 24 March 1682.[10] He married probably at Harbury, Warwickshire, ca. November 1635 Jane White.[11]

---

[7] Jay Mack Holbrook, *Massachusetts Vital Records: Boston, 1630–1849* (Oxford, Mass.: Holbrook Research Institute, 1985) "Boston Marriages 1689–1720" from the section "Marriages entered from Anno 1689 to 1695" unpaginated; records are grouped by the first letter of the surname of the groom. It looks to be a copy made in the eighteenth century. (hereafter Holbrook, *Boston Vital Records*)

[8] *Vital Records of Nantucket, Massachusetts, to the Year 1850* (Boston: New England Historic Genealogical Society, 1925), 1:465, citing the William C. Folger records at the Nantucket Historical Association.

[9] Genealogical chart of the Franklin family, drawn by Benjamin Franklin, "The Historical Society of Pennsylvania Collection of Benjamin Franklin Papers," Historical Society of Pennsylvania, Collection 215: Flat File 1. The chart was published in John W. Jordan, "Franklin as a Genealogist" *The Pennsylvania Magazine of History and Biography* (Philadelphia: Historical Society of Pennsylvania, 1877–) 23[1899]:17, as well as a transcript of insert opposite page 16, a facsimile of a handwritten document by Benjamin Franklin listing dates of birth and death for Josiah Franklin's children (hereafter Jordan, Franklin List). Chart drawn by Benjamin Franklin inserted between pages 2 and 3.

[10] Franklin, "Short Account" 3 [see Appendix B]. Church of England, Banbury St. Mary, Oxfordshire, Parish Registers, 1580–1708. Oxfordshire History Centre PAR21/1/R1/2. "Oxfordshire, England, Church of England Baptism, Marriages, and Burials, 1538-1812" database online at www.ancestry.com. (Lehi, UT, USA: Ancestry.com Operations, Inc., 2016). Unpaginated, records in chronological order.

[11] Feoffment in Trust, Thomas Franklin of Ecton to Nathaniel Brimley of Olney, Taylor, and Robarte [Robert] Wellford of Earls Barton, Yeoman. 3 November 1635. Northamptonshire Archives E(S)/464.

3. JANE WHITE was baptised at Grendon, Northampton-shire, 30 November 1617.[12] She was buried at Ec-ton 30 October 1662.

GENERATION THREE

4. HENRY FRANKLIN was baptised at Ecton, 26 May 1573. He was buried there 23 October 1631. He married there 30 October 1595 Agnes Jones.

5. AGNES JONES was baptised at Ecton 22 November 1573. She was buried there 29 January 1646.

6. GEORGE WHITE was baptised at Easton-Maudit, Northamptonshire, 29 June 1582.[13] He was buried at Grendon 25 February 1622. He married there 15 September 1607 Priscilla (Brimley/Bromley) Warner.

7. PRISCILLA BRIMLEY/BROMLEY married first —?— Warner.

GENERATION FOUR

8. THOMAS FRANKLIN was born say 1535 (estimating age 25 at marriage). He was buried at Desborough, Northamptonshire, February 1619.[14] He married at

---

[12] All references to baptisms, marriages, and burials at Grendon from Church of England, Grendon St. Mary, Northamptonshire, Parish Registers, Baptisms, Marriages, and Burials, 1559–1695, Northamptonshire Record Office, 141P/1. [FHL Microfiche #6,127,571; DGS #100,430,932]. Unpaginated, in chronological order

[13] All references to baptisms, marriages, and burials at Easton-Maudit from Church of England, Easton-Maudit Sts. Peter and Paul, Northamptonshire, Parish Registers, Baptisms 1539–1812, Marriages 1539-1755, and Burials, 1561–1812, Northamptonshire Record Office, 111P/1. [FHL Microfiche #6,127,352; DGS #100,624,328]. Records in chronological order.

[14] All references to baptisms, marriages, and burials at Desborough from Church of England, St. Giles, Desborough, Northamptonshire, Parish Regis-ters, Baptisms 1571–1649, Marriages 1571–1649, Burials 1571–1649; North-amptonshire Record Office 103P/9 [FHL Fiche #6,127,261]. Baptisms, 1648–1681; Northamptonshire Record Office 103P/10 [FHL Fiche #2,127,262]. Baptisms 1686–1748, Marriages 1695–1736, Burials 1695–1734; Northampton-shire Record Office 103P/11 [FHL Fiche #6,127,263].

Earls Barton, Northamptonshire, 20 November 1560 Margery Meadows.[15]

9. **MARGERY MEADOWS**, bur. at Desborough October 1629.

10. **WILLIAM JONES** is possibly the man of that name buried at Ecton, Northamptonshire, 23 November 1615. He married Margaret —?—.

11. **MARGARET** —?— was buried at Ecton 20 January 1592.

12. **NICHOLAS WHITE** was buried at Grendon, Northamptonshire, 4 April 1619. He married first Joanne — ?—. He married second at Easton-Mauditt, Northamptonshire, 7 August 1589 Alicia "Alice" Riding. She was buried there 10 March 1604.

13. **JOANNE** —?— She was buried at Easton-Mauditt 21 May 1588.

14. —?— **BRIMLEY/BROMLEY**
15. **ELIZABETH** —?—.

GENERATION FIVE

16. **ROBERT FRANKLIN** was buried at Earls Barton, 11 December 1752.

17. **KATHERINE** —?—.

---

[15] All references to baptisms, marriages, and burials at Earls Barton from Church of England, Earls Barton All Saints, Northamptonshire, Parish Registers, Baptisms 1558–1724, Marriages 1559–1728, Burials 1558–1725. Northamptonshire Record Office 110P/11 [FHL Fiche #5,127,339]. Book is unpaginated but records are in chronological order.

PART I

THE FAMILY OF BENJAMIN FRANKLIN

Chapter 1
REVIEW OF PREVIOUS RESEARCH

Before writing about any family, no matter how famous, it is helpful to first review what has already been published about the subjects. While countless books have been published about Benjamin Franklin over the years, no major work of compiled genealogy has ever been published on the Franklin family. This is most likely because most complied genealogies in the past focused on descendants of a single surname, and there are no known individuals who carry the surname Franklin. The last proven descendant of Benjamin Franklin's great-grandfather Henry to carry the surname of Franklin was William Temple Franklin, son of New Jersey Governor William Franklin and grandson of patriot, publisher, and inventor Benjamin Franklin. Temple Franklin died in Paris between 1823 and 1824.

The earliest known family compilation is a small manuscript written by Josiah's brother, Benjamin. The Revolutionary War patriot is his namesake. Josiah's brother is referred to here as Benjamin the Elder to avoid confusion with his far more famous nephew. Benjamin the Elder immigrated in 1715, following his only surviving son Samuel who had come earlier.

"A short account of the Family of Thomas Franklin of Ecton in Northampton Shire." was written 21 June 1717. It focuses primarily on his parents Thomas Franklin and Jane White and their children (and some of their grandchildren). He does speak a little about Thomas' ancestry, but this information is quite limited. A transcription of the "Short Account" is included here in Appendix B. The original manuscript story of his family now resides with the Franklin Papers in the Beinecke Library at Yale University. While it has been consulted and cited in numerous works, the only place where it was found published in its entirety previously is in Nian-Sheng Huang's biography of Josiah published in 2000 (see p. 8).

Benjamin the Elder starts his account by saying that "I have a dark Idea of the Granfather of Tho. Franklin my Father, that his name was Henery."[16] He admits to his memory not necessarily being as accurate as it could be. In this statement itself, for example, he is confusing generations. His father Thomas was a son of Henry, and Henry was son of another Thomas. The confusion is understandable given that Benjamin the Elder was in his late six-tiess when writing, and that he was born twenty years after his grandfather Henry died. Indeed, Henry died years before Thomas and Jane White were even married. In addition to time, he was now living in Boston, and the only family member left he could was his brother Josiah, seven years his junior.

In the spring of 1758, Benjamin Franklin took a holiday to the midlands with his son William. Together they visited Franklin's cousin Mary at Wellingborough in Northamptonshire. Mary was the only child of Josiah's brother Thomas. She married Richard Fisher and removed from Ecton to Wellingborough. From her Franklin obtained information about the family. His visit was very well-timed. By the end of the year, both Mary and Richard passed away.

After leaving the Fishers, father and son visited Ecton. There they spent quite some time visiting with the Rev. Eyre Whalley, rector of St. Mary Magdelene. An account of this visit, taken from Franklin's journal and from correspondence, was written by John W. Jordan and published in the *Pennsylvania Magazine of History and Biography* in 1899.[17]

In 1771, on a summer holiday, Franklin wrote the first part of his autobiography in less than two weeks. In it he states that "I have ever had pleasure in obtaining any little anecdotes of my ancestors. He goes on to say that "The notes of one of my uncles (who had the same kind of curiosity in collecting family anec-

---

[16] Benjamin Franklin, "A short account of the Family of Thomas Franklin of Ecton in Northamptonshire. 21 June 1717." Beinecke Rare Book and Manuscript Library, Yale University Library, Uncat MS Vault Franklin, 1 (hereafter Franklin, "Short Account") [see Appendix B].

[17] John W. Jordan, "Franklin as a Genealogist" The Pennsylvania Magazine of History and Biography (Philadelphia: Historical Society of Pennsylvania, (1877 –) 23 [1899]: 1 – 22. Benjamin and William also visited Birmingham in nearby Warwickshire on this trip. Birmingham was the birthplace of his mother-in-law, Deborah (White) Read. The information on this was published in Francis James Dallett, "Doctor Franklin's In-Laws" *Pennsylvania Genealogical Magazine* 21 (1958): 297–302.

dotes) once put into my hands, furnished me with several particulars relating to our ancestors."[18] He is no doubt referring to Benjamin the Elder's "Short Account." He also clearly incorporates information that he received from his visit with the Fishers and the village of Ecton.

When Benjamin Franklin lay down his pen from writing his autobiography, he had no way to know that it would be more than two centuries before anyone else would look with interest at his family's origins in England. With the exception of a single letter from Josiah written in 1743 to a great-nephew in England that appeared in Justin Winsor's 1881 *The Memorial History of Boston*, the next published work to include original research on the family would not appear until Arthur Bernon Tourtellot's *Benjamin Franklin: The Shaping of Genius, The Boston Years* in 1977.[19]

Jared Sparks, in his *The Life of Benjamin Franklin*, repeats only the information from the autobiography.[20] In 1854, William Bache and his cousin William Duane, great-grandsons of Benjamin Franklin, published a chart of his descendants in the *New England Historical and Genealogical Register*.[21] Bache later sent a transcription of the Franklin genealogy to the New England Historic Genealogical Society, where it was published in the *Register* in January 1857.[22] This genealogy includes information from Benjamin Franklin's research into the family, and discusses more of Thomas

---

[18] Van Doren, *Autobiographical Writings*, 216–7. [see note 1]

[19] George Makepeace Towle "Franklin, The Boston Boy" in Justin Winsor, *The Memorial History of Boston, Including Suffolk County, Massachusetts. 1630–1880* (Boston: James R. Osgood and Company, 1881), 269–296 (transcribed letter appears at 270–1).

[20] Jared Sparks, *The Life of Benjamin Franklin, Containing the Autobiography, with Notes and a Continuation* (Boston: Tappan and Dennet, 1844). The book was published by Franklin's great-nephew, Charles Tappan, and his business partner Charles F. Dennet.

[21] William Duane, Esq. and William Bache, Esq. "Descendants of Dr. Franklin" *New England Historical and Genealogical Register* (Boston, New England Historic Genealogical Society, 1847 –) 8 [1854]: 374.

[22] William Bache, "Franklin Family" *New England Historical and Genealogical Register* (Boston, New England Historic Genealogical Society, 1847 –) 11 [1857]: 17 – 20.

Franklin's descendants (including a list of Josiah's known progeny). It does not appear that any new research was conducted.

In the first half of the twentieth century, historian Carl Van Doren published a number of works about Benjamin Franklin and his family:

Benjamin Franklin (New York: The Viking Press, 1938)

Benjamin Franklin's Autobiographical Writings (New York: The Viking Press, 1945)

Jane Mecom: The Favorite Sister of Benjamin Franklin : Her Life here first fully narrated from their entire surviving correspondence. (New York: The Viking Press, 1950)

The Letters of Benjamin Franklin and Jane Mecom (Philadelphia: The American Philosophical Society, 1950)

Van Doren was awarded the Pulitzer Prize for Biography or Autobiography in 1939 for his 1938 *Benjamin Franklin*. The bit that discusses Josiah's family origins comes from the Capt. Benjamin Franklin letter and the *Autobiography*.[23]

The first volume of *The Papers of Benjamin Franklin* was published by Yale University in 1959. The beginning part of the book contains genealogical information on the English Franklins, the Folgers, descendants of Benjamin, and other descendants of Josiah. Unfortunately, the editors made a conscious decision not to include all known individuals: "This genealogy is selective, concentrating on those relatives of Benjamin Franklin with whom he was most closely associated or who appear in his papers." From the beginning, it appears, there was no major attempt to determine all members of the family.

The editors developed their own numbering system rather than using one of the established standard genealogical systems. Because of that, it is a bit clunky to navigate but serviceable. The information on the English Franklins is limited to Josiah's father Thomas; grandfather Henry; great-grandfather Thomas; and Josiah's siblings and their progeny, with little detailed information on

---

[23] Carl Van Doren, *Benjamin Franklin* (New York: The Viking Press, 1938) 3–4.

any of them. All of this is clearly a repeat of previously published information.[24]

P.I. King, archivist at the Northamptonshire Record Office in the 1960s, was fascinated by the Franklins and did much research in original records. Although he never directly published information about the family, his notes have been referenced by others, such as Arthur Bernon Tourtellot. His research notes are preserved at the Record Office, today the Northamptonshire Archives.

King used a personal shorthand in his notes. He abstracted only the barest of details. The notes include some attempts at rough descendencies. Some are more accurate than others. Visiting the archives, the staff was knowledgeable and very friendly and helpful. But even they had a difficult time understanding his source references, which sometimes impaired their ability to locate original documents he referenced. Unfortunately, like many other government archives, there is insufficient funding to properly process the collections, which can make retrieving documents even more complex for staff. Nick Bunker, in his *Young Benjamin Franklin: The Birth of Ingenuity* published in 2018, states that "King's notes seem to have been lost, and so I had to start again from the beginning."[25] Like many archives, Northamptonshire is very underfunded, leaving the devlopment of cataloging and collections processing with insufficient time. Unless lost in the last few years, the notes are still extant. But they are not cataloged under King's name. Instead they are contained in a folder of general correspondence about individuals named Franklin received by the archives.

Arthur Bernon Tourtellot was a writer, producer, and vice-president of CBS. He was also an amateur historian, with several books to his credit. His last was *Benjamin Franklin: The Shaping of Genius, The Boston Years.* Chapter two, "The Franklin Heritage," contains perhaps the best treatment of the English origins in print

---

[24] Leonard W. Labaree, ed. *The Papers of Benjamin Franklin* Volume 1: January 6, 1706 through December 31, 1734 (New Haven, Conn.: Yale University Press, 1959) lxiv – lxxv.

[25] Nick Bunker, *Young Benjamin Franklin: The Birth of Ingenuity* (New York: Penguin Random House, 2018) Chapter One, Note 9 (hereafter Bunker, *Young Benjamin Franklin*).

prior to Nick Bunker's work. Tourtellot personally visited the Northamptonshire Record Office and consulted with archivist Patrick I. King. He included information from King's research notes in his book.[26]

More recently, bestselling author Walter Isaacson (author of *Einstein* and *Steve Jobs*) wrote *Benjamin Franklin: An American Life*, published in 2003. Like many other biographies of the famed intellectual, few pages are devoted to his English ancestry (in this instance, only 5 of the work's 500 pages deal with the Franklins in England). And, as with the others, there is a simple summary of information about his roots. According to the source citations, the information is summarized from the *Autobiography* and Tourtellot.

In 2000, Nian-Sheng Huang wrote the only major work to date concerning Josiah, "Franklin's Father Josiah: Life of a Colonial Boston Tallow Chandler, 1657–1745," published by the American Philosophical Society.[27] While putting together an excellent analysis of Josiah's life, he broke no new ground with the English ancestry, referring instead to Tourtellot and the other previously published works.

Jill Lepore published *Book of Ages: The Life and Opinions* of Jane Franklin in 2013. Brief genealogical information is placed in the back of the book. It was designed into charts that do not follow standard genealogical format, making them more challenging to follow. The work contains only previously published information, including older errors that have since been corrected. The information on some family members is inconsistent (sometimes naming spouses of women and sometimes not). The information on English ancestry is very sparse.

George Goodwin published *Benjamin Franklin in London: The British Life of America's Founding Father* in 2016.[28] He is a Fellow of the Royal Historical Society and author in residence at the Benja-

---

[26] Arthur Bernon Tourtellot, *Benjamin Franklin: The Shaping of Genius, The Boston Years* (Garden City, N.Y. Doubleday and Company, Inc., 1977) 10 – 20.

[27] Nian-Sheng Huang, "Franklin's Father Josiah: Life of a Colonial Boston Tallow Chandler, 1657–1745" *Proceedings of the American Philosophical Society*, Volume 90, Part 3 (Philadelphia: APS, 2000).

[28] George Goodwin, *Benjamin Franklin in London: The British Life of America's Founding Father* (London: Orion Books, 2017).

min Franklin House on Craven Street in London. It does a very good job of describing Franklin's life back in England, but the information on the English relatives is very brief, and consists only of previously known information.

Most recently, Nick Bunker published *Young Benjamin Franklin: The Birth of Ingenuity*[29] He deals with the younger Benjamin Franklin, ending when Franklin turned forty-one years old. He focuses on the influences that worked on Benjamin and his family to make him into the man he became.

He does an excellent job of exploring not just the Franklin's ancestors, but the political and religious realities of the times in which they lived. These, of course, had a tremendous influence on the family. The book includes a great deal of original information, detailing, for example, the apprenticeships of Josiah Franklin and his brothers in London. While a great deal of discussion is dedicated to the family, it is focused on the generations from Henry Franklin to Josiah, focusing primarily on the direct ancestors with less discussion of the cousins.

These are just a few of the multitude of works about Benjamin Franklin published over the last two centuries. But few contain extensive biographical information on his family history. It is very apparent, however, that after Benjamin Franklin wrote his autobiography, nobody published any information based on original research until Tourtellot's biography was published two hundred years later. Given the fascination with Franklin and his contributions to both American and world history, it is truly remarkable that no additional original research was performed.

The work done by Benjamin Franklin the Elder and Benjamin Franklin created a strong foundation. P. I. King had some additional theories based on that foundation. Arthur Tourtellot and Nick Bunker built great foundations with additional work. New research, however, corrects some of the previous errors and extends the ancestry back further as well as opening up new branches for future research.

---

[29] Nick Bunker, *Young Benjamin Franklin: The Birth of Ingenuity* (New York: Penguin Random House, 2018)

Chapter 2
ROBERT^D FRANKLIN OF EARLS BARTON

Although the Franklins were purported to be at Ecton for hundreds of years, the first record in the parish there was for the baptism of Henry's brother Robert in 1563. Expanding the circle of research slightly shows us where Thomas^C Franklin originted. The village of Earls Barton is immediately adjacent to Ecton. Three parish records there show the likely origin of Benjamin Franklin's ancestry: [30]

> xi [11] day of Novembr [1560] Thomas Franklin Single and Margerie Meadowes Single were married.

> [1560/1] 4to die februarij baptiz fuit Christiana filia Thos Franklin ^pastor^

> Robert FrankLin the xith [11] of December was buryed Ao Dni 1571

Robert Franklin's will fills out more of the family.

Will of Robert Franklin of Earls Barton, probated 15 January 1573 [31]

[page1]
In the name of god Amen A° dm 1573 the xjth Daie of September in the yeare of the reigne of our Soveigne Ladie Elizabeth the xvth I Robert franklyn of Earles Barton in the countie of Northampton

---

[30] Church of England, Earls Barton All Saints, Parish Registers, Baptisms 1558–1724, Marriages 1559–1728, Burials 1558–1725. Northamptonshire Record Office 110P/11 [FHL Fiche #5,127,339]. Book is unpaginated but records are in chronological order.

[31] Church of England, Archdeaconry of Northampton Court, Registry Copy of Wills, vol. T, fol. 83, Will of Robert Franklyn of Earls Barton, 1573 [FHL Film #187,586, Item 2; DGS #8,098,669].

husbandman Sicke in bodie now nevertheless whole in mynde & of good and pfct remembrence Laude and praise be given to almightie god Doe ordene and make this my psent wyll & Last testam^t in manner & forme followynge that ys to saye First I bequethe my soule to almightie god my savyo^r onelye & redemer and to all the glorius and celestyall co[m]panye in heaven, and my bodie to be buryed wthin the pyshe churchyard of Earles Barton aforesaid imprmis I give to the poore mans boxxe iiij^d It[e]m I give & bequithe to Katheren my wyffe a godde cowe a baye mare foale a burroo hogge an aker of barley readie season that y^s to saye, a Roade and a gaffe in Stymkynge Lande iij woods in Thorpe Ryter, It[e]m I geve to the foresaid Katheren haffe an aker of rye benenthe ~~xxx~~ myll hyll halffe an aker of pease lande readye saison lyenge on great waye furlonge a potte & a posnett wch she brought with her, a newe tubbe a newe paile, Lymen whele a table in the house, the best barrell a chare & a bedsted, and tht to remayne and dwell wth my sonne Edward untyll Michaelmas next, It[e]m I geve unto Ales my daughter & maurie a bryndledd cowe between them, and she to be delyved unto them at micha^e next comynge It[e]m I geve to Ales my Daughter aforesaid a flaxen shete & a garden xv^s viij^d in money to be payde unto her at christmas come xij monthe, also the bigger brasse pott to be delyved at any tyme wthin two yeares after the makinge hereaft It[e]m I geve to maurie my daughter aforesaid a paire of harden shetes the Lesser brasse pott to be delyved at the feast of christmas before named It[e]m I give to margerye my daughter halffe an aker of rye lyenge at

[page 2]

tuffe stone wthin the fyelde of barley aforesaid It[e]m I geve to Agnes [xx]he halffe a quarter of barlye to be delyved at mich^amas next It[e]m I geve to Marie Carson a styke of barley to be delyv^red at the feast aforesayde It[e]m I geve to Elnor Carson a stryke of barlie to be delyv^red in manner aforesaid It[e]m I geve to Thomas Franklyn my sonne a blynde mare be be delyv^red unto him at the feast of michae next cōmynge so that he must suffer Edmond his brother to have her sould yf she geve [xxxx] All my other goode moveable & immoveable unbequethed I geve unto Edmond my sonne whome I make Sole Executor of this my psent will & last testam^t so that he must see the same trulye pformed & acco[m]plyshed accordinge to the true intent & meanynge [xxx] [x] he to see my debtes payed and my legacies pformed & my bodye brought honestly to the grounde, and I make smytysse [xxxxx] John Henrye & Thomas Fenno & to same for their paynes takinge [xxxx] eche of them a stryke of feede barlye, wytnes hereof Henrie wyhocke [xxx] th^t wth other m[xx] /.

The will shows a family unit of Robert, his wife Katherine, and children Edward, Alice, Marie, Margery, Thomas, and Edmond. Given that these are the only Franklins mentioned in Earls Barton at this time, the son Thomas mentioned in the will is almost certainly the man of that name who married Margery Meadows there 11 November 1560 (for more on Margery's ancestry see "Margery^C Meadows, wife of Thomas Franklin," on p. 203). Christiana Franklin baptized there 4 February 1560[/1], daughter of Thomas, is without doubt a child of this couple. The child was baptized less than three months after the marriage. No further record has been found for Christiana.

Parish registers during this period are notoriously incomplete, especially for burials, so the lack of information is not immediately disconcerting. Given that Edmund was made executor of Robert's estate, he was likely the eldest son. The order in which the children were mentioned probably closely matches the order of their birth, making Margery and Thomas were likely the youngest children. The Earls Barton parish registers only start in 1558, two years before the marriage of Thomas. It is quite likely that the others married prior to the start of the registers.

There is no evidence of Edward or Edmund having children at Earls Barton. Edmund was buried at Holcot, Northamptonshire (about six miles from Earls Baroton), 28 October 1601. There are no records of any marriage or children for him there, and he did not leave a will in Northamptonshire.

No evidence has been found of the ultimate fate of Edward. He cannot be identified anywhere in Northamptonshire. The sisters Alice and Marie may have remained at Earls Barton or moved with the family, but with no evidence of whom they married, it is impossible to know for certain. Thomas and Margery, however, clearly relocated to the town next door, Ecton.

CHAPTER 3

THOMAS^C FRANKLIN AT ECTON

Following Benjamin Franklin's return to London after his visit to the Midlands, the Rev. Whalley sent him a list of all records he could find in the parish for anyone named Franklin. The youngest children, Thomas and his sister Margery, start appearing in the Ecton parish registers shortly after the baptism of Christiana in Earls Barton in February 1561. The following records were found at St. Mary Magdelene:[32]

Baptisms

William the sonne of John Walch was christened the xxjth [21] of March Anno pdict [1561/2]

Agnes the Daughter of John Walch was christened the xxvth of Februarye Ann pdict [1562/3]

Roberde Franklyn, the son of Thomas Franklyn was bapt viijth [8] of Aprill [1563]

Jane, the daughter of Thomas Francklyn was bapt. First Augu[st] [1565]

John, the son of Thos Franklyne was bapt, The xvjth [16] of Maye [1567]

James Franklyn, the son of Thom^s Franklyn, was bapt ixth. [9] May [1570]

Henrye the Son of Thom^s Franklyn was Bapt, the xxvj^t [26] of Maye [1573].

---

[32] Church of England Parish Register, St. Mary Magdelene, Ecton, Northamptonshire, 1559 to 1584, 1592 to 1598, Northamptonshire Record Office 114P/201 [FHL Fiche #6,127,380; DGS #101,392,523]. Book is unpaginated; records are in chronological order, grouped by record type.

Marriages

John Walche and Marjery Franklin were marr. the vth [5th] Febra^y Anno pdt [10th]. [1560/61]

John Walche and Margerye Franklin were marryed the vth [5th] of February Anno pdict [1560/61] [duplicate entry]

Burials

Jane Franklyn the daughter of Thom^s Franklyn was bury the xxix^th [29] of the sad [August] [1565]

Jane the Daughter of Thomas Franklyn was buryed the xxix^th [29] of August Anno pdict [1565] [duplicate entry later in book]

There is some question concerning the occupation followed by Thomas. The family tradition is that Benjamin came from a long line of blacksmiths. Josiah Franklin wrote to his son Benjamin in 1739:

> The first that I can give account of, is my great grand father, as it was a custom in those days among young men too many times to goe to seek their fortune, and in his travels he went upon liking to a taylor; but he kept such a stingy house, that he left him and travelled farther, and came to a smith's house, and coming on a fasting day, being in popish times, he did not like there the first day; the next morning the servant was called up at five in the morning, but after a little time came a good toast and good beer, and he found good housekeeping there; he served and learned the trade of a smith.[33]

Josiah's great-grandfather was Thomas^C Franklin. There is no corroborating evidence that he was a blacksmith. The baptismal record of his daughter Christiana states that he was a shepherd. If he did later become a smith, it was not by visiting tradesmen as a young man and choosing a smith to teach him a trade. It is possible

---

[33] "To Benjamin Franklin from Josiah Franklin, 26 May 1739," Founders Online, National Archives, accessed September 29, 2019, https://founders.archives.gov/documents/Franklin/01-02-02-0048. [Original source: *The Papers of Benjamin Franklin*, vol. 2, January 1, 1735, through December 31, 1744, ed. Leonard W. Labaree. New Haven: Yale University Press, 1961, pp. 229–232.]

that he raised sheep as well as working as a smith. It is also possible that the smith was one of his other great-grandfathers. If it were William Jones, for example, the story would still have travelled down through the Franklin family.

Thomas may have moved to Ecton after the birth of his daughter Christiana to join his sister Margery who had married there the previous year. The baptisms of only two children of John and Margery (Franklin) Walch were recorded at Ecton: son William in March 1561/2, and daughter Agnes a year later in February 1562/3. There are no marriage records for the children, nor are there burial records for the couple or their children, indicating that the family may have relocated. The name John Walch/Walsh, however, is so common as to currently prevent positive identification of the family in another parish.

Thomas' sojourn in Ecton appears to be longer, but also temporary. He had five more children baptized at Ecton over the course of the following decade: Robert in 1563, Jane in 1565, John in 1567, James in 1570, and Henry in 1573. Jane was less than a month old when she died.

When Benjamin Franklin and his son William visited Northamptonshire and Warwickshire in 1758, they had the chance to visit Ecton and meet with the Rev. Eyre Whalley, rector of St. Mary Magdelene. Later he wrote to Benjamin with an abstraction of the records for anyone names Franklin. He wrote that:

> I have very carefully examined the Registers of this Parish, and the above are all I can find either Baptized, Married, or Buried, of the Name of Franklin: you, Sir, are descended from Henry the youngest Son of the first Thomas mentioned in the Register. Thomas, the only Surviving Son of which Henry was your Grandfather. Elizabeth daughter of Josias Franklin and Anne his wife, Baptized 10th of Mar. 1677. I Suppose was the eldest Child of your Father. The Omissions from the year 1641. to the year 1650. common in most Registers, were probably owing to the Confusions of those times.[34]

---

[34] "To Benjamin Franklin from Eyre Whalley, 25 July 1758," Founders Online, National Archives, accessed September 29, 2019, https://founders.archives.gov/documents/Franklin/01-08-02-0026. [Original source: *The Papers of Benjamin*

One wonders why Whalley was able to see that records were missing from the period during the Civil War, but omits any mention of the 1584–1592 gap. Eight years is a considerable time to be missing records. This is especially important as the records are missing during the period when Thomas's children were likely to be getting married.

After the baptism of Henry, the registers go silent for decades. Whalley incorrectly interpreted that to mean that Henry was the only surviving child. The gap is an indication that the family had relocated again. The trail is clear, and leads us to the nearby parishes of Desborough and Rothersthorpe.

Franklin, vol. 8, April 1, 1758, through December 31, 1759, ed. Leonard W. Labaree. New Haven and London: Yale University Press, 1965, pp. 114–117.]

CHAPTER 4

FRANKLINS OF DESBOROUGH

The parish of Desborough lies about twelve miles north of Ecton. Records there show us that Thomas[C] Franklin and at least some of his family ended up there. P.I. King's notes about the Franklin family include the following notation:[35]

> 29 5 20 J I   Th Symes of Barbara & Jacob Allen [xx] Allen
> E[xx] his wife marie of Barbara & [xxxc] wife of Jn Roughead
> to Hy F 2 <u>Desborough</u>   mess close & barn.

This indenture, dated 29 May 1622 [20 James I], establishes that Henry (Hy F in the note) was residing at Desborough. Unfortunately, archives staff were unable to locate the original indenture that King references in his notes.

This is not the only evidence we have, however. Examination of St. Giles parish registers establishes another strong link between the Franklin family and that village:[36]

Baptisms
Ellin Franklyn the Daughter of Robart Franklin was baptized
    the 6t Day [August] [1600]
Thomas Franklin the son Robert Fraklyn was baptized the
    xxvth [25] Day [September] [1602]

---

[35] Notes of P.I. King. Northamptonshire Archives, Franklin family c.1514–c1790, Biographical notes.

[36] All references to baptisms, marriages, and burials at Desborough are from Church of England, St. Giles, Desborough, Northamptonshire, Parish Registers, Baptisms 1571–1649, Marriages 1571–1649, Burials 1571–1649; Northamptonshire Record Office 103P/9 [FHL Fiche #6,127,261]. Baptisms, 1648–1681; Northamptonshire Record Office 103P/10 [FHL Fiche #2,127,262]. Baptisms 1686–1748, Marriages 1695–1736, Burials 1695–1734; Northamptonshire Record Office 103P/11 [FHL Fiche #6,127,263].

Ann the daughter of Thomas Franklin and his wife was baptized the eight day of December being Sundaye [1633] [marginal note says 18 under December, but this is the only note with a number and may mean something else]

Ann the daughter of Thomas Franklin and Mary his wife was baptiz the 12th of April being Teusday [1636]

Robert the sonne of Thomas Franklin and Mary his wife was bapt. the second of May beinge [Tues]day [1638]

Thomas the sonne of Thomas Franklin and mary his wife was baptiz the 30th of May being Sathurday [1640]

Mary Franklin the Daughter of Thomas Franklin and Sarah his wife was Baptized this 21th Day of March 1651

Ferdinando the son of Thomas Franklin & Sarah his wife of Desborough was bapt: Aug: 3 [1662]

Marriages

Robert Franklin of Earles Barton and Joane Wright were married the ixth [9] day July 1599

Burials

Thomas Franklin an ould man was [buried] the [difficult to read, duplicate entry elsewhere crossed off says xxvth (25)] Day [February] [1619]

Margerye Franklyn the wife of Thos Franklin was bure the xxxiith Day [October] [1629]

Anne the wife of Thomas Franklin was bur [6?] of maye being a Sundaye [1634]

Robert Franklin of the age of 80 years or there a[torn] was buried the 23th of June being Frydaye [1637]

Joane Francklin aged 80 or there abouts was buried the Fyst day of June being Frydaye [1640]

Probate records also provide valuable information. Although there is no record of a will for Thomas Franklin, there is one for his son Robert.

Will of Robert Franklin of Desborough, probated 10 September 1637[37]

In the name of god amen I Robard Franklin of Desbooro In the Counti ^of Northamton^ being Sycke in body but of good and parful memory thanks bee given to god Dooe make this my last will and testament In maner and forme following fierst I give and ba~~equet~~queth my Sooule to god that made it and my body to Christan bauryall in decent and orderly manar

It I give to Joane my wife the usage of her thurds and tooe beast and hur offer and that that is in it and that bed that shae lyes in and furnytur so if my will is that the good bease shall bee maynetayne as well as my wife can and to be renewed if they was old and after the deses of my wife to be returnd to my dafter Eling againe

It I give to my Sonne Thomas franklin tenn pounds to bee payde syx mounth after my deces

It I give Henry Right xxx3 Shillings 4 penc and ~~xxxxxg~~ to his children d five Shilling 8 pence It I give to Robard Right ten Shiling and to his children 6 pence a peace to bee payd 3 month after my desec

It I give to Thomas Yeomane 2 Shilings and to the rest of his brethren and Sisters twelve pence apeace

It I give to John Rightes Children 6 pence apeace

It I give ~~Lfe~~ to Goerge tallbut fourty Shiling to bee payd when hee cometh to the age of on and twenty

It I give to alse her sonne i Shilling

It I give to my sonne Thomas his child i Shiling

---

[37] Church of England, Archdeaconry of Northampton Court, Series 2, Original Wills, vol. H, no. 265, Will of Robert Franklin of Desborough, 1673 [FHL Film #187,603; DGS #7,904,798]. Also, Register Copy Wills, vol. AE, pt. 2, fol. 26 [FHL Film #187,593; DGS #8,.098,670].

All the rest of my goods I give to Nickleas Braine and his wife unbeegethed whom I dooe make my sole executors and I doe make Steven Watson and Isack Kent overseers and I doe appoint them [I give — shillings apeace for their paines]

It I dooe give to my Sonne Thoms Frankelin the bond and the covenants wich I have of Edward Right that hee may receve the money wich he oeth mee

Of all the goods and chatels wich I have made nickeolas Braine executor of I doe refeund the bands and covenants wich I have of Edward Right unto my Sonne Thomas.

These records leave little doubt that Thomas and Margery relocated to Desborough with at least some of their family. The parish registers and probate show son Robert marrying Joane Wright there in 1599 and having two children: Ellen, born 1600, and Thomas, born 1602. No marriage records can be found for either of the children, but baptismal records show children of Thomas with three different wives.

Daughter Ann was baptized there 8 December 1633. His wife Ann was buried six months later, in May 1634. Ann "the daughter of Thomas Franklin and Mary his wife" was baptized two years later, on 12 April1 1636, indicating that Thomas remarried. Two more children of the couple followed: Robert in 1638 and Thomas in 1640.

There is a gap of eleven years, then "Mary Franklin the Daughter of Thomas Franklin and Sarah his wife" was baptized 21 March 1651. Ten years later, a son of the couple, Ferdinando, was baptized in 1662.

In his will Robert left a legacy of one shilling "to my sonne Thomas his child." Given that both of Thomas' first two children were named Ann, it is likely that the first one died in infancy. The second one daughter, baptized in 1636, would then be the only child of Thomas living and fit perfectly with the will.

Thomas was older when the last two children with Sarah were born: 49 at the baptism of Mary and 59 for Ferdinando. But that was not unusual. Older men often married younger women.

There is another interesting Thomas Franklin will dated at Earls Barton 3 October 1670.

Will of Thomas Franklin of Earls Barton, probated 13 January 1670[/1]:[38]

In the Name of God Amen this third of October 1·6·7·0·1·Thomas Franklin of Earles Barton in the County of Northampton Sheepheard beeing sicke in body but of sound & perfect memory thanks bee to god For itt doe make & ordayne this my last will & testament In manor & forme following /. First I give & bequeath my soule into ye hands of Allmighty god my maker hopeing by ye pation of Jesus Christ my redemer I shall Inheritt Eternall life / . And For that worldly estate which itt hath pleased ye lord to bles me with I dispose of ett as Follows / First I give unto richard Jeames one shilling of good & lawfull money of England to bee payed within one year After my deacease Itm I give unto widow wright one yeare after my decease. Itm I give unto ^wydow^ wade one – – of like lawfull money of England Itm I give unto widow Smith one shilling of like lawfull ^money^ to bee paid within one yeare after my decease / Itm I give & bequeathe unto Sarah my loving wife one messuage or tenament ^with all ye appurtenancies^ wherein I doe now Inhabitt & dwell to hir & hir heirs and Asignes For ever Itm all my goods & Chattells my debts being paid legacies performed & Funeralls discharged I give unto my said loving ^wife^ Sarah & doe makie & ordaine hir the sole executor of this my last will & testament in witnes whereof I have hereunto set my hand & seale ye day & yeare First above written

Thomas signed the will with his mark. It was witnessed by Will Whitworth, who signed, and John Wright, who also made his mark.

---

[38] Church of England, Archdeaconry of Northampton Court, Original Wills, Series 4, vol. 6, no. 210, recto and verso, Will of Thomas Franklin of Earls Barton, 1670 [FHL Film #187,640, Item 2; DGS #8,047,395].

This may or may not be Thomas Franklin, the son of Robert. There is no mention of any children in the will. While the older children would be adults in their 30s and settled by 1670, the youngest children were 19 and 8 at the time the will was made, certainly young enough to deserve mention.

CHAPTER 5

FRANKLINS OF ROTHERSTHORPE

A likely candidate for John, son of Thomas^C Franklin, is found in the parish of Rothersthorpe, about ten miles west of Ecton and slightly southwest of the city of Northampton. The following records for individuals named Franklin were found in the Church of England parish registers at Rothersthorpe, which start in 1562:[39]

Baptisms

Sarah Francklyn the daughter of John Francklin was baptised the xix[th] [19] of March [1590/1]

Joseph Franklyn the Sonne of John Franklyn was baptized the xth [10] daye of March 1593[/4]

John Franklyn the Sonne of John Franklyn was baptized the xxij[th] [22] daye of August [1595]

Catherine Francklyn the daughter of John Franklyn was baptized the xj[th] [11] daye of March 1598[/9]

Alice Franklyn the daughter of John Franklyn was baptized the xxiiij[th] [24] daye of Janvarie [1601]

John Franklyn the sonne of John Franklyn was baptized the iiij[th] [4] daye of Maye [1606]

Henry Frankelin the sonne of Joseph Francklin and Agnes his wife was baptised January 15 1625[/6]

Sara Francklyn the daughter of Joseph Franck[illegible] and Agnes his wife was baptized April 15 [1627].

Briget Franckeline the daughter of Joseph Frank[illegible] Agnes his wife was baptized January 20 [1628]

Willyam Franklin the Sonne of John Franklin Alice his wiffe was Baptised the xx[th] of August [1630]

Anni Franklin the daughter of Joseph Franklyn and his wife was baptized the xxij[th] [22] of october [1632]

---

[39] Church of England, Rothersthorpe, Saints Peter and Paul, Northamptonshire, Parish Registers. Baptisms, marriages, and burials 1562–1659, Northamptonshire Archives 283P/1/1 [FHL #6,128,799].

Elizabeth Franklin the daughter of John Franklin and Alice his wiffe was baptized the xth [10] day of March [1632/3]

Thomas Franklyn the Sonne of Joseph Franklyn and Agnes his wife was Baptized the xxj[th] [21] daye of January [1633/4]

Thomas Franklin the Sonne of John Franklin and Alice his wife was baptised the forth Daye of February [1636/7]

Samuel Franklin the sonne of Samuel Franklin and Elizabeth his wife was baptized the ii [2] day of february [1652]

Marriages

John Franklyn and Agnes Ingram were married the First of Maye [1590]

Henry Symance & Ane Franklyne was marryed the xxviijth daye of Aprill [1605]

Edward Clarke and Sara Franklyn were married the xxi[th] [21] daye of november [1622]

Burials

Alice the daughter of John Franklyn was buried the xxvth daye daye [*sic*] of August [1602]

John Franklyn was buried the xxx[th] [30] daye of october [1602]

Joseph Franklin was buried the fore and twentie daye of Aprill [1635]

Agnes Franklin widow was buried the xviij[th] [18] Day of May [1638]

Samuel Franklin the sonne of Samuel Franklin and Elizabeth his wife was buried the xiiij of February [1652]

John the son of Thomas[C] Franklin is the only known man of that name in this area of Northamptonshire who is of the right age to be the John who married Agnes Ingram in 1590. John and Agnes had five children: Sarah, baptized in 1590/1, Joseph in 1593/4, John in 1595, Catherine in 1598/9, and Alice in 1601. John was buried in October 1602, and his widow married second Henry Symance 21 November 1605.

There is also the curious record of "John Franklyn son of John Franklyn" who was baptized 4 May 1606. Thomas's son John died four years previously, and his son with Agnes named John was only 11 years old at the time of this birth. There is no other known John Franklin in Northamptonshire at this time to whom this child can be assigned. Franklin is a very common name, however, and an unrelated John Franklin may have moved to the village from outside of Northamptonshire.

A John Franklyn and his wife Alice later had three children baptized at Rothersthorpe: William in 1630, Elizabeth in 1632/3, and Thomas in 1636/7. No record of the marriage of John and Alice has yet been found. While these may be the children of 1595 John, they may also be children of 1606 John, which would make them unrelated to the family of Benjamin Franklin. There is insufficient information to determine which John is the father.

John and Agnes (Ingram) Franklin's son Joseph and his wife Agnes had five children at Rottersthorpe: Henry, baptized in 1625/6, Sarah, baptized in 1627, Bridget, baptized in 1624, Anne, baptized in 1632, and Thomas, baptized in 1633/4. Joseph was buried 24 April 1635, leaving a widow with five children aged between 2 and 10 years old. Joseph was the only member of this branch of the family who left a will. It was dated two weeks before his death.

Will of Joseph Franklin of Rothersthorpe, probated 2 May 1635:[40]

In the name of God Amen the Tenth Daye of Aprill Anno Domin: 1635 I Joseph Franklin of Rotherstorpp Sick in bodye but perfect in memori thankjes be given to god for it doe make and ordayne this my Last will and testament in maner and Forme following my bodye to be buried in the churchyeard of Rothersthorpp

First I give and bequeath unto my Sonne Henri Franklyn — xij[d]

Item I give and bequeath unto my Daughter Sara Franklyn — xij[d]
Item I give and bequeath unto my Daughter Bridgit Franklyn — xij[d]

---

[40] Church of England, Archdeaconry Court of Northampton, Wills and Administrations, Series 2, Original Wills, C: 31-32, Will of Joseph Franklin of Rothersthorpe, 1635 [FHL #187,599; DGS #8,047,425].

Item I give and bequeath unto my Daughter Agnis Franklyn — xij^d

Item I give and bequeath unto my Sonne Thomas Franklyn — xij^d

All the Rest of my Goods catteles and cattle unbequeathed I give and beqeath unto my Wiffe Agnis Franklin whom I do make my whole Executror of this my Last will and Testament : witness to the same supervisors

Thomas Baylie
Jasper Sheardlye

Joseph's widow Agnes did not long survive him. She had no will or probate when she was buried at Rothersthorpe three years later, on 13 May 1638. She left five children age 5 to 13.

CHAPTER 6

HENRY^B FRANKLIN

Henry was the first of Benjamin Franklin's direct-line ancestors born at Ecton. He was baptised there at St. Mary Magdelene 26 May 1573, the youngest child of Thomas^C and Margery (Meadows) Franklin.[41] The following additional records related to mary were found at Ecton St. Mary Magdelene:

Baptisms
> Thomas the Sonne of Henry Frankline was christened the xxviijth [28] of February anno pdict [1595]
> Thomas the Sonne of Henry Frankline was christened the viijth [8] of October Anno pdict [1598]

Marriages
> Henrye Frankline and Annis Joanes were married the xxxth [30th] of October anno pdict [1595].
> Henry Franklin and Agnes Joanes were marryed the xxxth [30th] of October Anno first [1595] [duplicate entry later in book]

Burials
> Thomas the Sonne of Henry Franklyn was buryed the xjth [11th] of August Anno Dom first [1598]
> Henry Franklyn Husbandman was buried Octobr xxiijth [23d] [1631]
> 1646 Janu. 29 _____ Franklin an aged widow

Henry and Agnes were married on 28 October 1595. Not quite four months later, their first child, Thomas, was baptised. He was two years old when he died in the summer of 1598. Their

---

[41] Church of England, St. Mary Magdelene, Ecton, Northamptonshire, Parish Registers, 1559 to 1637, Northamptonshire Record Office 114P/202 [FHL Fiche #6,127,381], and 1638 to 1754, Northamptonshire Record Office 114P/203, [FHL Fiche #6,127,382]. Books are unpaginated; records in chronological order.

next child was also named Thomas when he was baptised 11 August 1598.

Benjamin Franklin the Elder in his *Short Account* says of Henry "that he was an Atturney and lived at Houghton two Miles from Northampton, and that he had an Estate there of about Eighty pounds a year."[42] Henry was not an attorney. He did partner with Michael Jones to purchase property. The exact nature of the relationship (if any) between Henry's wife Agnes and Michael Jones is uncertain, although siblings is a possibility (see "Agnes[B] Jones, Wife of Henry Franklin" on page 193).

Thomas was only an infant when his parents moved with Michael and his family to Houghton Magna (now Great Houghton). There the family added one more to their ranks:

> Easter Franklen y[e] Daughter of Henrie Franklyn was baptised the six & twentieth day of September, Anno Regin Eliz 44· Anno Dmi 1602 :: 1602:[43]

England at the time was embroiled in a systemic change that was causing much social unrest. Wealthy landowners wanted to remove small farmers from the land, converting their fields of crops into grazing land for goats and sheep that would be fenced and hedged in smaller oblongs of land. This process was called enclosure, and Northamptonshire and the midlands were heavily involved in the process.[44]

In 1604 Ferdinando Baude purchased the land holdings of the Tresham family in Houghton Magna. He started erecting hedges to enclose the land, but the villagers, including Henry and Michael, were opposed to it. They joined villagers in frequently tearing down the hedges to plow their fields and plant their crops. Baude

---

[42] Franklin, "Short Account" 1 [see Appendix B].

[43] Church of England, Great Houghton St. Michael and All Angels, Northamptonshire, Parish Registers, Baptisms 1559–1677, marriages 1558–1673, Burials 1562–1673, Northamptonshire Record Office 175P/1 [FHL #6, 127,824; DGS #100,430,829].

[44] For more on the process of enclosure, see Briony McDonagh and Stephen Daniels, "Enclosure stories: narratives from Northamptonshire" *Cultural Geographies* (London: Sage Publications, 1994–) 19 [2012]: 107–21.

hired men to attack Henry, but he would not back down. Baude ended up filing a suit in chancery, which despite a valiant effort on the parts of Henry and Michael he won. Nick Bunker goes into even greater detail on Henry's experiences and motivations during this time.[45]

After his loss, Henry moved to Desborough to be with his family. It is not until 1620 that he returned to Ecton (where his in-laws still lived) with his wife and two children. He set up a forge there and practiced his trade as a blacksmith for another decade before he died in 1631. Agnes survived him. She is almost certainly the aged widow Franklin who was buried there on 29 January 1646.

ESTHER FRANKLIN

Benjamin Franklin the Elder in his *Short Account* says of Henry that "his son was put to a blacksmith and settled at Ecton but wether the Atturney had any other child I know not . . ."[46] Other accounts have stated that Thomas^A had a sister without identifying her.

The only baptisms at Ecton are for two sons named Thomas. But the parish records of Great Houghton (Houghton Magna) contain a single record for someone named Franklin during this period:

Easter Franklen th^e Daughter of Henrie Franklyn was baptised the six & twentieth day of September, Anno Regin Eliz 44· Anno Dmi 1602 :: 1602:[47]

---

[45] Nick Bunker, *Young Benjamin Franklin*, 14–17 [see note 25].

[46] Franklin, "Short Account" 1 [see Appendix B].

[47] Church of England, Great Houghton St. Michael and All Angels, Northamptonshire, Parish Registers, Baptisms 1559–1677, marriages 1558–1673, Burials 1562–1673, Northamptonshire Record Office 175P/1 [FHL #6, 127,824; DGS #100,430,829].

Esther was twenty-nine years old when she married Robert Ryde at Northampton St. Peter:[48]

Robert Ryde of Ladbrok in the County of Warwick[shire] and Hester Franklyn of Ecton mariedthe xij[th] Day of Januarie: 163i [1]

The following records from Ladbroke All Saints tell us more about the Ride family:[49]

Baptisms

Joh[ann]es Ride, filius Rob[er]ti [baptized] Decembeis prime [1607]

Robert the sonne of Richard Ride and Katherine his wiffe babtized the 20 of October [1633]

Hester the daughter of Richard Ryde & Katherine his wiffe babt. the j [1] day of February in Ao Pdict [1634].

John Ride son of Richard & Catherine his wife Feb: 20 [1636]

Robert, Sarah, & Catherine children of Richard Ride and Catherine his wife feb: 2[x] [1639] [second digit buried in fold and illegible]

John Ride sone of Richard & Katherine his Wife Ap[ll] 18 [1641]

John and Abraham the sonnes of Rich: Ride & Katherine his wife [baptized] Deceb [day buried in fold and illegible] [1643]

Burials

Robert Ride sōnne of Richard & Katherine his wife July 2[x] [second digit buried in fold and illegible] [1638]

Ester the wife of Robert Ride th[e] 18th day of April [1646].

Robert Ride buried the 11th day of September [1647].

---

[48] Church of England, Northampton St. Peter, Northamptonshire, Parish Registers, 1578–1737, Northamptonshire Record Office 240P/1 [FHL #6, 128,350; DGS #101,392,543].

[49] Church of England, Ladbrook All Saints, Warwickshire, Parish Registers, 1559–1762Warwickshire Record Office, DR0085/1 [FHL Film #549,656, Item 2; DGS #4,290,822]. Unpaginated, records in chronological order.

Robert Ride [buried] the 20th day of october [1649]
Richard Ride the 5th day of October [1653]
Katherine Ride September 3 [1657]

Interestingly, there are no marriage records for the Ride family in Ladbrooke. Although Robert and Esther died at Ladbroke, there are no baptisms for any children there. The only baptisms are a single one for a child of Robert in 1607, and nine children of John Ride and his wife Catherine. That Richard and Catherine named children Robert and Hester indicates that this he could be a brother of Robert.

Robert the father of John in 1607 could also be the father of Robert and Richard, born elsewhere. Since no father was named, the burials for men named Robert Ride were likely for adults. Richard's son was too young, so they are likely the father of John, and Esther's husband. No will was found for any of them. There is no way to tell which record is for which man.

In his "Short Account," Benjamin the Elder wrote that his mother Jane (White) Franklin had:

> one sister who married m[r] Ride in Warwickshire, and had by him one son Named Samuel Ride to whom he left about 60l per An: free land which he in a few years spent & sold and became a Gent. Servant and afterward a Labourer in building the city of London after that Great and Dreadful fire that burn'd it on the 2, 3, and 4 of sep 1666, which did destroy 13300 houses, This Samuel Ride had oneley one daughter who married a butcher in Clare Market, Westminster[50]

He was writing decades later, and there is no doubt that he confused his father's sister for his mother's sister.[51]

The timeline for the story fits perfectly for Esther. She and Robert married in January 1631/2. If their son was born within a few years of their marriage in 1631/2, he would have been in his early thirties at the time of the great fire, certainly of sufficient age

---

[50] Franklin, "Short Account" 1–2 [see Appendix B].
[51] See the discussion of Jane's family that corrects the confusion in "Jane[A] White, Wife of Thomas Franklin" on page 135.

to have gone from working a farm to a gentleman's servant. The massive destruction in London in 1666 presented many opportunities for work.

No baptismal or marriage record has been found for Samuel. Clare Market, Westminster, was located close to the parish of St. Clement Danes, but no marriage can be found for a woman named Ride (or spelling variants thereof) in the appropriate timeframe. Although the groom was from that area, Samuel could have been living elsewhere in the city, where the marriage would have taken place as the home parish of the bride. Complicating the search is the lack of a first name for Samuel's daughter. There is also the question of the husband's name. Was butcher the man's occupation, or was that his actual surname? The story could have gotten confused over time.

CHAPTER 7

THOMAS[A] FRANKLIN

After spending his youth in Houghton Magna and Desborough, Thomas[A] Franklin returned to Ecton with his parents and spent decades there. As reported by Ezra Whalley to Benjamin Franklin, the parish registers of St. Mary Magdelene have numerous records for his family:[52]

Baptisms

Thomas the Sonne of Henry Frankline was christened the xxviij[th] [28] of February anno pdict [1595]

Thomas the Sonne of Henry Frankline was christened the viij[th] [8] of October Anno pdict [1598]

Thomas the Sonn of Thomas Franklyn and Jane his wife was baptized the xi [11] day of March. [1637]

Samuel the son of Thomas Franklin baptised November 7 1641

1650 March 23 Benjamin son of Thomas Franklin and Jane his wife

Hannah the Daughter of Thomas Franklin and Jane his wife was borne the three and twentieth of october and baptized the 29 of the same [1654]

Josia the Sonne of Thomas Frankline and Jane his wife was borne 28: Day of December and baptized the third Day of January : 1657:

[1673.] Octob 24 Mary daughter of Thomas Franklin jun. and Helen his wife

---

[52] Church of England Parish Register, St. Mary Magdelene, Ecton, Northamptonshire, 1559 to 1584, 1592 to 1598. Northamptonshire Record Office 114P/201 [FHL Fiche #6,127,380; DGS #101,392,523]. 1559–1637. Northamptonshire Record Office 114P/202 [FHL Fiche #6,127,381]. Baptisms and Burials 1638–1754, Marriages 1638–1753. Northamptonshire Record Office 114P/203 [FHL Fiche #6,127,382; DGS #100,430,949] 1653–1658. Northamptonshire Record Office 114P/204 [FHL Fiche #6,127,383; DGS #100,430,966] Books are unpaginated; records are in chronological order, grouped by record type.

[1677][/8] March 10 Elizabeth daughter of Josias Franklin and of Anne his wife.

Burials

[1662] Oct 30 Jane wife of Thomas Franklin sen

[1702] Jan 7th. Thomas Franklyn Clerk to the comissioners for Taxes. Affid: Before Mr. Walker Rd 13th.

[1711] March 16th. Helen Widow of Thomas Franklyn deceas'd Jan:7th 1702. Affid: before Mr. Whaley. Rd 21th.

Thomas Franklin and Jane White Feoffment in Trust[53]

1635. to all xtian people to whom this presente everything Indented shall come Thomas Franklin of Ecton in the country of Northampton yeoman doth sende gretinge in our Lord God everlastinge Knoew yee That the said Thomas Franklin aswell for and in consideration of a marriadge by the grace of God shortly to be had and solemnized Betweene him the said Thomas Franklin and Jane White of Harbery in the county of Warwicke the daughter and heire of George White late of Grendon in thaforesaid County of Northton yeoman deceassed so allso for and in consideration of all such lande and goods and other things which he the said Thomas Franklin shall have holde and enjoy of the Inheritance and freehold of hir the said Jane White and otherwyse is to have and receive by or wth the marriadge of hir and for some recompense to be made unto hir for the same and for divers other good causes and considerations him the said Thomas Franklin thereunto especially movinge hath given granted and enfeiffed and confirmed and by theise prsents doth give grante enfeeffe and confirme unto Nathaniel Brimley of Olney in the county of Buck taylor and to Robarte Wellford of Earles Barton in the county Northton aforesaid yeoman and to their heirs All that messuage or tenemente with the yard gardaine and orchard on the south and weste pte thereunto adioyninge scituate and beinge in the towne of Ecton aforesaid wherein the said Thomas Franklin Doth nowe inhabitt and Dwell and all those prells of arable lands leys

---

[53] Feoffment in Trust, Thomas Franklin of Ecton to Nathaniel Brimley of Olney, Taylor, and Robarte [Robert] Wellford of Earls Barton, Yeoman. 3 November 1635. Northamptonshire Archives E(S)/464.

meadowe pasture and grass grounde scituate lyinge and beinge
disposed in the territories feilds meadowes parish and perinofe
of Ecton aforesaid beinge the freehold and Inheritance of the
said Thomas Franklin wth the said messuage nowe used occu-
pied or enjioyed And all houses edifics buildings com[m]ons
and com[m]on of pasture for hallfe yardlande wayes passags
easements proffitts com[m]odities hereditaments appten[a]ncs
whasoever unto the said messuage or tenemente and premisses
or any of them of to my pte member or prell of them be-
longinge or in anywyse apptayninge and nowe in the tenure or
occupation of the said Thomas Franklin or of his assignee or
assignes And also all the estate right tytle interest rente use
reverc[i]on and reverc[i]ons remayndor and remayndors clayme
and demande of him the said Thomas Franklin thereunto or to
any pte member or prell therof with thappten[a]ncs as aforesaid
whatsoever To have and to holde the said messuage or tenemente and premisses wth all and singular their and every of their
righte members and appten[a]nce and every pte and prell thereof unto the said Nathaniel Brimley and Robert Wellford and
their heirs to the use uses and behoofe herein hereafter speci-
fyed and exp^essed and to none other use intente or ppose whatsoever that is to say to the use and behoofe of the said Thomas
Franklin for and duringe the terme of his naturall lyfe wthout
impeachment of or for any manner of waste and after the deceasse of the said Thomas Franklin then to the use and pte thereof any stoyle or willfull waste for and duringe the naturall lyfe of
the said Jane if there shall happen to be noe sonne of the boddy
of the said Thom' to be begotten of the boddy of the said Jane,
but if there shalbe a sonne begotten of their boddies Then the
said p^emisses to be to the use and behoofe of the said Jane
Wha[crease, illegible]y do aforesaid untill such sonne as aforesaid shall accomplish the full adge of twenty and one years and
afterwrd the moytie or one hallf of the sid p^emisses do of every
pte and prell thereof to be to the use and behoofe of teh said
Jane for and duringe the terme of hir naturall lyfe in mann^e and
fourme aforesaid and after hir deceasse then to the use and be-
hoof of the heirs and assignes of the said Thomas Franklin forever And the other moytie or one hallfe of the said premisses
and of every [crease, illegible] and prell thereof to be to the use
and behoofe of such sonne of the boodyes of the said Thomas
and Jane lawfully to be begotten and of his heirs and assignes

forer To be Holden of the cheife Lord or Lorde of the fee or
fees thereof by the rents and service therefore to become dewe
and of righte a[xxxx]omes to be done And to said Thomas
Franklin and his heirs the said messuage or tenemente and all
other the premesses wth all and singular their appten[a]ncs and
every [crease, illegible] and prell thereof unto the said Nathaniell
Brimley and Robert Wellford and their heirs to the use uses and
behoofe herein before mentioned against him th[crease, illegi-
ble] said Thomas Franklin and his heirs and again if all and every other pdon and psons whatsoever lawfully claminge by from
or under him or his of fate righte tytle accordinge to the trewe
intente and meaninge hereof shall and will warr[a]nte and be
theise presents defende forevermore In wittnesse whereof the
said Thomas Franklin unto both pte of theise psents indented
(the one of them to be and remayne in the hands and custody
of one of the testtees above menconed and the other of them to
be and remayne in the hands and custody of the said Thomas
Franklin) hathe sett his hand and seale the thirde d[crease, illeg-
ible]ye of November in the eleventh yeare of the raigne of o^r
Sou^raigne Lord Charles by the grace god of England Scotland
France & Irelande kinge defender of the fayth

Tho: Franklin

Sealed & Delyve^red & all so quiett & peaceable possession &
sioson of the w^thin menconed messuage in the name of all the
within granted lands tenements & hereditaments was given &
delyuefed the very day of the date w^thin written by the w^thin
named Thomas Franklin in his [xxxx] pson unto the w^thin
named Robart Wellford one of the testtees w^thin named To
Holde accordinge to the uses enour pporte forme and effecte
w^thin written in the p^rsence of us :·/

Mychaell Jones
Will^am Mustore
Thomas Skamer

A dexigraph copy of Thomas^A Franklin's will is in the collections at the Northamptonshire Record Office. There is no prove-
nance for the copy and where it came from. No original or regis-

tered copy of has been found in indexes for probate jurisdictions covering Oxfordshire and Northamptonshire, so it is likely the original was never probated. It is a two-page document. Neither of the verso sides were included in the dexigraph copy.

Will of Thomas^A Franklin, unprobated:[54]

[page 1]
In the name of God Amen the Eighteenth day of March Anno Dom 1681° And in the foure & thirtieth yeare of the Reigne of our Souvaigne Lord King Charles the Second over England &tc I Thomas Franklin Holder of Banbury in the County of Oxon Blacksmith being weake in body but of sound memory minde and understanding Doe make & ordayne this my last will & testament in manner & forme following (that is to say) First & principally I doe Committ my soule into the hands of Allmighty God my maker & Redeemer And my body I commit to the earth to be buryed in decent & Christian Buriall att the discretion of my Executor hereafter named First I give devise & bequeath unto my eldest sonne Thomas Franklin & his heires & assignes forever All my two yard lands of arable meadow & pasture ground wth thapptenancs lying & being in the parish & feilds of Ecton in the County of Northton in a syde there called the ~~Bug~~ Badgers Hide [xx]th Said two yard lands I purchased of one Thomas Ball ^nevertheless subject to the paymt & chargable with the legacies as hereafter I shalle charge the sayme^ And alsoe I give devise & bequeath unto my said ^sonne^ Thomas Franklin & his heires & assignes for ever All other my lands tenemts & hereditamts whatsoever scituate lying & being in the parish & feilds of Ecton aforesaid Also I give unto my sonne John Franklin twenty shillings Also I give & bequeath unto my sonne Joseph Franklin the sume of twenty pounds to be paid unto him by my sonne Thomas Franklin wthin one yeare next after my decease Also I give & bequeath unto my sonne Benjamine Franklin the sume of Forty pounds to be paid him by my sonne Thomas Franklin wthin two years next after my decease Alsoe I give & bequeath unto my daughter Hannah Franklin the sume of one hundred pounds of lawfull English money to paid

---

[54] Will of Thomas Franklin, Northamptonshire Archives, Franklin family c.1514–c1790 Biographical Notes.

her by my said sonne Thomas wthin one yeare next after my decease Also I give & bequeath unto my sonne Josia Franklin the sume of Twenty pounds to be paid him by my said sonne Thomas wthin six months next after my decease And for the [xx]ne paymt of all & every the said bequeaths & legacyes before given & bequeathed unto my said Sonnes John Joseph Benjamine & Josia & my said daughter Hannah [?]^I^ Charge my said two yard lands in Ecton soe given & devised unto my said xx sonne Thomas as aforesaid And my will & meaning further is & I doe herby declare, that if it shall happen, the said John Joseph Benjamine Hannah & Josia or either or any of them shall dye & depart this life before his her or their porton or legacy herein before given & bequeathed shal be come & payable that then the porton or legacy of him her ^or^ them soe dyeing as aforesaid shall be equally devided amongst the survivors of them share & share alike Alsoe I give & bequeath unto my Grandson Samuel Franklin my sonne Josia's sonne the sume of Five pounds to be paid him by my said sonne Thomas when he shall attaine the age of one & twenty yeares & in the meane time to pay him the said Josia interest for the same for the use of the said Samuel after the wale of six pounds pcent. And for the said paymt thereof I charge my said two yard lands And my will & meaning further is & I doe

    Tho Franklin

[page 2]

hereby declare That if in case my said Grandson Samuel shall dye & depart this life before his said legacy shalbe come due & payable, That then my will & meaning is & I doe hereby give & bequeath the same unto my said sonne Josia & for the said paymt thereof I also charge my said two yard lands Also I give & bequeath unto my Grandaughter Mary Franklin my sonne Thomas Franklin's daughter the sume of Tenn pounds Also I give & bequeath unto my said daughter Hannah & Thomas Franklin all my household goods of what nature or kind soever the same and equally to be divided ^betweene^ & amongst them share & shall share like Alsoe [long string of illegible crossed out text] I give & bequeath unto the poore of Ecton aforesaid for the time being the sume of twenty five shillings yearely to be paid for twenty yeares next my decease to the Overseers of Ecton aforesaid for the time being yearly upon the fifth day of November they giving acquittainces unto my said sonne Thomas for the receipt of the same & for the true payment thereof yearely as aforesaid I charge my said two yard lands Also all the rest & residue of my goods chattels & personall estate whatsoever & not herein before given & bequeathed, by debts legacys & funerall expenses being first discharged I give & bequeathe unto my said Sonne Thomas whome I make sole Executor of this my last my last Will & Testament desiering [xxxx] as my trust in [xxxxxx] & to see the same duly & truely performed And I doe herby revoke all former wills by me att any time heretofore made. In witness whereof to this my last will and testament contayned in two sheets of paper to the first of them I sett my hand & to this last my hand & seale the dayes ^&^ yeares first above written. :/:

Signed sealed & published, but their words nevertheless subiect to the paymt chargable wth such legacyes as hereafter I shall charge the same same, were first outelyned in the pdect
Tho: Mettcalfe
Tho: Mohollsey
Abraham Clarke
        His mke
Will Adams

Tho Franklin
Tho Franklin
[signed twice]

The prenuptual feoffment in trust for the marriage of Thomas Franklin and Jane White contains critical information for understanding the family. First is the date of the contract, 3 November 1635. The marriage, which was impending, likely took place not long after the contract was made. There is no record of the marriage at Ecton or Grendon, but the agreement states that Jane was living at Harbury, Warwickshire, at the time of the marriage. Unfortunately, there are no extant marriage records there for 1631 to 1652. This is exactly when Thomas and Jane were married, and the likely reason why no record of the marriage has ever been found.

The agreement also makes clear that Jane's father was George White of Grendon. (See "Jane[A] White, wife of Thomas Franklin" (page 173) for further discussion of Jane's ancestry.) Benjamin Franklin the Elder wrote of his mother:

> His Wife Jane (my Mother whose name as much as his) I shall ever love and Honr, was a tall fair comly person Exact in her morals, and as she was Religiously Educated & also Religiously Inclin'd and kept up a Thursday meeting of her godly woman Neighbours, In which they spent in prayer, conference, and repletion of the forebgoing Lords day serm, and singing, about 2 hours time which things I being a child an admited into their company, had the greater opportunity to know. Two things with relation to this I yet remember, her singing the 4 psalm in the old metre for we then know no other, and her speaking with a great deale of pleasure and pressing with a great deal of Earnestness the meditation of the 3 last verses of the 3 chap. of Malachy upon them that were p'sent. And I remeber once she severly chid me for my Backwardness in learning the Lords prayer, and sd If I went to Hell I should there remember that she had warn'd me of my danger and told and Instructed me in my duty. [55]

Thomas and Jane had five children baptised at Ecton: Thomas in 1637, Samuel in 1641, Benjamin in 1650, Hannah in 1654, and Josiah in 1657. Benjamin Franklin the Elder wrote that in addition to the children who lived, his parents

> had two sons more, Twins, born before benjam— but tis tho't they dyed unbaptized because their names are not found in the church Register at Ecton where we were all born & brought up.[56]

This trend comes from Jane White's family. At least three couples in her family had twins. Her grandparents, Nicholas[C] and Joanne—?—, had twins Margery and Joanne. Her cousin Elizabeth (White) Hutton had twins Thomas and Jane. And her cousin Jane (White) Houghton had twins Thomas and Paul.

---

[55] Franklin, "Short Account" 3–4 [see Appendix B].
[56] Franklin, "Short Account" 2 [see Appendix B].

Besides the twins, no baptismal record could be found in Northamptonshire for either John, born in 1643, or Joseph, born in 1646. Six of Thomas and Jane's children who lived to adulthood married and had children of their own. None of them, however, were married at Ecton. Benjamin the Elder wrote that

> She had a Long time of Languishing I think I have heard my father say nere seven years undr. that flattering Lingering distemper, a consumtion, which with other Afflictions she bore with much christian patience and resignation, she dyed and was buried in Ecton church-yard on the North-east side, about 4° November 1662 or 3.[57]

Jane was 45 years old when she died after a long battle with consumption and was buried in the churchyard at Ecton St. Mary Magdelene 30 October 1662. Three of her children predeceased her. Her six surviving children ranged in age from 5 to 25.

Thomas^A Franklin made certain that each of his younger sons was apprenticed in a trade, setting them up as well as he could. Son Samuel died before he could finish. But John, Benjamin, and Josiah were all apprenticed to members of the Worshipful Company of Dyers in London. Joseph was apprenticed to Joseph Titcomb of the Armourers Guild to become a joiner.[58] His eldest son Thomas "about the year 1665 persuaded my father to let his land and leave off Husbandry which in a year or two after he did, and his own trade alsoe, and boarded with him for a while but his Temper being passionate did not suite wth my fathers so he went to banbury" where his sons John and Josiah would later join him.[59] Benjamin the Elder reports that his father's death "fell out on the 21 of March 1681[/2]."[60] Parish registers show "Mr. Franklin buried the 24" of March 1681/2 in the Banbury churchyard.[61]

---

[57] Franklin, "Short Account" 3–4 [see Appendix B].

[58] Bunker, *Young Benjamin Franklin*, 27–29, 386 (note 1) [see note 25].

[59] Franklin, "Short Account" 4 [see Appendix B].

[60] Franklin, "Short Account" 3 [see Appendix B].

[61] Church of England, Banbury St. Mary, Oxfordshire, Parish Registers, 1580–1708. Oxfordshire History Centre PAR21/1/R1/2. "Oxfordshire, England, Church of England Baptism, Marriages, and Burials, 1538-1812" database

A Thomas Franklin Mystery

Josiah Franklin's first wife was Anne Child, daughter of Robert and Debora (—?—) Child of Ecton (for a more complete discussion of this family, see "Anne[1] Child, wife of Josiah[1] Franklin" starting on p. 153). Researching the Child family reveals a Thomas Franklin mystery.

Robert Child's sister Anne died unmarried in 1631. The was buried at Ecton 11 October 1631. Her will was dated 9 October and was probated on 22 October. The inventory is dated 14 October, showing that the two documents were created only a few days apart.[62] A Thomas Franklin witnessed her will and another was one of the men who took the inventory. The signatures do not match, and were undoubtedly written by two different men.

It is very clear that every letter in the name Thomas was written differently. The capital "T" hooks in opposite directions, the letter "h" is styled completely differently, the letter "o" hooks down lower in the will, the letter "m" tails higher in the will, the letter "a" has a sharp upward hook in the will but not in the inventory, the letter "s" is styled completely differently.

Thomas[A] Franklin gave bond to Nathaniel Brimley (called Bromley in George White's will) and Robert Wellford on 3 November 1635 at his marriage to Jane White, just a few years after Anne's death. Although not identical, there are many similarities to the man who conducted the inventory. The T is very similar, as is the double-f in Franklin. Unfortunately, Thomas[A] used the abbreviated form Tho. when signing the bond, so we cannot compare the lowercase "s." It is, however, significantly different from the man who witnessed the will.

The big question is "To whom does the other signature belong?" While Anne's will was written in a single hand, it was not her own. She signed the will with her mark, indicating that she

---

online at www.ancestry.com. (Lehi, UT, USA: Ancestry.com Operations, Inc., 2016). Unpaginated, records in chronological order.

[62] Church of England, Archdeaconry Court of Northampton Wills and Administrations, Series 2, K:14–15, Will and Inventory of Anne Childe of Ecton, 1631 [FHL #187,605; DGS #8,047,430].

could not even write her name and therefore it is reasonable to say that she could not have written it herself. Of the three witnesses, John Hensman appears with Thomas Franklin on both documents. His signatures, however, match each other. The signatures on both documents (as well as the marks of Anne Child and Nathan Prisse) appear to be original and not copies made by a clerk.

There is no evidence of any other men named Thomas Franklin at Ecton around 1631. Indeed, there are few Franklins in Ecton at all during this time. Thomas^A was still a few years from marrying Jane White. His father, Henry^B and Agnes (Jones) Franklin are still there, although Henry^B died just days after Anne Child. Henry had no siblings named Thomas. Henry's brother John, however, in his 1637 will names his son Thomas. Perhaps Henry's nephew had followed him to Ecton from Desborough for awhile, and was there to witness the will.

Another possibility is that this mystery Thomas is related to Nicholas Franklin, the only documented Franklin in Ecton who is not related to Josiah. He may also be a random man who tarried in the village for a time. But the signatures on the will of Thomas^A and on Anne's inventory would indicate that he was acquainted with the Child family, which no doubt contributed to the marriage of his son to Anne Child.

THOMAS^A FRANKLIN'S SECOND WIFE

Many individuals have ascribed a second wife, Elizabeth, to Thomas. Benjamin Franklin, himself, seems to have believed this. In a letter to his cousin Mary (Franklin) Fisher in 1758 he wrote:

> His first Wife and Mother of his Children, was named Jane; she was buried at Ecton Oct. 30. 1662. but I think he married again, for I find in the Register a Widow Elizabeth Franklin, who was buried at Ecton Sept. 1. 1696. aged 79. Perhaps she return'd to Ecton after his Death. I do not remember ever to [have] heard of her, but suppose my Father nam'd his first Child, after her, Elizabeth, who is yet living; she was born Mar. 10. 1677. If this

Widow Elizabeth was our Grandfathers second Wife, you probably may remember her.[63]

This conjecture was based on the burial record. Thomas mentions no wife in his will. And Benjamin the Elder, in his "Short Account," mentions no second wife for his father. The will of the mysterious Nicholas Franklin provides the solution to this problem.

---

[63] "From Benjamin Franklin to Mary Fisher, 31 July 1758," Founders Online, National Archives, accessed September 29, 2019, https://founders.archives.gov/documents/Franklin/01-08-02-0027. [Original source: *The Papers of Benjamin Franklin*, vol. 8, April 1, 1758, through December 31, 1759, ed. Leonard W. Labaree. New Haven and London: Yale University Press, 1965, pp. 117–119.]

CHAPTER 8

THE EXCEPTION: NICHOLAS FRANKLIN OF ECTON

There is often a presumption that if there are a limited number of individuals in a parish of a particular surname, they should
be related. While this is often true, it is not always true. That is the
case here in Ecton, something that has eluded many individuals
before. There are four parish records at Ecton for whom there is
no ready connection to Benjamin Franklin's family:[64]

Marriage
Nicholas Franklyn and Awdrey Bett were marryed the fourth day of
February [1630]

Burials
1663 Febr.3. Awdrey wife of Nicolas Franklin

1674. Aug·16. Nicolas Franklin yeoman aged about 80.

[1696] Sept: 1st. Elizabeth Franklyn Widow. aged 79
        Affid. before Mr. Lettice Rd 7th

The first three records are very clearly linked as Nicholas and
his wife. There are no other marriage records at Ecton, nor can
any baptismal record there for either of them there or in indexes
to the other parishes of Northamptonshire. There are no baptismal records for any children of the couple either.

The third record, for the burial of the widow Elizabeth Franklin has often been misinterpreted. This includes Benjamin Franklin

---

[64] Church of England Parish Register, Ecton St. Mary Magdelene, North-
amptonshire, 1559–1637; Northamptonshire Record Office 114P/202 [FHL
Fiche #6,127,381]. Baptisms and Burials 1638–1754, Marriages 1638–1753.
Northamptonshire Record Office 114P/203 [FHL Fiche #6,127,382; DGS
#100,430,949] 1653–1658. Northamptonshire Record Office 114P/204 [FHL
Fiche #6,127,383; DGS #100,430,966] Books are unpaginated; records are in
chronological order, grouped by record type.

and other family mermbers who ascribed this individual to being a second wife of Thomas[A] Franklin. Nicholas left a will that is extremely informative, and helps to clarify all the relationships, and confirms that Nicholas had no surviving children:

Will of Nicholas Franklin of Ecton, probated 22 August 1674[65]

> In the name of god amen This Twelfth day of August Anno Dmi 1671 and in the six and Twentyeth yeare of the Raigne of o[r] sovaigne Lord Charles the second by the grace of King of England and Scotland offraine of Ireland defend[e] of the faith I Nicholas Franklin of Ecton in the County of Northton yeoman being sick in body but of compeleat understanding and memory doe make this my last will and testam[t] in maner following First I comit my soule into the hands of Almighty God my maker and redeemer and my bodiy I comit to the Earth to be buryed in decent and Christianlike manet at the discression of my Executrix hereafter named Also I give unto my Cozen Robert Wiseman of Buckingham the sume of Twenty pounds twelve months after my decease Also I give to Humphry Pratt of Ecton my best suite of Cloathes, And my next suite I give to Robert Allen of Moulton And to Thomas Martin of Ecton my old Coate Alsoe I give unto my Godson Thomas son of the said humphry Pratt Five Shillings To my Godson Nicholas Allen Five Shillings. And to the rest of my Godchildren hereafter named vizt Richard Malerd of Ecton, Anne now wife of David Palmer of Earles Barton, Elizabeth Daughter of John Housman of Ecton, and William sonne of William Barker of Ecton, I give Twelve pound a peace Twelve Monthes after my decease Also I give to Anne Brire of Hasham Twenty Shillings Twelve monthes after me decease Also after the decease of my wife =2=2 I give my Cupboard in the Hall to Elizabeth daughter of

---

[65] Church of England, Archdeaconry Court of Northampton. Register Copy Wills, Series 3, L:20, Will of Nicholas Franklin of Ecton, 1674 [FHL #187,626; 8,047,413].

George Bett of Ecton. Also I give to the nine Children of George Bett of Ecton Tenne Shillings To be paid Twelve monthes after my decease Also I give to the Foure Children of Pearsy Eagleston of Lamport Two Shillings and six pence when they shall come to their respective age of one and Twenty years. Also I doe desire John Morris late of Billingand Thomas Franklin the Young[E] of Ecton aforesaid that they will be overseers of the performance of this my last will and Testament, To whom I give Twenty Shillings apeace yet my mind and will is that if more debts shall be charged upon my Execute[r] then I now thinke of or by casually mistake or otherwise howsoed my money goods and chattels (houshold goods Excepted) shall fall short of Raising money to pay my debts legatyes and funeral expenses That then soe much as they shall fall short shall be deducted and abated out of the legacyes aforesaid And I doe hereby make my wife sole Executrix of this my last will and Testam[t] And if any doubt question or Controversy shall happen to arise between my Executrix legataryes of any of them Touhing my Intent in any Clause or sentence herein contained shall be Judged and finally determined by my said ovrseers or such umpire as they =2= or the survivo[r] of them shall shoose. In Witnesse whereof I the said Nicholas Franklin have hereunto put my hand and seale the day and yeare first above written.

Nicholas Franklin
His X Mark

Signed sealed and declared to be the last will
of the testato[r] in the presence of
Jonathan Langdall
Richard Housman
his X mark

It was probated 22 August 1674 by Elizabeth Franklin, the "relict and executrix" of Nicholas. This solves, once and for all, the longstanding mystery of the widow who was buried at Ecton in 1674. She was not married to Thomas, but to Nicholas.

Although Nicholas choose Josiah's brother Thomas to be an overseer, he does not name a familial relationship. Thomas was well-known in the community and it would not be unusual for him to be selected as an overseer for someone who had no relations in the village. The other overseer was "John Morris late of Billing." While Thomas's younger sister Hannah married a John Morris at Great Billing, that marriage did not take place for another decade, so even if this is the same John Morris, he was not related to the Franklin family at the time.

Despite his presence at Ecton, there is no reason to believe that Nicholas has any relationship to Benjamin Franklin's family. Ecton lies only four miles from the county border with Buckinghamshire, and about twenty miles from the town of Buckingham. The fact that Nicholas has a cousin Robert Wiseman living there raises the possibility that he may have originated there himself.

CHAPTER 9
JOSIAH[1] FRANKLIN AND HIS SIBLINGS

Of the Thomas[A] and Jane (White) Franklin's children, only Benjamin Franklin the Elder and his brother Josiah immigrated to America. The rest of the siblings died in England. Benjamin the Elder's "Short Account," written decades before his namesake nephew became wealthy and successful, provides details we wouldn't ordinarily know about the family.

There are no baptimal records for four of the siblings: John, Joseph, and the twins who did not live long. This is not surprising. There is a gap for baptismal records at Ecton. There are no baptisms for 1643, only a single baptism for 1644, and two baptisms in 1646. This is not unusual, for the births fell during the Civil War. Northampton was a focal point of Puritanism at the time, and many of the lords were opposed to King Charles. The Catesby family owned the manor of Ecton at the time, allowing them to select the leader of the chuch. In 1641 they appointed John Palmer (who married Bridget Catesby) as rector of the parish. He followed the Presbyterian form of Puritanism, which the Franklins agreed with. He was also quite involved in science as well. Blacksmith Thomas Franklin was very helpful to him with the tools that he needed for his work.[66] This is quite likely the reason for the missing records. Rectors often had to hide their registers during the conflict. And Palmer may have avoided recording activities during this time when King Charles was actively opposed to the Puritan revolution.

In a 1759 letter to her cousin Benjamin Franklin, Anne (Franklin) Farrow, daughter of John and Anne (Jeffes) Franklin, wrote:

---

[66] Bunker, *Young Benjamin Franklin*, 19–22 [see note 25].

> As to my Fathers been Born at Ecton I always thought he was till
> 2 years ago I was at Wellingbourgh and our Cousin Fisher said
> som'thing of his coming from some other Town to Live at Ecton
> and Named the Place but I quit forgot for my Memory has failed
> me some years but my Eye Sight is good.[67]

Mary (Franklin) Fisher, daughter of the eldest son, was twelve years older than John Franklin's daughter. She told Anne that her father was born somewhere other than Ecton. Given the mobility of his father Henry, it is certainly possible that Thomas[A] Franklin left Ecton for a time before returning. This could also be the reason for the missing baptismal records for Joseph and the twins. There is not enough evidence, however, for us to conclusively say which of these two circumstances is the true explanation.

THOMAS FRANKLIN

Thomas, born at Ecton 9 March 1637, was the eldest of the siblings.[68] He was baptised there two day later.[69] He was very well-known and a successful man in Ecton. Of him, Benjamin the Elder wrote:

> Thomas about the year 1665 persuaded my father to let his land
> and leave off husbandry which in a year or two after he did, and
> his own trade alsoe, and boarded with him for a while but —
> his temper being passionate did not sute wth my fathers and so
> he went to banbury. after and for some time before bro. Tho.
> kept a school and sold tobacco, but when his business of writ-

---

[67] "To Benjamin Franklin from Anne Farrow, 19 January 1759," Founders Online, National Archives, accessed September 29, 2019, https://founders.archives.gov/documents/ Franklin/01-08-02-0068. [Original source: *The Papers of Benjamin Franklin*, vol. 8, April 1, 1758, through December 31, 1759, ed. Leonard W. Labaree. New Haven and London: Yale University Press, 1965, pp. 237–239.]

[68] Franklin, "Short Account" 2 [see Appendix B].

[69] All references in this section to baptisms, marriages, and burials for Ecton from Church of England, Ecton St. Mary Magdelene, Northamptonshire, Parish Register, 1559–1637; Northamptonshire Record Office 114P/202 [FHL Fiche #6,127,381]. Baptisms and Burials 1638–1754, Marriages 1638–1753, Northamptonshire Record Office 114P/203 [FHL Fiche #6,127,382; DGS #100,430,949]; 1653–1658; Northamptonshire Record Office 114P/204 [FHL Fiche #6,127,383; DGS #100,430,966] Books are unpaginated; records are in chronological order.

ing Bills, and bonds and Deeds &c was Increased he left off his schoole to Samuel Roberts his Neighbour. and so his business still Increasing he at length be–came a Noted scrivener, and having the advantage of the Arch Deacon and Esqʳs Catesby two rich mens purses at comand he raised an Estate of about two Thousand pounds. He had by Elenor his wife one Daughter only, her name is Mary, she was married to Mʳ Richard Fisher of Welingborough in Northamptonshire who has sould all she had at Ecton, that was left by her father and mother. Thomas dyed at Ecton ^in com[m]ission for receiving the land tax for the King in that country.^ on 6 Janʳ. 1702. and his widdow dyed there about 10 years afterward. He was a black thin man of very mean appearance, but of great understanding and quick appʳhension, very passionate, soon reconciled, & Just in his dealings, Highly for the church of Eng. yet wanted a cordial love for its Ministers and toward his end had almost turn'd dissenter.[70]

No marriage record has been found for Thomas and his wife. She is referred to as both Helen and Eleanor in various records. There are four records for the family at Ecton two baptisms and two burials:

Baptisms
Thomas the Sonn of Thomas Franklyn and Jane his wife was baptized the xi [11] day of March. [1637]
[1673.] Octob 24 Mary daughter of Thomas Franklin jun. and Helen his wife

Burials
[1702] Jan 7ᵗʰ. Thomas Franklyn Clerk to the comissioners for Taxes. Affid: Before Mr. Walker Rᵈ 13ᵗʰ [buried]
[1711] March 16ᵗʰ. Helen Widow of Thomas Franklyn deceas'd Jan:7ᵗʰ 1702. Affid: before Mr. Whaley. Rᵈ 21th

No record for the marriage of daughter Mary and Richard Fisher of Wellingborough has been found. In his first autobiography, Benjamin² Franklin wrote:

---

[70] Franklin, "Short Account" 4–5 [see Appendix B].

Thomas was bred a smith under his father; but being ingenious, and encouraged in learning (as all my brothers were) by an Esquire Palmer, then the principal gentleman in that parish, he qualified himself for the business of scrivener; became a considerable man in the county; and much taken notice of and patronized by the then Lord Halifax. He died in 1702, January 6, old style, just four years to a day before I was born. The account we received of his life and character from some old people at Ecton, I remember, struck you as something extraordinary, from its similarity to what you knew of mine. "Had he died on the same day," you said, "one might have supposed a transmigration."[71]

When touring his ancestral home in 1758, Benjamin Franklin visited with the Fishers. He wrote to his wife:

at Wellingborough; on inquiry we found still living Mary Fisher, whose maiden name was Franklin, daughter and only child of Thomas Franklin, my father's eldest brother: she is five years older than sister Douse, and remembers her going away with my father and his then wife, and two other children to New England, about the year, 1685. We have had no correspondence with her since my uncle Benjamin's death, now near 30 years. I knew she had lived at Wellingborough, and had married there to one Mr. Richard Fisher, a grazier and tanner, about fifty years ago, but did not expect to see either of them alive, so inquired for their posterity; I was directed to their house and we found them both alive, but weak with age, very glad however to see us; she seems to have been a very smart, sensible woman. They are wealthy, have left off business, and live comfortably. They have had only one child, a daughter, who died, when about thirty years of age, unmarried;[72]

---

[71] *Autobiography of Benjamin Franklin* (New York: John B. Alden, 1892) 7 [see Appendix A].

[72] "From Benjamin Franklin to Deborah Franklin, 6 September 1758," Founders Online, National Archives, accessed September 29, 2019, https://founders.archives.gov/documents/Franklin/01-08-02-0034. [Original source: *The Papers of Benjamin Franklin*, vol. 8, April 1, 1758, through December 31, 1759, ed. Leonard W. Labaree. New Haven and London: Yale University Press, 1965, pp. 133–146.] See also Appendix A.

Franklin was very lucky to have visited when he did in the summer of 1758. On 31 July, he wrote to his cousin Mary telling her more about his trip. On 14 August, she wrote back to him:

> We have received your kind Letter as also your Present of most excellent Madeira, which was the more agreeable to us as Mr. Fisher was seized with an Illness soon after you left these Parts, under which his Physicians have obliged him to drink a greater Quantity of generous Wine than before he was used to. His ail is a Mortification in his Foot, which considering his Age will I fear prove fatal: It has hitherto got the better of all Medicines that have been applied, and we have not wanted for the best Physicians and Surgeons this Country affords.

She added a post script on 18 September:

> This Letter has been wrote above a Month but was neglected to be sent to You on the Account of Mr. Fisher's Illness, who has been so bad that we expected nothing but Death for some Weeks; tho' now have the Pleasure to inform You that his Mortification is entirely stopp'd, and on that Account have Hopes of his Recovery.

This seems to be the last communication between the two. The Fishers died within two weeks of each other that December:[73]

Mr. Richard Fisher 16th [December 1758]
Mrs. Mary Fisher 30th [December 1758]

Richard left a will and there is a bond for administration of Mary's estate, both in 1758.

Will of Richard Fisher, Probated 18 December 1758[74]

---

[73] Church of England, Wellingborough All Hallows, Northamptonshire, Parish Register, Baptisms and Burials 1702–1774, Marriages 1702–1754, Northamptonshire Record Office 350P/647 [FHL Fiche #6,129,278; DGS #100,430,944].

[74] Church of England, Archdeaconry of Northampton Court; Original Wills, Administrations, Inventories, 1758; Will of Richard Fisher of Wellingborough, 1758 [FHL Film #187,746; DGS #8,473,627].

[page 1]

I Richard Fisher of Wellingborough in the County of Northampton Gentleman, Revoking all former Wills by me made, do
for the settling and disposing of all my Worldly Estate which it
hath pleased God to bestow upon me make this my Last Will
and Testament in Manner and Form following Viz^t First I give
and devise all that Land lying dispersedly in the Fields of Wellingborough aforesaid which I lately purchased of M^rs. Mary
Cleaver Widow and which then was and now is in the Tenure
or Occupation of Ephraim Pattison Junr with all the Appurtenances thereto belonging. My House wherein I dwell with the
Yard Orchard Garden Edificies Buidings Barnes Stables Hovels
and Appurtenances belonging thereo, The Yard and Barnes
with all the Appurts which were John Hootons. The five
Sellions of Land on the Backside of my House and Premises
with the Hedges on both Side belonging thereto late Dennets,
And also all that half Yard Land late Dennets which George
Barwick lately rented of Me, and all that half Yard Land late
Halfords (Copyhold) and all that Quartern of a Yard Land
(Copyhold) late Harrises, and all that Quarternof a Yard late
Collis's, and all that Quartern of a Yard Land (Freehold) that
was my Fathers and all that Parcell of Land Freehold late Pea-
cocks with their and every of their Appūrts unto my Nephew
the Reverend M^r. William Fisher Rector of Newton Bromswold
Clerk his Heirs and Assignes for ever. On Condition nevertheless that he the said William Fisher his Heirs and Assignes do
and shall from Time to Time and at all Times from and after
my Decease permit and suffer my dear Wife Mary Fisher pea-
cably and quietly to live and reside in my said Dwelling House
and to have all Manner of Conveniencies and Priviledges in teh
Premises there for her own private Use for and during the
Term of her natural Life both Rent and Tax free vizt. without
her Paying any Rent or Acknowledgment or any Taxes Rates
Levies or Impositions of any Kind that shall be charged set or
imposed upon my s^d House and Premises or any Part therof. All
of which he the said William Fisher his Heirs and Assignes shall
pay bear and defray Secondly I give and devise all my Houses at
the Top of Harriots Lane in Wellingborough afores^d. with the
Yards Buildings Barns Stables Orchards Gardens [cross out]
Premises and Appurtenances whatsoever severally and respec-

tively belonging, My two Houses in the Yard at the South End of the Town of Wellingborough afores^d. late Coxes with a little Close or Price of a Close belonging to them which Houses are now in the several Tenures or Occupations of William Webb and Craddock and are Coppyhold, My two other Houses with the Barns and Appūrts belonging to them at the same End of the Town now in the several Tenures or Occupations of George Harding and John Barker, My Close there which is Freehold and in the Occupation of John Crane All that Parcel of Land Coppyhold late Deaters, and all those five Sellions of Land late Killingworths Unto my Neice Elizabeth the Wife of M^r. James Gibbs and to her Heirs and Assignes for Ever. And Thirdly I give and devise my Copyhold House in the East End Quarter of Wellingborough afores^d. with all the Appūrts now in the Occupation of Bury an Officer in the Excise, All that three Quarters of a Yard Land Freehold late Dennets, all that half Yard Land Freehold late Pinkards, All

[page 2]
that half Yard Land Freehold late Browns unto my Neice Eleanor Fisher Spinster her Heirs and Assignes for ever And for a decent Provision Support and Maintenance for my s^d. Wife I do give and Grant unto her and her Assignes during her Life Three several clear Annuities or Yearly Rent Charges of fifteen Pounds of lawful Money of Great Britain to be Isuing out of the three several Estates respectively by me above given and devised unto my said Nephew Willim Fisher, and my s^d Neices Eliz: Gibbs and Eleanor Fisher, and to be paid by them respectivly that is to say Each of them to pay to my s^d. Wife and her Assignes out of their respective Estates fifteen Pounds Yearly without any Deduction or Abatement whatsoever by two equal half Yearly Payments during her natural Life at the two most usual Times of Payment vizt. The Feasts of the Annunciation of the blessed Virgin Mary and St. Michael the Arch Angel, The first Payment whereof shall become due and be made, at which of the s^d. two Days or Feasts as shall first next happen after my Decease, And for Nonpayment respectively of the said Annuities or Rent Charges as the same shall from Time to Time become due it shall and may be lawful to and for my s^d. Annuities or Rent Charges in such Manner as the Law directs. And I give and bequeath the Use of all and Singular my Goods and Furni-

ture of my said dwelling House unto my said Wife for her Life And my Will is that no Inventory or Account shall be had taken or made thereof until after her Decease. And after her Decease I give my said Household Goods unto my three Neices Mary Fisher Elizabeth Gibbs and Eleanor Fisher to be equally divided between them Share and Share alike. And I moreover Give and bequeath unto my said Wife the Sum of One Hundred Pounds to be paid to be paid to her by my Executor within three Kalendar Months next after my Decease. And Lastly, all the Rest and Residue of my Goods Chattells and Personal Estate of what Nature or Kind soever after Payment of my just Debts Legacies and Funerl Expences I give and bequeath unto my said three Neices Mary Fisher Elizabeth Gibbs and Elanor Fisher to be equally divided among them Share and Share alike. And I do hereby nominate Constitute and appoint my said Nephew William Fisher Clerk the sole Executor of this my Last Will and Testament. In Witness whereof I have hereunto set my Hand and Seal this Seventeenth Day of October in the Year of Our Lord One Thousand Seven Hundred and Fifty Eight.

Signed Sealed Published and Declared
by the s^d. Richard fisher for and as his   Richd Fisher
Last Willand Testam^t. in the Presence
of us who have hereunto subscribed
our Names as Witnesses in the Presene
of the s^d Testator and also in the Presence of each other

Tho: Holms
Thos Maul
Martha Coles

The Rev. William Fisher was baptized at Irchester St. Katharine, Northamptonshire, 16 November 1724, son of William and Elizabeth (—?—) Fisher. Another son, Jeffery, was baptised there 20 June 1723. The only other record for a Fisher at Irchester in this period is the burial for the widow Mary Fisher 25 November 1723.[75] No connection back to Wellingborough and possible parents for Richard has been found.

In the bond, "Ann Farrow of the Parish of Castlethorpe in the County of Bucks Widow and William Fisher Rector of Newton Bromswold in the County of Northampton Clerk and John Doe" gave bond of 200£ to the Lord Bishop of Peterborough on 29 December 1758, the day before she was buried. Ann was next of kin and administrator of Mary's estate. She was ordered to deliver an inventory at or before "the Twenty Eighth Day of December next." Anne and William signed the bond in the presence of Peter Matthews and Thos Holms.[76] No inventory was found. Ann was Mary's cousin, a daughter of John Franklin. In a letter to her cousin Benjamin Franklin, Anne wrote:

> our Cousin Fisher is dead and their is a Small matter to come amongst us First cousins so the[y] fetch me over to Administer being I Lived the nearest but Mr. Fisher. Mr. Fishers Executor Pays all charges for when I come the[y] would have her buried as grand as her Husband. So my Daughter was force to Stay to Look after my School the while. The Sum was a hundred Pound But the Funeral Charges before I came away came to between thirty and forty Pound for Mr. Fisher Paid the Bills for it was not in my Power to do it and I Should be glad to know how many first Cousins thier is. I would have buried her in a Neat Manner but the[y] complled me to Buirey her as her Husband was.[77]

---

[75] John Venn and J. A. Venn, comp. *Alumni Cantabrigienses* (London: Cambridge University Press, 1922) 144. Church of England, Irchester St. Katharine, Northamptonshire, Parish Registers, Baptisms 1673–1740, Marriages 1676–1740, Burials 1675–1740; Northamptonshire Record Office 177P/2 [FHL Fiche #6,127,834; DGS #100,614,771]. Books are unpaginated; records are in chronological order.

[76] Church of England, Archdeaconry of Northampton Court; Original Wills, Administrations, Inventories, 1758; Administrator Bond of Mary Fisher of Wellingborough, 1758 [FHL Film #187,746; DGS #8,473,627].

[77] "To Benjamin Franklin from Anne Farrow, 19 January 1759," Founders Online, National Archives, accessed September 29, 2019, https://founders.archives.gov/documents/Franklin/01-08-02-0068. [Original source: *The Papers of Benjamin Franklin*, vol. 8, April 1, 1758, through December 31, 1759, ed. Leonard W. Labaree. New Haven and London: Yale University Press, 1965, pp. 237–239.]

Benjamin later informed her that he would forego his share and have it distributed to the other cousins.

SAMUEL FRANKLIN

Samuel was the second of Thomas and Jane's children, born at Ecton 5 November 1641.[78] He was baptised there two days later. Of his brother Samuel, Benjamin the Elder wrote:

> Samuel, was put Aprentis to M[r] Wilkinson a silk weaver in maid lane southwark. he dye din the time of his Aprentiship. of a dropsy. He is s[d] to be very Ingenious, the most comly person in the family and religiously Inclin'd. He and John Loved on the other Entirely In So much that when one had done a fault the othe would plead, and procure his pardon before he came in sight. He was burried in st. Mary overy · (alis) st saviours southwark church yeard about the year 1659 or so.[79]

On 24 July 1656, fourteen-year-old Samuel went to the Dyers' Company in London and started his apprenticeship.[80] The parish registers of St. Saviour show that he died a bit earlier than his brother remembered. Samuel's burial at St. Saviours occurred two years later, when he was just sixteen years old:

[1657/8] March 13 Samuel Franklin s. of Thomas a weaver[81]

---

[78] Franklin, "Short Account" 2 [see Appendix B].

[79] Franklin, "Short Account" 5 [see Appendix B].

[80] Bunker, *Young Benjamin Franklin*, 27 [see note 25].

[81] Church of England, Southwark St. Saviour, Surrey, Parish Registers, 1644–1673; London Metropolitan Archives, P92/SAV. Accessed at Ancestry.com. "London, England, Church of England Baptisms, Marriages and Burials, 1538-1812" database on-line. (Provo, UT, USA: Ancestry.com Operations, Inc., 2010). Original data: Church of England Parish Registers, 1538-1812. London, England: London Metropolitan Archives.

JOHN FRANKLIN

The third son of Thomas and Jane was born 20 February 1643.[82] His place of birth is uncertain. There is no baptismal record at Ecton, but there is a gap in the records. His daughter Anne, writing in 1759, said that:

> As to my Fathers been Born at Ecton I always thought he was till 2 years ago I was at Wellingbourgh and our Cousin Fisher said som'thing of his coming from some other Town to Live at Ecton and Named the Place but I quit forgot for my Memory has failed me some years but my Eye Sight is good.[83]

In 1660, like his brother Samuel, John went to the Dyer's Company in London to start his apprenticeship.[84] Benjamin wrote of his brother John:

> John served his time to mᵣ Glover a cloth Dyer at 3 crans in Thames street London. and being Importun'd to set up in the country by mᵣ Warren of Warmington weaver, and not hving his health in the city, he setled at Banbury in Oxfordshire, he lived a batchelor long and wa a sutor to many young women whose love he seldom miss'd of gaining, but then some trifle or other turn'd his affections from them and I tho't he did not fairly leave them. at last he Married Mᵣˢ Ann Jeffs of Marson in warwickshire with whom he had about 250 £ by whom he had severall children whose names follow in order.

Thomas Born on 15 Sept 1683

Hannah	
Ann · ·	They were all born at Banbury
Mary · ·	and when their father and
Jane · ·	mother dyed they became the
Elenor ·	care of my bro. Thomas.

---

[82] Franklin, "Short Account" 2 [see Appendix B].

[83] "To Benjamin Franklin from Anne Farrow, 19 January 1759," Founders Online, National Archives, accessed September 29, 2019, https://founders.archives.gov/documents/Franklin/01-08-02-0068. [Original source: *The Papers of Benjamin Franklin*, vol. 8, April 1, 1758, through December 31, 1759, ed. Leonard W. Labaree. New Haven and London: Yale University Press, 1965, pp. 237–239.]

[84] Bunker, *Young Benjamin Franklin*, 27 [see note 25).

While John lived in the city he was as a father to me and helped me thro' my troubles with my Mr Pratt · to whom I served 5 years of my time. He was of a very pleasant conversation, could sute himselfe to any company, and did when he pleaded Insinuate himself into the good opinion of persons of all Qualities and conditions, in Marrying he missed it as to one maine designe he aymed at, which was the having a Wife that would Assist in his business, but she proved neither capable nor carful in that point and soe B^r Thomases prediction was in a great measure verified, who once in my hearing, reproving him for courting and for such little causes leaving, soe many whose Affections he has gained, Told him that it would return upon him, that he would be not with, and take up with the Worst at last and Indeed soe he did, according to his own consession when he thus Express'd himselfe. If my Wife was but like — other women, If she was but liek my sister Benjamin, (that is to say my wife) I should ever Adore her, but then he checkt himselfe and s^d: but, may be, It is best, it should be [crossout] as it is, for I should a been apt to set her in the first place. He was a dyer, lived in good repute at banbury many years. the cause of his death was a boyle or sweling which came by a hurt which he got in mounting his horse, It being in his privities (and thinking to keep it secret) he ^o^pened it with a Needle beforee it was ripe which caused it to Gangrene up into his body it killed him in 3 dayes time, He dyed I think in June 1689. Much lamented of rich and poor in Banbury in Banbury for he was a peace maker and a frind to the poor. [85]

John had a reputation for sowing his wild oats. He was thirty-eight years old before he finally chose a woman to marry, at Fawsley St. Mary the Virgin, Northamptonshire:

John Francklin & An Jeffes were Married June 23. 1681.[86]

---

[85] Franklin, "Short Account" 5–7 [see Appendix B].

[86] Church of England, Fawsley St. Mary the Virgin, Northamptonshire, Parish Registers, Baptisms 1583–1731, Marriages 1587–1731, Burials 1591–1731, Northamptonshire Record Office 125P/1 [FHL Fiche #6,127,462; DGS #100,624,431].

Fawsley lies about 15 miles northeast of Banbury. No mention is made of either being from another parish, but there is no evidence that either lived there either. John was only known to live at Ecton, London, and Banbury. No other records for individuals named Jeffes could be found in St. Mary the Virgin in this period.

Benjamin the Elder states that she was "of Marson in warwickshire." The village of Marton lies about twenty miles north of Banbury. There are no baptismal records for Anne there, but there is an interesting entry at Banbury. An entry was squeezed in at the end of April 1661 for "Ann Jeffes, daughter of John Jeffes of Grimsbury".[87] It was clearly not recorded at the same time as the others, as it is squeezed into existing space, and the ink is a bit different. The entry was later crossed out. There were other baptisms for individuals named Jeffes a decade earlier, but no others near 1662. Grimsbury was a hamlet in Warkton, Northamptonshire. Today it is now the eastern part of Banbury.

It is possible that the family was mobile and that they resided at Marton about the time of the marriage. Marton lies about 15 miles northwest of Fawsley, which itself is about 15 miles northeast of Banbury.

Based on Benjamin the Elder's description of her, Anne was in some ways a disappointment to John. Benjamin looked on her as the fulfillment of their brother Thomas's warning to John that he would someday regret having turned down so many other women. John hoped to marry a woman who would help him in his business, but Anne was apparently not suited to the work.

By 1692 John had risen in the social ranks of Banbury. He was friendly with the village leaders and clergy. He was also friendly with minister Samuel Welles. John played matchmaker between his brother Benjamin and Samuel's daughter Hannah.[88] He had become a landowner, with a house and a cottage let out to a ten-

---

[87] Church of England, Banbury St. Mary, Oxfordshire, Parish Registers, 1580–1708. Oxfordshire History Centre PAR21/1/R1/2. "Oxfordshire, England, Church of England Baptism, Marriages, and Burials, 1538-1812" database online at www.ancestry.com. (Lehi, UT, USA: Ancestry.com Operations, Inc., 2016). Unpaginated, records in chronological order.

[88] Bunker, *Young Benjamin Franklin*, 41–42 [see note 25].

ant in addition to the tools of his trade. In September 1690 he was appointed a constable.

There is conflicting information about the exact date of John Franklin's death. Shortly after Benjamin Franklin finished his tour of the midlands with his son William in 1758, he wrote a letter to his cousin Mary (Franklin) Fisher, wrote that he had visited Banbury and:

> In the Church Yard we found a Gravestone expressing that Thomas Franklin was buried there March 24. 1681/2, and also John the Son of the said Thomas Franklin, who died June 11. 1691.[89]

John's brother, Benjamin Franklin the Elder, wrote about the circumstances of his death, saying that:

> the cause of his death was a boyle or sweling which came by a hurt which he got in mounting his horse, It being in his privities (and thinking to keep it secret) he ^o^pened it with a Needle beforee it was ripe which caused it to Gangrene up into his body it killed him in 3 dayes time, He dyed I think in June 1689. Much lamented of rich and poor in Banbury in Banbury for he was a peace maker and a frind to the poor. [90]

Neither of the Benjamins was entirely correct. Examination of John's will, and the Banbury parish registers, show us the truth.

Will of John Franklin, probated 20 May 1692[91]

> In the Name of God Amen I John Franklin of Banbury in the County of Oxon Dyer being weake of body but of perfect mind

---

[89] "From Benjamin Franklin to Mary Fisher, 31 July 1758," Founders Online, National Archives, accessed September 29, 2019, https://founders.archives.gov/documents/Franklin/01-08-02-0027. [Original source: *The Papers of Benjamin Franklin*, vol. 8, April 1, 1758, through December 31, 1759, ed. Leonard W. Labaree. New Haven and London: Yale University Press, 1965, pp. 117–119.]

[90] Franklin, "Short Account" 5–7 [see Appendix B].

[91] Church of England. Peculiar Court, Banbury, Oxfordshire, Original Wills, Administration Bonds, and Inventories, (surname E) 1557–1675 and (surname F) 1683–1799. Will and Administration of John Franklin, 1692 [FHL #173,596; DGS #8,472,405].

and memory praysed be God for the same and Considering the
uncertainty of this life doe make and constitute this my last will
and testament in manner following First and principally I
Commend my soule unto God my Creator trusting through the
uneik passion and death of my redeemer Jesus Christ to have
Free pardon of all my sins and to inheritt Eternall life and my
body to the earth to be decently buryed by my executrix herein-
after named and as touching such worldly Estate as the Lord in
mercy hath sent me y dispose thereof as followeth Item I give
devise and bequeath unto my son Thomas Franklin All that my
now dwelling house in Banbury together with all outhouses Ed-
ifices buildings bowries stables gardens orchards bastfields and
appurtenances there unto belonging unto him and his heirs forever imediately after the decease of my loving wife Anne Franklin And alsoe my will is that my debts and funeral charges being
paid and discharged that all my persoinal estate of goods and
chattells household stuff debts bills bonds and all other utensills
belonging to my trade shall be equally shared among my four
daughters Hannah Anne Mary and Jane Franklin when they
shall attaine to the age of one and twenty years or day of marriage which shall first happen and if it happen that either or any
of them dye all my Estate as aforesaid to be divided equally
amongst the survivor or survivors of them And further my will
is that my said daughters continuing under my wife Anne
Franklin her care and tuition shee my said wife shall have the is-
sues and proffitts of all my Estate and goods for and towards
the maintenance and breeding up of my four daughters And
whereas my said wife Anne Franklin is great with child and if
shee be delivered of a living child my will is that that child alsoe
shall have an equall share with the rest of my said foure daughters And alsoe I give the Lease of my house or tenemᵗs in Sugar
Bow Street unto my Executrix herein named in trust either to
sett or to sell as to her shall be thought most needfull and convenient and the moneys soe raysed thereby to be disposed as
aforesaid And if it shall happen that my said wife Anne Franklin
shall mairy my will is that my said wife Anne Franklin shall give
good and sufficient senuity for the several shares for the use
and benefitt of my four daughters unto my brother Thomas
Franklin Mʳ: Nathaniell Wheatly and Mʳ Joseph Hams or to the
survivior or survivors of them whome I appoint overseers of this
my last will and testamᵗ: for all the closse and estate then in her

hands intreating them to be ayding and assisting unto my said wife Anne in gathering in all my debts due to me And my will is that if my said wife Anne Franklin depart this left that then my sonne Thomas Franklin shall be under the Guardianship of his uncle Thomas Franklin And I Doe make and ordaine my said loving wife Anne Franklin sole Executrix of this my last will and testament in witnesse whereof I have herunto sett my hand and seale this sixth day of June in the year of our Lord one thousand six hundred ninety and one Anno Dom[ini] 1691

In the presence of the testator
sealed signed published
and declared in the presence
of us   John Franklin
Edw Thomp:
the marke of
Abraham Clarke
Jacob Gascoigne

John Franklin by his last will dated June 26 [*sic*] 1691 devised all his psonall estate debts and utensills of his trade after his debts p[ai]d to his 5 young[r] children, — And made Anne his then wife Executrix of the sd will, — Anne Takes upon the the Executrix of the sd will, Receives [x]eid all of the dects debts & payes [illegible] owing by him —

July 25[th] 1694 th[e] sd Anne th Exec[er] Maryes one Moulder, who now Ab[xxx]ds

May   1696 The said Anne the Executries dyed leaving 6 children. by the said Jō Franklin decd: but [illegible] by Moulder, the oldes being a sonne is heire in [illegible] by virture of his mothers Joynture of a house in Banbury and is of the age of 14 or threabouts and Tho Franklin [illegible] huole is by his fathers will appoynted his guardian —

Now there remains about 50£ of the debts of the said John Franklin on Bond unp[ai]d, and its said there may be some small debts of his ~~of p~~ on psonall contracts — And a great p[c] of the goods and Chattells of the s^d John Franklin and are now remaining the pperty [xxxx]erd

And Thomas Franklin of Ecton in the County of North[hamp]ton ~~the [xxx]~~ ^Eldest^ Br of the s[ai]d John Franklin and Guardian to the said Infants who also hath taken care to pvide ^for^ the said ~~younge~~ young^r Children desire that he may either in his own Right or the Right of the s^d 5 young^r children have [x]d[xxx]dron de bonis non. If the psonall Estate of the s^d Jō F dcn^t the prperty whereof is not altered to be granted to him

of the 5 ~~younger~~ young^r Children the Eldest is sd to be about 12 years old, and the youngest about 5.
If Administracōn may not be granted to the sd Tho Franklin and if the principall Credit^r may not take it[92]

John wote his will 6 June 1691. Banbury parish registers show "John Franklin Dyer buryed th^e 9" June 1691.[93] The dates of the will and burial agree with Benjamin the Elder's statement that John died in three days' time. But the year was two years off. When their nephew Benjamin stated that the gravestone shows a death date of 11 June 1691, the year is correct, but the day is off. He reported that the date came from John's gravestone. Either his notes were wrong, or the stone was carved incorrectly. The stone is no longer extant, so it is impossible to determine which is the correct situation.

John's will was not probated until almost a year later, in May 1692. There are additional papers in the handling of his estate filed 2 October 1696 with the will. According to these papers, Anne Jeffes married second to a man named Moulder 24 July 1694.

---

[92] Church of England. Peculiar Court, Banbury, Oxfordshire, Original Wills, Administration Bonds, and Inventories, (surname E) 1557–1675 and (surname F) 1683–1799. Will and Administration of John Franklin, 1692 [FHL #173,596; DGS #8,472,405].

[93] Church of England, Banbury St. Mary, Oxfordshire, Parish Registers, 1580–1708. Oxfordshire History Centre PAR21/1/R1/2. "Oxfordshire, England, Church of England Baptism, Marriages, and Burials, 1538-1812" database online at www.ancestry.com. (Lehi, UT, USA: Ancestry.com Operations, Inc., 2016). Unpaginated, records in chronological order.

There is no record of the marriage at Banbury, and the exact location has not been found. She died about May 1696. A statement is made about whether she had children with Moulder, but it is unfortunately illegible. There are no baptisms at Banbury for any such children.

Thomas Franklin was awarded administration of the estate after Anne's death and guardianship of the children. His brother-in-law John Morris was one of the men who provided bond for the proper administration of the estate. Rector Thomas Franklin and Thomas Sheppard were witnesses to the signatures.

As Nick Bunker points out, at the time of his death, John was set set for a political career in Banbury if he wanted one. But the question is whether it was something he wanted. It appears, however, that he didn't want it. His daughter Anne, writing to her uncle Benjamin in 1759 stated that "He died of a Mortification of else if he had Lived he Designed going into New England."[94]

Despite his success, John apparently wanted to leave Banbury and England. His brother Josiah had been in Boston for eight years by the time of John's death. He had found success as a tallow chandler, and was well-respected in the community. Although his first wife and two of their children had died, he was happily remarried and raising his six surviving children. It is not surprising, then, that John desired to join him there with his own wife and five (soon to be six) children.

Benjamin the Elder wrote that John's son Thomas was born 15 September 1683.[95] There is no baptism for him at Banbury, but there are baptisms for the next three children:

Hannah Franklin Daughter of John Franklin bapt the—26 [November 1683]
Anna Franklin, daughter of John: Franklin bapt the 3 [February 1684/5]

---

[94] "To Benjamin Franklin from Anne Farrow, 8 January 1759," Founders Online, National Archives, accessed September 29, 2019, https://founders.archives.gov/ documents/Franklin/01-08-02-0063. [Original source: *The Papers of Benjamin Franklin*, vol. 8, April 1, 1758, through December 31, 1759, ed. Leonard W. Labaree. New Haven and London: Yale University Press, 1965, pp. 223–224.]

[95] Franklin, "Short Account" 5–7 [see Appendix B].

Mary Franklin the Daughter of John Franklin bapt the 3 [April 1687][96]

The birth date Benjamin gives for Thomas is contradicted by the baptismal date for Hannah. This is clarified by the administration papers, which indicate that Thomas was 14 years old "or thereabouts" in May 1696. If Benjamin was correct about the day, Thomas was born 15 September 1681. This would have made Anne six months pregnant at the time of the marriage. It is also possible that Thomas was born 15 September 1682, which would make him just shy of his fourteenth birthday, fitting the phrase "or thereabouts" in the administration papers.

There is no baptismal record for daughter Eleanor at Banbury, and she is not named in the will. Anne was "great with child" when John died. This was likely Eleanor, who would have been born not long after her father's death. This would fit the administration papers which stated that in May 1696 the eldest of the younger children (Hannah, baptised in November 1683) was about twelve years old and the youngest (Eleanor, born in the summer of 1691 after John's death in June) about 5. Benjamin the Elder wrote about his nieces and nephew in 1717:

His son Thomas is a dyer, lives at Lutterworth in Leicester-shire, Hanª. and Mary are at London, in service there, the other three are Lacemakers and live, Ann at Hartwell with a ginger-bread baker, Jane with David blunt at Ashton, and Nelly at Mr. Davis's a famer at Warden, Hannah lived at Mr Keat a banker's near Hungerford market in the strand, Westminster, at the unicorn. Tho. is married and has one son, the 3 tones above named I take to be in Northampton-shire.[97]

At the time Benjamin was writing, Thomas was 35, Hannah 34, Anne 33, Mary 30, Jane 28, and Eleanor "Nelly" 26. Thomas is

---

[96] Church of England, Banbury St. Mary, Oxfordshire, Parish Registers, 1580–1708. Oxfordshire History Centre PAR21/1/R1/2. "Oxfordshire, England, Church of England Baptism, Marriages, and Burials, 1538-1812" database online at www.ancestry.com. (Lehi, UT, USA: Ancestry.com Operations, Inc., 2016). Unpaginated, records in chronological order.

[97] Franklin, "Short Account" 5–7 [see Appendix B].

the only one of the children said to be married. Hannah and Mary were in service (i.e., working as servants) in London. Anne, Jane, and Eleanor, were living in towns in Northamptonshire.

Only Thomas, Anne, and Jane are known to have married. "Robert Page and Jane Francklin both of this Town were Marr[d]. wth Banns th[e] 16." April 1727."[98] After touring Northamptonshire and Warwickshire with his son William, Benjamin Franklin wrote to his cousin Mary (Franklin) Fisher that "When we return'd from the North we call'd at Banbury, and there found Robert Page, who had married our Cousin Jane Daughter of John Franklin; she is dead and left no Children."[99] Robert Page, "(Garter Weaver) was Buried th[e]. 16t[h]. Day" of April 1776.[100]

We know that John's son Thomas Franklin had two, and likely three, children, although no record of his marriage or their births has been found. First is a letter written by Josiah Franklin in Boston dated 11 January 1743/4. A letter had been written to him by an English relative, but was lost at Benjamin Franklin's home in Philadelphia before it could be delivered to Josiah. He wrote back to the sender, Captain Benjamin Franklin, a surveyor at Blenheim Palace. Josiah wrote that "by what intelegence I have rec[d] from my son at philadelphia and what intelligence of have had by the a gentlman that comes pretty often to dine[r] hear I and I am pretty much inclined to think that you are my Brothers Grandson that I

---

[98] Church of England, Banbury St. Mary, Oxfordshire, Parish Registers, 1723–1801, p. 180. Oxfordshire History Centre PAR21/1/R1/4. "Oxfordshire, England, Church of England Baptism, Marriages, and Burials, 1538-1812" database online at www.ancestry.com. (Lehi, UT, USA: Ancestry.com Operations, Inc., 2016).

[99] "From Benjamin Franklin to Mary Fisher, 31 July 1758," Founders Online, National Archives, accessed September 29, 2019, https://founders.archives.gov/ documents/Franklin/01-08-02-0027. [Original source: *The Papers of Benjamin Franklin*, vol. 8, April 1, 1758, through December 31, 1759, ed. Leonard W. Labaree. New Haven and London: Yale University Press, 1965, pp. 117–119.]

[100] Church of England, Banbury St. Mary, Oxfordshire, Parish Registers, 1723–1801, p. 272. Oxfordshire History Centre PAR21/1/R1/4. Oxfordshire, England, Church of England Baptism, Marriages, and Burials, 1538-1812" database online at www.ancestry.com. (Lehi, UT, USA: Ancestry.com Operations, Inc., 2016).

Lived with 11 years. . . your Grandfathers name was John and his eldest was Thomas after his grandfather Thomas."[101]

Josiah stated that it was his father's will that his land would go to his male heirs, and that since his brother Thomas had no son that it must have gone to John (the next eldest surviving son), and thus to Benjamin's father Thomas. In reality, the land at Ecton went from the brother Thomas to his daughter Mary, who with her husband Richard Fisher sold it out of the family. Josiah went on to say that "I understand by the gentleman above mentioned that you sold land to the value of 500 £. Sterling, which I suppose is about the valut of what my father was posesed of which became yours by your great grandfathers will." Benjamin likely came into the property that his grandfather John owned by the mill in Banbury which he left to his son Thomas. This would indicate that he was deceased by 1743, and that Benjamin is most likely his eldest son.

Blenheim Palace in Woodstock, Oxfordshire, is one of the largest houses in England. Built between 1705 and 1722, it is the ancestral home of the Churchill-Spencer family, ancestors of Sir Winston Churchill and Lady Diana Spencer, later Princess Diana, wife of Prince Charles. The palace is surrounded by miles of parkland and gardens. As a surveyor, Benjamin may have been working on the gardens at the time. The library at Blenheim has no records of those who worked there at the time. The British Library has materials from Blenheim and the first Duchess of Marlborough in its collections, but none of the material contained any information about Benjamin. The family has a chapel in the palace, but Blenheim itself is extra-parochial. Nothing in the surrounding parishes showed any records of Benjamin Franklin or any potential family members.

---

[101] Josiah Franklin to Maj. Benjamin Franklin, Blenheim, dated 11 January 1743/4. Boston Public Library, Rare Books and Manuscripts, K.10.24. A transcription of the letter appears in George Makepeace Towle "Franklin, The Boston Boy" in Justin Winsor, *The Memorial History of Boston, Including Suffolk County, Massachusetts. 1630–1880* (Boston: James R. Osgood and Company, 1881), 269–296 (transcribed letter appears at 270–1).

The title of captain indicates that Benjamin might have been in the British Army at some point. So far there is not enough information to identify Benjamin's connection to the British Army.

The second son, Thomas, was a dyer at Lutterworth, Leicestershire. The younger Thomas corresponded with his father's cousin Benjamin Franklin during his time in London. Lutterworth parish registers show the following records:[102]

Baptisms
John son of thomas franklin Bap June the 12 [1747]
Sarah daughter of thomas franklin Bap June the 5 [1752]

Burials
John the Son of thomas franklin Buried OCT the 7 [1729]
John son of thomas franklin Buried Feb the 4 [1747]
Sarah the wife of tho franklin April the 20 [1748]
John Son of thomas franklin Bur Apr the 25 [1749]
Ann Daughter of Tho: Franklin buried April the 21 [1758]
Mary Wife of Thos Franklin Buried Augt. 31 [1765]
Thomas Franklin aged 87 years of this Parish was buried Janry 20th 1803 Registered Janry 21st 1803 by me C. Coaton Parish Clerk.

There is no burial record at Lutterworth for John's son Thomas. The *Papers of Benjamin Franklin* states, with no source, that he died around 1752 at Birmingham, Warwickshire.[103] No burial record has so far been found in any of the Birmingham parishes. His branch of the family was not as financially successful, so it is no surprise that no will or administration could be found for him either.

---

[102] Church of England, Lutterworth St. Mary, Leicestershire, Parish Registers, 1635–1736, 1737–17922, and 1793–1812, Record Office for Leicestershire, Leicester, and Rutland, DE2094/1 [FHL DGS # 102,112,506], DE2094/2 [FHL DGS #102,115,006], DE2094/3 [FHL DGS# 102,113,993].

[103] Leonard W. Labaree, ed., and Whitefield J. Bell, Jr., assoc. ed., *The Papers of Benjamin Franklin, Volume I: January 6, 1706 through December 31, 1734* (New Haven: Yale University Press, 1959) li.

Benjamin Franklin died in Philadelphia 17 April 1790. On 6 September 1791 Aulay Macaulay, Anglican curate at Claybrook, Leicestershire, wrote a letter to George Washington:

> I beg leave to appeal to your humanity on behalf of a poor old man in this neighbourhood whose name is Thomas Franklin— and who stands in the relation of first cousin to the late Dr Benjamin Franklin—His Father and Dr F.'s Father were Brothers— He is now in indigent circumstances—and sinking under the pressure of age and infirmities—Dr Franklin once took some notice of him tho' he made no mention of him in his will—At the time that the Doctor first heard of his having so near a relation in Leicestershire—the poor man happened to be imprisoned for debt—but Dr F. released him[104]

It is virtually impossible for this to be Thomas, son of John, as he would have been 100 years old when the letter was written. The author almost certainly missed a generation, and was clearly discussing Thomas' son Thomas. That son was buried at Lutterworth 20 January 1803 at the age of 87, putting his birth around 1715. He would have been 76 years old at the time the letter was written. No other source corroborates the story of Benjamin getting Thomas out of debtor's prison. Macaulay was writing to try to get financial assistance for Thomas, but was unsuccessful.

The John Franklin buried at Lutterworth in 1729 cannot be his son, but is possibly a brother. The younger Thomas was married twice. His first wife, Sarah, was buried in 1748. His second wife, Mary, was buried there in 1765. No record has been found for either wife. The John who was baptized and buried in 1747 is obviously a child of Sarah. The son John buried in 1749 and daughter Ann buried in 1758 could belong to either wife.

Sarah, baptized in 1752 is the only child of the younger Thomas known to have lived to adulthood. After his second wife's death, Thomas brought Sarah to London, where she lived with Benjamin Franklin. In the summer of 1773 Benjamin wrote

---

[104] Mark A. Mastromarino, editor, and Jack D. Warren, Jr., assistant editor, *Papers of George Washington, Presidential Series (24 September 1788–3 March 1797)*, (Charlottesville: University of Virginia Press, 1999), pp. 497–99 (hereafter Mastromarino, *Papers of George Washington*).

to his cousin Samuel back in Boston that "Sally Franklin is lately married to Mr. James Pierce, a substantial young Farmer at Ewell, about 13 Miles from London; a very sober industrious Man, and I think it likely to prove a good Match, as she is likewise an industrious good Girl."[105] They were married in the parish of Ewell, Surrey:

> James Pearce of this Parish Bachelor and Sarah Franklin of the Parish of St. Martin in the Fields London were married in this Parish by Banns this seventeenth Day of April in the year One Thousand seven Hundred and seventy three by me Charles Burch Curate. In the presence of B. Franklin Chas Bunny[106]

The record states that James was of the parish, but there is no baptismal record for him there. Sarah's cousin Benjamin Franklin was a witness at the wedding, but the identity of Charles Bunny is unknown. Four baptisms for children of the couple were recorded at Richmond, Surrey:[107]

> Margaret the Daur of James and Sarah Pearce 17 [April 1775]
> Mary the Dagr of James and Sarah Pearce 25 [January 1777]
> Ths. James the son of James and Ann Pearce 10 [November 1778]
> Frances the Daur of James and Sarah Pearce 19 [August 1780]

The record for Thomas James Pearce has a mother's name of Ann instead of Sarah. That is likely an error. This is the only record of James and "Ann" Pearce at Richmond. And Mary Hewson

---

[105] "From Benjamin Franklin to Samuel Franklin, 7 July 1773," Founders Online, National Archives, accessed September 29, 2019, https://founders.archives.gov/documents/Franklin/01-20-02-0154. [Original source: *The Papers of Benjamin Franklin*, vol. 20, January 1 through December 31, 1773, ed. William B. Willcox. New Haven and London: Yale University Press, 1976, pp. 276–277.]

[106] Church of England, Ewell St. Mary the Virgin, Surrey, Parish Registers, 1754–1837, Surrey History Centre 2374/1/b p. 33, no. 132. *Ancestry.com*, "Surrey, England, Church of England Baptisms, Marriages and Burials, 1538-1812" database on-line (Provo, UT, USA: Ancestry.com Operations, Inc., 2013).

[107] Church of England, Richmond St. Mary Magdelene, Surrey, Parish Registers, 1760–1812. Surrey Hisotry Centre P7/1/5. [FHL #991,696, Item 5; DGS #7,907,707].

confirmed that James and Sarah had recently had a son when she wrote to Benjamin Franklin on 30 May 1779 that:

> The Pearces are well, they have now a son to their two daughters. I hope they will thrive, for I believe indeed he is a very industrious good man, and she does as much as she can. Mrs Wilkes has lately taken a house at Richmond for the accommodation of young ladies, and as there was a detached apartment sufficient for Pearce's family and business she offered it to him rent-free, this will be a help to them.[108]

This letter places the birth of James and Sarah's son between early 1778 (a year after the baptism of daughter Mary in January 1777) and May 1779. It continues to locate the Pearces at Richmond. It is almost certain that the mother's name on the baptism of Thomas James Pearce was recorded incorrectly, and that this is the child of James and Sarah (Franklin) Pearce.

The *Papers of Benjamin Franklin* gives a death date for Sarah of 22 October 1781, but no source is given for the information.[109] Reading through the parish registers of Richmond St. Mary Magdalene and Lutterworth for the period 1780 through 1783 shows no burial record for Sarah. Aulay Macaulay wrote about Benjamin Franklin:

> besides other marks of kindness and generosity he took his kinsman's daughter under his protection—and gave her a good education—This young Lady was married by Dr Franklin's consent to a Mr Pearce, who went to America in 1783 (his wife having died a year before) and left his Son—who was then about four years old under the care of his Grandfather Thomas Franklin—He has never heard from the Boy's Father, but once since he left England—The letter was dated Annapolis in Maryland—July 1784—The Boy is still with his Grandfather—He has no other relation or protector in this part of the world—

---

[108] "To Benjamin Franklin from Mary Hewson, 30 May 1779," Founders Online, National Archives, accessed September 29, 2019, https://founders.archives.gov/documents/Franklin/01-29-02-0470. [Original source: *The Papers of Benjamin Franklin*, vol. 29, March 1 through June 30, 1779, ed. Barbara B. Oberg. New Haven and London: Yale University Press, 1992, pp. 578–579.]

[109] Labaree, Papers of Benjamin Franklin 1: lii [see note 24].

and when the old man dies—he will be in a very pitiable situation.[110]

James's emigration to America is curious. The American Revolution formally ended with the signing of the Treaty of Paris on 3 September 1783, certainly perhaps not the most opportune time for an Englishman to be emigrating. Also, in 1783 his children ranged in age from 3 to 8 years old. Thomas James was 4–5 years old at the time, too young to be apprenticed. And while we know that he was left with his grandfather, no mention is made of his sisters. If they were living with Thomas, Macaulay would most likely have mentioned them as well. Perhaps James left them with his own parents? It seems unlikely that he would have brought them to Maryland with him and left his son behind in England. It is also possible that they died.

No record can be found for James at Annapolis. It is possible that he died after writing the July 1784 letter. There are no records of burial or marriage for any of the children at Lutterworth. Thomas James Pearce was just shy of his thirteenth birthday at the time Macaulay wrote his letter to George Washington. He was approaching the age when boys were sent out to apprentice, and my have gone elsewhere to learn a trade.

John Franklin's daughter Anne is the only other of his children known to have had children. She married Henry Farrow, but no record of the marriage has been found. She was deceased by the summer of 1767 when Benjamin Franklin wrote to his cousin Samuel in Boston, listing Anne's daughter Hannah as among the living relatives in England, but does not mention Anne herself.[111]

Their daughter Hannah was baptised at Castlethorpe, Buckinghamshire, 9 August 1724.[112] She was married there shortly before her thirtieth birthday:

---

[110] Mastromarino, *Papers of George Washington* 8:497–99 [see note 104].

[111] "From Benjamin Franklin to Samuel Franklin, 17 July 1767," Founders Online, National Archives, accessed September 29, 2019, https://founders.archives.gov/documents/Franklin/01-14-02-0127. [Original source: *The Papers of Benjamin Franklin*, vol. 14, January 1 through December 31, 1767, ed. Leonard W. Labaree. New Haven and London: Yale University Press, 1970, pp. 215–216.]

[112] Church of England, Castlethorpe Church of St. Simon and St. Jude, Buckinghamshire, Bishop's Transcripts, 1600–1837; Buckinghamshire Record

Marriages 1754

No. 1 Banns of Marriage between Thomas Walker and Hannah Farrow were published on the 12, 14 and the 26 day of May one thousand seven hudred and fifty four by me Moses Agar Vicar The said Thomas Walker of this parish and the said Hannah Farrow of this parish spinster were married in this Church by Banns this third ^{day} of June in the year one thousand seven hundred and fifty four by me Moses Agar Vicar This marriage was solemnized between us Thomas Walker Hannah Farrow now Hannah Walker

In the presence of us John Walker John Harris.[113]

Hannah and her family were quite poor. Benjamin Franklin helped them out considerably. Only two of their children are discussed in their correspondence, but Benjamin does reference a third son in a letter to his cousin Samuel back in Boston.[114] They were parents to six children, all boys, baptised at Castlethorpe and the nearby town of Westbury:

Castlethorpe[115]
Baptism
John Son of Thomas and Hannah Walker March 4 [1755]
Henry Son of Thos. and Hannah Walker Decer. 26th. [1756]

Office D/A/T/34, 210/2 [FHL #1,999,133; DGS #4,010,424]. Books are unpaginated, in chronological order.

113 Church of England, Castlethorpe Church of St. Simon and St. Jude, Buckinghamshire, Bishop's Transcripts, 1600–1837; Buckinghamshire Record Office D/A/T/34, 210/2 [FHL #1,999,133; DGS #4,010,424]. Books are unpaginated, in chronological order.

114 "From Benjamin Franklin to Samuel Franklin, 17 July 1767," Founders Online, National Archives, accessed September 29, 2019, https://founders.archives.gov/documents/Franklin/01-14-02-0127. [Original source: *The Papers of Benjamin Franklin*, vol. 14, January 1 through December 31, 1767, ed. Leonard W. Labaree. New Haven and London: Yale University Press, 1970, pp. 215–216.]

115 Church of England, Castlethorpe Church of St. Simon and St. Jude, Buckinghamshire, Bishop's Transcripts, 1600–1837; Buckinghamshire Record Office D/A/T/34, 210/2 [FHL #1,999,133; DGS #4,010,424]. Books are unpaginated, in chronological order.

Westbury[116]
Baptisms
Thomas son of Thomas and Hannah Walker was Baptised December 26° [1759]
Benjamin Franclin son of Thomas and Hannah Walker was Baptised May 4th [1762]
Wm Francklin Walker son of Tho: and Hannah Walker was Baptiz'd May 13 1764
Wm Franclin Walker was Baptised May 13th [1765]

Burials
Benjamin Francklin Walker was buried May 9 1763.
Wm Francklin Walker buried Nov. 20th 1764
Wm Franclin Walker was buried Novr 16th [1765]
Hannah Walker Widow Buried January the 9 1787

The *Papers of Benjamin Franklin* provides birth dates for John (4 March 1755) and Henry Walker (29 November 1756) without providing any source information.[117] The dates do not conflict with the baptismal dates.

The first surviving letter from Hannah (Farrow) Walker to Benjamin Franklin is dated at Westbury 18 December 1764, in response to a letter from him to her on two days earlier which does not survive.[118] Her mother's cousin, Eleanor Morris, was residing with the family.

Thomas and Hannah named a son after Benjamin Franklin in 1762, and the next two sons after William Franklin in 1764 and 1765. Perhaps this was out of gratitude for the help that Benjamin had provided to them, or perhaps to add motivation for him to continue to help them. Their eldest son, John, had a problem with

---

[116] Church of England, Westbury St. Augustine, Buckinghamshire, Parish Registers, 1558–1812. Buckinghamshire Record Office PR223/1/1 [FHL #1,999,918; DGS #7,909,425]. Books are unpaginated, in chronological order.

[117] Labaree, *Papers of Benjamin Franklin*, 1:lii [see note 24].

[118] "To Benjamin Franklin from Hannah Walker, 18 December 1764," Founders Online, National Archives, accessed September 29, 2019, https://founders.archives.gov/documents/Franklin/01-11-02-0152. [Original source: *The Papers of Benjamin Franklin*, vol. 11, January 1, through December 31, 1764, ed. Leonard W. Labaree. New Haven and London: Yale University Press, 1967, pp. 524–525.]

his eyesight. In a letter from Hannah to her cousin Benjamin in June 1768 she wrote:

> Honoured Sir I humbly beg your Pardon for being so ungratful in not returning you Answar for Such a Favour no Sooner but I will give you the Reasons and then I hope you will not take it ill as I was never so guilty before nor never will again if I am well but there is a very famais gentlewoman at Banbury for Eyes that People go for and great go for her Adivice for She takes Nothing for that nor undertakes none whithait [without] She Sees Some hopes of doing them good and People wondered I never went with my Johnny but it was not my fault for ever since his eye began to grow worse I beged and Intreated his Father with all the words and tears Night and Day but never could Pervail because it was not agreeable to his Friends however Resolved I was to have her Adwice as People said it was so little Trouble so at whitesuntide I took Henery and Johnney and went to Banbury it is but Nine Miles and my Husband as an Uncle at Midletan Chenney and we Stay there a Saturday Night and went on Sunday to Banbury but to my great Sorrow when the Gentlewoman saw him she said she was sorry to tell me but I had staid to long for she could do him no good which struck such a terror upon my spirits that I almost fainted away but the good Gentlewoman gave me somthing comfortable and very good Counsel as she said I had done my Endeavour to have help. She would have me content my self as well as Possible in my Affliction but it has put me under such Disconsalation that I have been quite ill to think of the Dismal condition of my Dear Child as long as he lives but I thank God I am much better. . .[119]

She was more successful at helping her next eldest son, Henry, however. On 1 April 1768, he sent a note to Benjamin's landlady,

---

[119] "To Benjamin Franklin from Hannah Walker, 16 June 1768," Founders Online, National Archives, accessed September 29, 2019, https://founders.archives.gov/documents/Franklin/01-15-02-0083. [Original source: *The Papers of Benjamin Franklin*, vol. 15, January 1 through December 31, 1768, ed. William B. Willcox. New Haven and London: Yale University Press, 1972, pp. 142–144.]

Margaret Stevenson, in care of the good Doctor Franklin.[120] Benjamin set up an apprenticeship for Henry.

Fifteen-year-old Henry went to Boston earlier that year, indentured to work for Josiah and Jonathan Williams, Jr., the eldest children of Jonathan and Grace (Harris) Williams. Grace was a daughter of Benjamin Franklin's sister Ann (Franklin) Harris. The brothers had been spending time with their uncle Benjamin in London. Josiah was blind as a result of a smallpox infection when he was a child. Henry may have felt a special affinity towards him because of his brother John's vision problems. Unfortunately, Josiah Williams died that summer, and there seems to have been a problem with Jonathan, which he communicated to Benjamin Franklin:

> In my last I acquainted you with the Death of my Brother, and in the same Letter gave you an Account of Henry's unfaithfulness; I have now the pleasure to acquaint You, that he is still content with his Situation, and his Master seems satisfied with him, when I recieve my Indentures and your approbation, I shall take care to fix him with every customary Advantage: as I thought best not to bind him, till I heard from You.[121]

In this letter, Jonathan accused Henry of being "unfaithful." He references an earlier letter that is no longer extant, so we do not know the circumstances of what happened.

Whatever the circumstances of the disagreement, they could not have been too serious, as Jonathan found another position for Henry, and continued to support him. The following summer, Hannah sent some letters for her son to Benjamin Franklin, who

---

[120] "To Benjamin Franklin from Henry Walker, 1 April 1768," Founders Online, National Archives, accessed September 29, 2019, https://founders.archives.gov/documents/Franklin/01-15-02-0052. [Original source: *The Papers of Benjamin Franklin*, vol. 15, January 1 through December 31, 1768, ed. William B. Willcox. New Haven and London: Yale University Press, 1972, p. 92.]

[121] "To Benjamin Franklin from Jonathan Williams, Jr., 13 October 1772," Founders Online, National Archives, accessed September 29, 2019, https://founders.archives.gov/documents/Franklin/01-19-02-0226. [Original source: *The Papers of Benjamin Franklin*, vol. 19, January 1 through December 31, 1772, ed. William B. Willcox. New Haven and London: Yale University Press, New Haven and London, 1975, pp. 337–338.]

forwarded them to his great-nephew Jonathan. In a letter to Benjamin that September, Jonathan acknowledged their receipt and delivery to Henry "who I take care to advise with regard to his Behaviour to his master and application to his Trade which I hope and believe he will be master of and as I hear no complaints I am inclined to think he behaves very well."[122]

Hannah last mentions her husband in a letter to Benjamin dated 20 June 1773.[123] He died sometime between then and 9 January 1787, when she was buried at Westbury as a widow.

JOSEPH FRANKLIN

Joseph was the fourth child and fourth son of Thomas[A] and Jane (White) Franklin. There is no baptismal record for him at Ecton, but Benjamin Franklin the Elder recorded his birthday as 10 October 1646.[124] Benjamin also wrote of this brother:

> Joseph was a carpenter, seved his time wth Mr Titcomb Just without Moregate London. that being one of the city Gates he helpt to build it, His time of Ap^rntis being Expired Mr Cogshall a Suffolk Gent. took him down to Aldborough to build him an house which when he had finished he went and setled at Knatshall a town 6 miles distant from Alboro · in the same county where he married Sarah Sawyer, Daughter of Mr Saw^er s to · · · · · He had by her one son named Joseph, born after is fathers death. He was facetious in his comon conversation, his Judgm^t was for the Church of England. but his wife was otherwise Enclin'd. He dyed on St Andrews day, the 30 Nov. 1683. She mar-

---

122 "To Benjamin Franklin from Jonathan Williams, Jr., [before 21 September 1773]," Founders Online, National Archives, accessed September 29, 2019, https://founders.archives.gov/documents/Franklin/01-20-02-0220. [Original source: *The Papers of Benjamin Franklin*, vol. 20, January 1 through December 31, 1773, ed. William B. Willcox. New Haven and London: Yale University Press, 1976, pp. 408–410.]

123 "To Benjamin Franklin from Hannah Walker, 20 June 1773," Founders Online, National Archives, accessed September 29, 2019, https://founders.archives.gov/documents/Franklin/01-20-02-0139. [Original source: *The Papers of Benjamin Franklin*, vol. 20, January 1 through December 31, 1773, ed. William B. Willcox. New Haven and London: Yale University Press, 1976, pp. 239–240.]

124 Franklin, "Short Account" 2 [see Appendix B].

ried againe to Mr Blackmore by blybrow near Dunwick in Suffolk, and there her son Joseph dyed about 21 year of his Age.[125]

No record of marriage for Joseph has been identified. The village of Knodishall is located in eastern Suffolk, about three miles
from the coast of the North Sea. The following records were transcribed from the parish registers at Knoddishall St. Lawrence:

Joseph Franklin ye son of Jos. Franklin & Sarah his wife was
baptiz. ye 7th of May 1682.[126]

Mary the D. of Rob. Blakemore & Sarah his wife bap. Nov. 25.
1688.[127]

[16] '87 Rob. Blakemoore & Sarah Franklin Marr. May 27th.[128]

Although there are Sawyer families at Knodishall early on, there
is no baptism for Sarah there, and her parentage remains unknown.
There is no burial record for Joseph at Knodishall, nor can any will
or administration be found. He would have been 35 years old when
his son was born. Benjamin the Elder said that he died on St. Andrews day, 30 November 1683, and that his son was born posthumously. But Joseph's son Joseph was baptised 7 May 1682. Thus,
either his son was not born posthumously or Joseph died prior to 7
May 1682.

The full name of his widow's second husband was Robert
Blakemore, whom she married 27 May 1687. They had a daughter
Mary, baptised at Knodishall a year later. The village of Blythburgh lies about ten miles north of Knodishall. Benjamin wrote
that his nephew died there when he was about 21 years old, or
about 1704. Unfortunately, the parish registers for Blythburgh
Holy Trinity for this period are missing and nothing further can
be discovered of the family.

---

[125] Franklin, "Short Account" 5 [see Appendix B].

[126] Arthur T. Winn, ed., The *Register of the Parish Church of Knodishall, Co. Suffolk, 1566–1705* (London: Bemrose & Sons, 1909) 45 (hereafter Winn, *Knodishall
Parish Register*).

[127] Winn, *Knodishall Parish Register*, 48.

[128] Winn, *Knodishall Parish Register*, 66.

BENJAMIN FRANKLIN

This Benjamin is referred to as Benjamin Franklin the Elder to differentiate him from his more well-known nephew. He was born at Ecton 20 March 1650, the fifth child of Thomas[A] and Jane (White) Franklin. As a sixty-five-year-old man he left England behind forever to join his son Samuel and his brother Josiah in Boston. Who better than Benjamin himself to tell us his story:

Benjamin served his time to M[r] Pratt 5 years, M[r] Paine 2 years. Dyers of skeyn silk black. which he practised for about 7 years after. and then learned to dye skeyn silk into collours, that he followed for about Eleven years more, then turn'd Ragg dyer as tis called in London, that is dying wr't silk in the peece and when made into Garments, this he did for about seventeen years, but not having the desired success he left off and went to New England and Landed at Boston on 10 Oct. 1715

Before this Benjamin there were born two sons more, Twins, which as I s sd (tis tho't) dyed unbatiz'd.

In the year 1683 on fryday 23 Nov. He Married M[rs] Hannah Welles, Daughter of M[r] Samuel Welles — minister of Banbury in Oxfordshire, this M[r] W. was wone of these 2000 that were turn'd out soon after King Charles 2[d] restoration, on 24 Aug 1662 comonly called, Black Bartholomew day. Dr Mather is another of them, who in England are called Dessenters, together with those that follow them, Benj. had By his wife Hannah Ten children, Namly

Samuel born on	15	Oct.	1684	
Benjamin · · · ·	6	Aug.	1686	dyed 22 Apr 87
Jane · · · · ·	14	feb.	1687	
Hannah · · · ·	18	Nov.	1689	dyed 31 Dec. 1710
Thomas · · · ·	31	Aug.	1692	dyed 2 Mar:94
Elisabeth · · ·	27	Oct	1694	
Mary · · ·	23	Apr.	1686	dyed 27 Aug 96
John · · · · ·	8	Apr.	1699	
Joseph · · · ·	27	Jan[r].	1700	
Josiah · · · ·	3	Jan[r].	1703	dyed 10 Jan[r].

Hannah the Mother of these dyed in princes street in st Ann's parish in Westminster on the 4° Nov· 1705 · and in her I lost the delight of – mine Eyes, the desire of my heart, and the comfort of my Life. she worte severall things for her own private use, some of them are in her son Samuels hands. Hannah My Daughter was of a weakly constituttion, as was her mother, and took after her as to writing, rediness of witt and curious working with her Needle, but was not soe happy in her Natural temper which was somwhat like her fathers. which he was apt to Impute to her sickly disposition when I had begun too much to set my Affections on her, as standing in her mother stead, and in good measure filling up her room, having a good understanding in the best things, of a discreet deportment toward others, and prudent houswifely neat and saving in all her managements. It pleased the holy God to take her (I hope) to himselfe on 31 Dec·1710 · bet. 11 and 12 at Night being the last day and the last hour of the old year. her brother Sam. has something that she wrote alsoe for her own private use.

Samuel who was born on wed. at 8 o clock in the evening in prescote street in Goodīns fields was baptiz'd by Mr James who used to preach near Nightingall Lane near Well Closs. who on that occasion did Exelently open and Apply that text in the 20 Ezek. 37 I will cause you to pass under the rod &c

Elizabeth was born Near the falcon staires in the parish of christs-church southwark on — saturday · and baptiz'd by mr Nathaniel Vincent It was sd of her by mrs polly a Doctoress that — betty was short lived she is of a good temper ^O dismal change for Father to reherse, his Daughter Turned unto the Just reverse.^ and week spirit yet knows how to resent an Injury, she is of a healthful constitution and is near the age of my Neece Mrs Mary Holmes

It pleased God to take away all the rest of my children in their Infancy, none except Ben. & Thomas lived twelve months if they lived soe long which I am not certaine of.[129]

---

[129] Franklin, "Short Account" 7–9 [see Appendix B].

Benjamin's wife Hannah Welles was a daughter of the minister at Banbury, where his father Thomas and brothers John and Josiah lived. His brother John seems to have played matchmaker in setting the two up. Hannah was the youngest of Samuel and Dorothy (Doyley) Welles's ten children. Dorothy's family was well-connected. Her brother, who served as an officer in Oliver Cromwell's army, was made the first English governor of Jamaica after Britain took the island from the Spanish.[130]

Benjamin and Hannah had ten children, but only Samuel and Hannah are known to have survived to adulthood. Hannah died when she was 21 years old. Their daughter daughter Elizabeth, however, is a curiousity.

In his Short Account written in 1717, Benjamin writes of her in both the past and present tense: "It was s^d of her by m^{rs} polly a Doctoress that — betty was short lived she is of a good temper . . . and week spirit yet knows how to resent an Injury, she is of a healthful constitution and is near the age of my Neece Mrs Mary Holmes."[131] Thus there is confusion as to whether she was still alive. She would have been just shy of 21 when her father emigrated to Boston. There is no mention of her at all in Boston. Would he have left her behind all alone? If she were alive in 1717, it is unlikely she was married, as Benjamin would most likely have mentioned it.

Samuel emigrated to Boston first, joining his uncle Josiah who had emigrated back in 1683. Benjamin the Elder joined him in 1715. Twelve years after arrriving in Boston, and almost a decade after writing his "Short Account," Benjamin Franklin the Elder died in Boston.

On Monday last was decently Interr'd the Remains of Mr. *Benjamin Franklin*, who dyed here on Fryday the 17th. Instant, in the 77th Year of his Age. A Person who was justly esteem'd and valu'd as a rare & exemplary Christian; one who lov'd the People and Ministers of CHRIST: His Presence in the House of GOD was always solemn & affecting; and tho' he courted not the Observation of Men, yet there were many that could not

---

130 Bunker, *Young Benjamin Franklin*, 41 [see note 25].
131 Franklin, "Short Account" 9 [see Appendix B].

but take notice of, and admire the peculiar Excellenties that so
vicibly adorn'd him.[132]

More details about Benjamin Franklin the Elder and his descendants can be found in Volume 2 of *Benjamin Franklin's Family*.

HANNAH FRANKLIN

Hannah "the Daughter of Thomas Franklin and Jane his wife
was borne the three and twentieth of october and baptized the 29
of the same" in 1654 at Ecton. She married at Great Billing,
Northamptonshire:

> Married 1684 Dec. 29. John Morris, Citizen of London, Dyer,
> & Hannah Franklin of Ecton.[133]

Percival Boyd created the largest work on Londoners in that
time frame. Formerly called "Citizens of London" and now
known as "Inhabitants of London," it contains information on
70,000 families between 1200 and 1946. Much of his work was
done from the records of the various livery companies in London.
Unfortunately, the Worshipful Company of Dyers was not included in his work, thus the absence of John Morris and his family
from Boyd's massive work. The contemporary reference to John
Morris being a citizen of London in the marriage record is no
doubt accurate.[134] Her brother Benjamin wrote of them:

> Hannah, of whom my father used to say, when any asked how
> many children he had, I have had seven seven sons, and they
> have every one a sister. she had several good offers, but as She

---

[132] Obituary of Benjamin Franklin. *New-England Weekly Journal* (Boston,
Massachusetts), No. 1, Monday, March 27, 1727, p. 2.

[133] Church of England, St. Andrews Great Billing Parish Registers, Baptisms
from 1662 to 1811 (wanting years 1736 to 1746), Marriages from 1664 to 1762,
Burials are from 1662 to 1810, Northamptonshire Record Office, 31P/1 [FHL
Fiche #6,126,700; DGS#101,392,526]. Records are not paginated, but are in alphabetical order.

[134] Boyd's Inhabitants, which was given to the Society of Genealogists, is
now available online on FindMyPast.com.

was a hinderance in brother John's closing with several good – offers, soe she her selfe refused severale and took up with what proved the worst she was married to John Morris son of Billing Morris of Ecton aforesaid who had with her 100P He was a zealous son of the church and made her soe, he had good and profitable business of his trade which was a rag dyer but his fancy lead him to building – whereby he Involved himselfe, and soon after dying he left his widdow 3 Daughters and six-hundred pounds in Debt out of which she never got all her life long · but dyed in debt to all and more than she dealth with {24 June 1712.

He dyed 17 June 1695 · and left 3 daughters whose names are as follows but their age I doe not know, they are all single and live in London she Dyed 24 June 1712 ·[135]

There is no man named "Billing Morris" in Northampton-shire. Benjamin likely confused the place of Hannah's marriage with the name of her father-in-law. There are two men named John Morris born in the right period to be her husband:

John the sonne of James Morris and Mary his wife was borne the fourteenth of October and baptized the 2jth of the same. [1655]

John Morris the Sonne of John Morris and Elline his wife was borne the i8 Day of Aprill and baptized the 25 of the same Aprill 1658

No other children of either couple can be found in North-amptonshire. No record of either of the marriages can be found there either.

John and Hannah had three daughters: Eleanor, Jane, and Hannah. No record of birth or baptism has been found for any of them. None of them is known to have married. Benjamin Franklin the Elder wrote of the girls:

---

[135] Franklin, "Short Account" 9–10 [see Appendix B].

Elenor   . Has a chaming tongue, is of a very obliging carriage free in her promises but far from endeavours to perform
them.

Jane   . is of few words, and many deeds, yet guilty of the
above named fault these two speak and write and read french
near as fluently as English, are redy witts and highly for the
church of England

Hannah   . is of very few words you – must draw them out ,
or goe without them of a bashful countenance and a weak constitution, they are all 3 of very smal Appetites, I know some on
wom[en] that would eat more than they all, they did all to gether
follow the dying silk garments and scouring since their mother's
death which happend 24 June 1712. but now they all goe to
Service.

The fates of Jane and Hannah are unknown, but when she was
older Eleanor went to live with her cousin Anne (Franklin) Farrow, and later with Anne's daughter Hannah (Farrow) Walker and
her family. A single letter from Eleanor to Benjamin Franklin sur-
vives. She wrote to him in January 1768 congratulating him on his
recent birthday:

I make bold hoping you will Excuse me my Cousins joyning me
once more to Congratulate you on that Happy Day which we
kept very joyfully for we had a Plumpuding for Dinner and the
Children and we Drank your Health in tea in the Afternoon
which Happy Day I may never live to see again but hope God
will be Pleased to Continue Health and Happiness to your Self
and all your Dear Family which I hope are all well. I Bless God
for my Age I Enjoy a very good State of Health tho the weather
has been so very severe I have been as comfortabe as my cousin
could make me[136]

---

[136] "To Benjamin Franklin from Eleanor Morris, 18 January 1768," Founders
Online, National Archives, accessed September 29, 2019, https://founders.archives.
gov/ documents/Franklin/01-15-02-0007. [Original source: *The Papers of Benjamin
Franklin*, vol. 15, January 1 through December 31, 1768, ed. William B. Willcox.
New Haven and London: Yale University Press, 1972, p. 20.]

Eleanor is likely the eldest child of John and Hannah. If she were born within a couple years of their marriage, she would have been in her early eighties when she wrote to Benjamin. There is another mystery surrounding her passing. There is a burial record for Eleanor Morris at Westbury 2 July 1768.[137] Benjamin and Hannah's cousin is the only person named Morris known to haved lived there at the time. But when Hannah wrote Benjamin in May 1769, she closed her letter with:

> My Cousin Morris is Suprizingly Hearty for one of her Agge I bless God and all my Family at Present are well which Blessing I hope God continues upon you and your good Family which is my continual Prayers. My cousin Morris and we joyn in begging the acceptance of our Humble Duty to you and your good Family and all our Humble Complements to mrs. Stevenson from your most Humble and most obdient Servant.[138]

If that burial record was for Hannah's cousin, she would hardly be conveying Eleanor's best wishes in a letter written almost a year later. But if Eleanor was dead, then who is the cousin Morris mentioned in the letter? Benjamin was clear after his 1758 that Eleanor was the only one of the sisters still alive.

JOSIAH FRANKLIN

Born at Ecton 3 January 1657, Josiah¹ was the youngest child of ThomasᴬA and Jane (White) Franklin. He emigrated to Boston in 1683 with his first wife, Anne Child, and their two young children. Years later, when his brother Benjamin Franklin the Elder emigrated to Boston, he chose to live with Josiah and his family rather than his own son Samuel who had also emigrated to the city. In the summer of 1717, Benjamin the Elder wrote his Short

---

[137] Church of England, Westbury St. Augustine, Buckinghamshire, Parish Registers, 1558–1812. Buckinghamshire Record Office PR223/1/1 [FHL #1,999,918; DGS #7,909,425]. Books are unpaginated, in chronological order.

[138] "To Benjamin Franklin from Hannah Walker, 24 May 1769," Founders Online, National Archives, accessed September 29, 2019, https://founders.archives. gov/documents/Franklin/01-16-02-0067. [Original source: *The Papers of Benjamin Franklin*, vol. 16, January 1 through December 31, 1769, ed. William B. Willcox. New Haven and London: Yale University Press, 1972, p. 136.]

Account while staying with the family at Josiah's house. Of his youngest sibling Benjamin said:

> Josiah was a dyer, served his Aprentiship to his Brŏ. John at banbury wher he married Ann child of Ecton the daughter of Robert Childe there. but things not succeeding there according to his mind, wth. the leave of his frinds and father he went to New England in the year 1683 • in order to which voyage he was come up to London at tht time when the Noble Lord Russel was murder'd

He had by his wife Ann seven children •

Elizabeth born •	2	Mar.	1677
Samuel • dead •	16	May	1681
Hannah • • • •	25	May	1683
Josiah • dead •	23	Aug	1685
Ann • • • •	5	Janr	1686
Joseph } dead	6	feb.	1687
Joseph 2d	30	June	1689

by his 2d wife Mrs Abiah Foulger

John born • •	7	Dec.	1690
Peter • • • •	22	Nov.	1692
Mary • • • •	26	Sept	1694
James • • • •	4	feb.	1696
Sarah • • • •	9	Jul	1699
Ebenezer } dead	20	Sept	1701
Thomas • • •	7	Dec.	1703
Benjamin • •	6	Janr.	1706
Lidia • • • •	8	Aug	1708
Jane • • • •	27	Mar 1712	

After he came to Boston in N. England, he made severall Essays, in several sorts of bussines, and at last fixed upon the trade of Tallow chandler, and Sope Maker, in which it has pleased God so to bless his diligence and Endeavours, that he has comfotably bro't up a Numerous family, providing for and disposing off almost halfe of them in a credible maner and himself lives in good repute among his frinds and Neighbours at the blue ball in union street Boston the place where this briefe account was written on the 1 • 2 •3 • of July 1717 by his brother[139]

Josiah became an active member of his congregation at the Old South Church. The date of marriage with his first wife Anne is estimated from baptism of their daughter Elizabeth. She, too, was from Ecton (see "Anne¹ Child, Wife of Josiah Franklin" on p. 153), baptised 21 January 1654, daughter of Robert and Debora (—?—) Child.[140]

According to Benjamin Franklin the Elder, their first child, Elizabeth, was born at Banbury, Oxfordshire, 2 March 1677/8. However, she was baptised at Ecton a week later, on 10 March.[141] Banbury is 35 miles away from Ecton. This would have been a long distance to travel to have a week-old baby baptised. It is possible that Josiah and Anne were already living at Banbury and that Anne went to her parents' home to give birth to her first child there. Shortly after their daughter Hannah was born in 1683, Josiah and his young family emigrated to Boston. He had four more children with his wife Anne before she died, most likely from complications of giving birth to her son Joseph in the summer of 1689.

Josiah was a thirty-two-year-old widower with five young children between 3 and 12 years old, but he did not remain so for long. Just four months later he married Abiah Folger, a decade his junior. Their marriage was a happy one and lasted for more than half a century.

---

[139] Franklin, "Short Account" 11–2 [see Appendix B].

[140] Church of England, Ecton St. Mary Magdelene, Northamptonshire, Baptisms and Burials 1638–1754, Marriages 1638–1753. Northamptonshire Record Office 114P/203 [FHL Fiche #6,127,382; DGS #100,430,949] 1653–1658. Northamptonshire Record Office 114P/204 [FHL Fiche #6,127,383; DGS #100,430,966] Books are unpaginated; records are in chronological order.

[141] Church of England, Ecton St. Mary Magdelene, Northamptonshire, Parish Register, 1559–1637. Northamptonshire Record Office 114P/202 [FHL Fiche #6,127,381]. Baptisms and Burials 1638–1754, Marriages 1638–1753. Northamptonshire Record Office 114P/203 [FHL Fiche #6,127,382; DGS #100,430,949] Books are unpaginated; records are in chronological order.

He had seventeen children with his two wives. Twelve of them lived to adulthood, but only nine of these had children of their own. However, their descendants represent the vast majority of the known living descendants of Thomas[C] Franklin. More information on Josiah Franklin and his descendants will be found in Volume 3 of *Benjamin Franklin's Family*.

1. **ROBERT^D FRANKLIN** was buried at Earls Barton, Northampton-shire, 11 December 1572.[142] He married **KATHERINE** —?—. No marriage record has yet been found, and Katherine's maiden name is still a mystery.

He left a will naming his wife Katherine and five children.[143] Robert's occupation is not given in his will, but from the legacies he appears to be a farmer. The children were likely born in the 1520s and 30s, prior to the start of parish registers. In the absence of contradictory evidence, Katherine is presumed to be the mother of his children. Edmund, as Robert's principal heir, is presumed to be the eldest son.

Children of Robert^D and Katherine (—?—) Franklin:

 i. EDMUND FRANKLIN, bur. at Holcot, Northamptonshire, 28 October 1601.[144]
 ii. EDWARD FRANKLIN.
 iii. ALICE FRANKLIN.
 iv. MARIE FRANKLIN.
2 v. THOMAS^C FRANKLIN, b. say 1536 (est. 25 at marriage) bur. at Desborough, Northamptonshire, February 1619; m. at Earls Barton 20 November 1560 MARGERY MEADOWS.

---

[142] All references to baptisms, marriages, and burials at Earls Barton from Church of England, Earls Barton All Saints, Northamptonshire, Parish Registers, Baptisms 1558–1724, Marriages 1559–1728, Burials 1558–1725; Northamptonshire Record Office 110P/11 [FHL Fiche #5,127,339]. Book is unpaginated but records are in chronological order.

[143] Church of England, Archdeaconry of Northampton Court, Series 2, Original Wills, vol. H, no. 265, Will of Robert Franklin of Desborough, 1673 [FHL Film #187,603; DGS #7,904,798]. Also, Register Copy Wills, vol. AE, pt. 2, fol. 26 [FHL Film #187,593; DGS #8,098,670].

[144] Church of England, Holcot St. Mary and All Saints, Northamptonshire, Parish Registers, 1559–1764; Northamptonshire Record Office 170P/4 [FHL Fiche #6,127,805; DGS #1,009,430,845].

3 vi. MARGERY FRANKLIN, b. say 1541 (est. 20 at marriage) m. at Ecton, Northamptonshire, 5 February 1561[/2] JOHN WALSH.

2. THOMAS[C] FRANKLIN (*Robert[B]*) was born say 1536, son of Robert and Katherine (—?—) Franklin. He was buried at Desborough, Northamptonshire, February 1619.[145]

Thomas married at Earls Barton, Northamptonshire, 20 November 1560 MARGERY MEADOWS. She was buried at Desborough October 1629.

There is conflicting information about Thomas's occupation. Daughter Christiana's baptismal record identifies him as a shepherd. Family tradition passed down by Josiah[1] Franklin to his son Benjamin states that Thomas learned the trade of a smith.[146] No corroborating evidence for the smith occupation has been found, and it is possible that there is some confusion as to which of his great-grandfathers was a smith by trade. Examination of Meadows families who left wills shows no connections between Margery and any of those Meadows families in Northamptonshire.

Children of Thomas[C] and Margery (Meadows) Franklin (all except first baptized at Ecton):

    i. CHRISTIANA FRANKLIN, bp. at Earls Barton 4 February 1560[/1].
4   ii. ROBERT FRANKLIN, bp. 8 April 1563;[147] bur. at Desborough 23 June 1637; m. there July 1599 JOANE WRIGHT.

---

[145] All references in the summary to baptisms, marriages, and burials at Desborough from Church of England, St. Giles, Desborough, Northamptonshire, Parish Registers, Baptisms 1571–1649, Marriages 1571–1649, Burials 1571–1649; Northamptonshire Record Office 103P/9 [FHL Fiche #6,127,261]. Baptisms, 1648–1681; Northamptonshire Record Office 103P/10 [FHL Fiche #2,127,262]. Baptisms 1686–1748, Marriages 1695–1736, Burials 1695–1734; Northamptonshire Record Office 103P/11 [FHL Fiche #6,127,263].

[146] "To Benjamin Franklin from Josiah Franklin, 26 May 1739," Founders Online, National Archives, accessed September 29, 2019, https://founders.archives.gov/documents/Franklin/01-02-02-0048. [Original source: *The Papers of Benjamin Franklin*, vol. 2, January 1, 1735, through December 31, 1744, ed. Leonard W. Labaree. New Haven: Yale University Press, 1961, pp. 229–232.]

[147] All references in the summary to baptisms, marriages, and burials at Ecton from Church of England Parish Register, Ecton St. Mary Magdelene,

iii. JANE FRANKLIN, bp. 1 August 1565; bur. at Ecton 29 August 1565.

5   iv. JOHN FRANKLIN, bp. 16 May 1567; m. at Rothersthorpe1 May 1590 AGNES INGRAM.

v. JAMES FRANKLIN, bp. 9 May 1570.

6   vi. HENRY[B] FRANKLIN, bp. 26 May 1573; bur. at Ecton 23 October 1631; m. there 30 October 1595 AGNES JONES.

3. **MARGERY FRANKLIN** (*Robert[D]*) was born say 1536, daughter of Robert[D] and Katherine (—?—) Franklin. She was buried at Earls Barton 12 August 1591. She married at Ecton 5 February 1561[/2] **JOHN WALSH**.

There appears to be only one John Walsh at Ecton during this time. Just six weeks after the marriage, "W[m] Walshe, the son of John Walshe was bapt, the xvi[th] Daye Marche." Robert Franklin names Agnes Walsh in his will but does not give the relationship.

Children of John and Margery (Franklin) Walsh:

i. WILLIAM WALSH, bp. at Ecton 16 March 1561[/2].

ii. AGNES WALSH, bp. at Ecton 30 February 1562[/3].

4. **ROBERT FRANKLIN** (*Thomas[C]*, *Robert[D]*) was baptized at Ecton, Northamptonshire, 8 April 1563, son of Thomas and Margery (Meadows) Franklin. He was buried at Desborough, Northamptonshire, 23 June 1637.

Robert married at Desborough July 1599 **JOANE WRIGHT**. She was buried there 5 June 1640.

In his will, Robert left his wife Joane her thirds, two beasts, her bed and other furniture. After her death they were to be re-

Northamptonshire, 1559 to 1584, 1592 to 1598. Northamptonshire Record Office 114P/201 [FHL Fiche #6,127,380; DGS #101,392,523]. 1559–1637. Northamptonshire Record Office 114P/202 [FHL Fiche #6,127,381]. Baptisms and Burials 1638–1754, Marriages 1638–1753. Northamptonshire Record Office 114P/203 [FHL Fiche #6,127,382; DGS #100,430,949] 1653–1658. Northamptonshire Record Office 114P/204 [FHL Fiche #6,127,383; DGS #100,430,966] Books are unpaginated; records are in chronological order, grouped by record type.

turned to his son Ellen. Son Thomas received ten pounds and Thomas child to receive one shilling. After some additional small bequests, the remainder of his goods were to go to Nicholas Braine and his wife. Braine may have been a creditor. There is no known familial connection.

Children of Robert and Joane (Wright) Franklin:

       i.   ELLEN FRANKLIN,   bp. at Desborough 6 August 1600.
7   ii. THOMAS FRANKLIN, bp. at Desborough 25 September 1602; m. MARY —?—.

5. **JOHN FRANKLIN** (*Thomas^C, Robert^D*) was baptized at Ecton, Northamptonshire, 16 May 1567, son of Thomas and Margery (Meadows) Franklin. He was buried at Rothersthorpe, Northamptonshire, 30 October 1602.[148]

John married at Rothersthorpe 1 May 1590 **AGNES INGRAM**. She was baptized there 11 December 1563, daughter of Nicholas Ingram.

Children of John and Agnes (Ingram) Franklin, baptized at Rothersthorpe:

       i.   SARA FRANKLIN, bp. 19 March 1590/1.
8   ii. JOSEPH FRANKLIN, bp. 10 March 1593/4; bur. at Rothersthorpe 14 April 1635; m. by 1625 AGNES HOUSE.
9   iii. JOHN FRANKLIN, bp. 22 August 1595; m. (1) ALICE —?—;
    iv. CATHERINE FRANKLIN, bp. 11 March 1598/9
     v. ALICE FRANKLIN, bp. 24 January 1601/2.

6. **HENRY^B FRANKLIN** (*Thomas^C, Robert^D*) was baptized at Ecton, Northamptonshire, 26 May 1573, son of Thomas and Margery (Meadows) Franklin. He was buried there 23 October 1631.

---

[148] All references in the summary to baptisms, marriages, and burials at Rothersthorpe from Church of England, Rothersthorpe Saints Peter and Paul, Northamptonshire, Parish Registers. Baptisms, marriages, and burials 1562–1659; Northamptonshire Archives 283P/1/1 [FHL #6,128,799].

Henry married at Ecton 30 October 1595 **AGNES JONES**. She was baptised there 22 November 1573, daughter of William and Margaret (—?—) Jones. She is likely the "aged widow" Franklin who was buried there 29 January 1646. (for more information about Agnes' ancestry, see *Agnes Jones, Wife of Henry*[B] *Franklin*, p. 193).

Children of Henry[B] and Agnes (Jones) Franklin, born at Ecton:

  i.   THOMAS FRANKLIN, bp. 28 February 1595; bur. at Ecton 11 August 1598.
10 ii. THOMAS[A] FRANKLIN, bp. 8 October 1598; d. at Banbury, Oxfordshire, 21 and bur. 24 March 1682; m. by 1637 (baptism of first child) JANE WHITE.
11 iii. ESTHER FRANKLIN, bp. at Great Houghton (Houghton Magna) 26 September 1602; m. at St. Peter's, Northampton, 12 January 1631/2, ROBERT RIDE.

7. **THOMAS FRANKLIN**, (*Robert, Thomas*[C]*, Robert*[D]) was baptised at Desborough 25 September 1602, son of Robert and Joane (Wright) Franklin.

Thomas was married three times. None of his marriage records have been found. He married first by 1633 **ANN —?—**. She was buried at Desborough 6 May 1634.

He married second ca. 1635 **MARY —?—**. He married third **SARAH —?—**.

Children of Thomas and Ann (—?—) Franklin, baptised at Desborough:

  i.   ANN FRANKLIN, bp. 8 December 1633.

Children of Thomas and Mary (—?—) Franklin, baptised at Desborough:

  ii. ANN FRANKLIN, bp. 12 April 1636.
  iii. ROBERT FRANKLIN, bp. 2 May 1638.
  iv. THOMAS FRANKLIN, bp. 20 May 1640.

Children of Thomas and Sarah (—?—) Franklin, baptised at Desborough:

> v.   MARY FRANKLIN, bp. 21 March 1651.
> vi. FERDINANDO FRANKLIN, bp. 3 August 1662.

8. **JOSEPH FRANKLIN** (*John, Thomas^C, Robert^D*) was baptized at Rothersthorpe, Northamptonshire, 10 March 1593/4, son of John and Agnes (Ingram) Franklin. He was buried there 14 April 1635.

Joseph married by 1625 (birth of first child) **AGNES HOUSE**. She was buried at Rothersthorpe 18 May 1638.

In his will, Joseph left twelve pence to each of his children. The remainder of his estate was to go to his wife Agnes, who was his executor. [149] She was buried there three years later, but left no will or administration.

Children of Joseph and Agnes (House) Franklin, baptized at Rothersthorpe:

> i.   HENRY FRANKLIN, bp. 15 January 1625/6.
> ii.   SARA FRANKLIN, bp. 15 April 1627.
> iii. BRIDGET FRANKLIN, bp. 20 January 1628/9.
> iv.   AGNES FRANKLIN, bp. 22 October 1632.
> v.   THOMAS FRANKLIN, bp. 21 January 1633/4.

9. **JOHN FRANKLIN** (*John, Thomas^C, Robert^D*) was baptized at Rothersthorpe, Northamptonshire, 22 August 1595, son of John and Agnes (Ingram) Franklin.

John married by 1630 (birth of first child) **ALICE** —?—.

Children of John and Alice (—?—) Franklin, baptized at Rothersthorpe:

> i.   WILLIAM FRANKLIN, bp. 20 August 1630.
> ii.   ELIZABETH FRANKLIN, bp. 10 March 1632/3.
> iii. THOMAS FRANKLIN, bp. 4 February 1636/7.

---

[149] Church of England, Archdeaconry Court of Northampton, Wills and Administrations, Series 2, Original Wills, C: 31-32, will of Joseph Franklin, 1635 [FHL #187,599; DGS #8,047,425].

10. **THOMAS**[A] **FRANKLIN** (*Henry*[B], *Thomas*[C], *Robert*[D]) was baptized at Ecton, Northamptonshire, 8 October 1598, son of Henry[B] and Agnes (Jones) Franklin. He died at Banbury, Oxfordshire, 21 March 1682 and was buried there three days later.[150]

Thomas married probably at Harbury, Warwickshire, about November 1635 **JANE WHITE**. She was baptised at Grendon, Northamptonshire, 21 March 1616/17, daughter of George and Priscilla (Brimley/Bromley) (Warner) White of Grendon, Northamptonshire.[151] She was buried at Ecton 30 October 1662. (for more information about Jane's ancestry, see "Jane[A] White, Wife of Thomas Franklin," p. 173)

Thomas signed a feoffment in trust with Nathaniel "Brimley" of Olney, Buckinghamshire (George White's will calls him Nathaniel Bromley), and Robert Wellford of Earls Barton, Northamptonshire, on 11 November 1635, "aswell for and in consideration of a marriadge by the grace of God shortly to be had and solemnized Betweene him the said Thomas Franklin and Jane White of Harbery in the county of Warwicke"[152] The exact date of the marriage is unknown, as the records of Harbury for that period are no longer extant.

Benjamin the Elder wrote that his mother was a very pious woman, holding regular prayer meetings. She was especially fond of the last three verses of the third chapter of Malachi in the Old Testament, which end with ""Then shall ye return, and discern between the righteous and the wicked, between him that serveth

---

[150] Franklin, "Short Account" 3 [see Appendix B]. Church of England, Banbury St. Mary, Oxfordshire, Parish Registers, 1580–1708. Oxfordshire History Centre PAR21/1/R1/2. "Oxfordshire, England, Church of England Baptism, Marriages, and Burials, 1538-1812" database online at www.ancestry.com. (Lehi, UT, USA: Ancestry.com Operations, Inc., 2016). Unpaginated, records in chronological order.

[151] Church of England, Grendon St. Mary, Northamptonshire, Parish Registers, Baptisms, Marriages, and Burials, 1559–1695; Northamptonshire Record Office, 141P/1. [FHL Microfiche #6,127,571; DGS #100,430,932]. Unpaginated, in chronological order.

[152] Feoffment in Trust, Thomas Franklin of Ecton to Nathaniel Brimley of Olney, Taylor, and Robarte [Robert] Wellford of Earls Barton, Yeoman. 3 November 1635. Northamptonshire Archives E(S)/464.

God and him that serveth him not." She died of consumption when he was only twelve years old.

Thomas[A] Franklin turned 64 years old just weeks before his wife died. He had six children ranging in age from 5 years to 25 years old. He never remarried. His eldest son Thomas "about the year 1665 persuaded my father to let his land and leave off Husbandry which in a year or two after he did, and his own trade alsoe, and boarded with him for a while but his Temper being passionate did not suite wth my fathers so he went to banbury," where his sons John and Josiah would later join him.[153] He died there 31 March 1681/2 and was buried in the churchyard three days later.

Children of Thomas[A] and Jane (White) Franklin, born at Ecton:[154]

12 i.   THOMAS FRANKLIN, b. 3 March 1637; bp. at Ecton 11 March 1637; bur. at Ecton 6 January 1702; m. ELEANOR/ HELEN —?—.

    ii. SAMUEL FRANKLIN, b. 5 November 1641, bp. at Ecton 7 November; d.s.p. and bur. at St. Saviours, Southwark, Surrey, 13 March 1657/8.[155]

13 iii. JOHN FRANKLIN, b. 20 February 1643; d. at Banbury 7 June 1691; m. at Fawsley, Northamptonshire, 23 June 1681 ANNE JEFFES.

14 iv. JOSEPH FRANKLIN, b. 10 October 1646; d. at Knodishall, Suffolk, 30 November 1683; m. there SARAH SAWYER.

    v.   —?— FRANKLIN, twin son, d. young.

    vi. —?— FRANKLIN, twin son, d. young.

15 vii. BENJAMIN[1] FRANKLIN, b. 20 March 1650; bp. at Ecton 23 March 1650; d. at Boston, Suffolk Co., Mass., 17 March 1727; m. 23 November 1683 HANNAH WELLES.

---

[153] Franklin, "Short Account" 4 [see Appendix B].

[154] All references in the summary to births of children of Thomas[A] and Jane (White) Franklin from Franklin, "Short Account" 2.

[155] Church of England, Southwark St. Saviour, Surrey, Parish Registers, 1644–1673; London Metropolitan Archives, P92/SAV. Accessed at Ancestry.com. "London, England, Church of England Baptisms, Marriages and Burials, 1538-1812" database on-line. (Provo, UT, USA: Ancestry.com Operations, Inc., 2010). Original data: Church of England Parish Registers, 1538-1812. London, England: London Metropolitan Archives.

16 viii. HANNAH FRANKLIN, b. 23 and bp. at Ecton 29 October 1654; d. at Ecton 24 June 1712; m. JOHN MORRIS.

17 ix. JOSIAH[1] FRANKLIN, b. 28 December and bp. 3 January 1657; d. at Boston 6 January 1745; m. (1) by 1677 ANNE CHILD; m. (2) at Boston 15 Aug 1667 ABIAH FOLGER.

11. **ESTHER/HESTHER FRANKLIN** (*Henry*[B], *Thomas*[C], *Robert*[D]) was baptised at Great Houghton, Northamptonshire, 26 September 1602, daughter of Henry[B] and Agnes (Jones) Franklin.[156] She was buried at Ladbroke, Warwickshire, 18 April 1646.[157]

She married at Northampton St. Peter, Northamptonshire, 12 January 1631/2, **ROBERT RIDE** of Ladbroke.[158] He was buried at Ladbroke either 11 September 1647 or 20 October 1649.

Little is known of this family. There were two burials for individuals named Robert Ride within two years of each other at Ladbrooke, and it is not possible to distinguish which of these was the husband of Esther. Benjamin Franklin described this family in his short account, but confused Esther's family of origin. He wrote of her as his mother Jane's sister, but there is no doubt that he was referring to his father's sister. According to Benjamin the Elder, Robert and Esther/Hesther had one son, Samuel.

Child of Robert and Ester (Franklin) Ride:

18 i. SAMUEL RIDE, res. London.

---

[156] Church of England, Great Houghton St. Michael and All Angels, Northamptonshire, Parish Registers, Baptisms 1559–1677, marriages 1558–1673, Burials 1562–1673; Northamptonshire Record Office 175P/1 [FHL #6, 127,824; DGS #100,430,829].

[157] All references in the summary to baptisms, marriages, and burials at Ladbrooke from Church of England, Ladbrook All Saints, Warwickshire, Parish Registers, 1559–1762. Warwickshire Record Office, DR0085/1 [FHL Film #549,656, Item 2; DGS #4,290,822]. Unpaginated, records in chronological order.

[158] Church of England, Northampton St. Peter, Northamptonshire, Parish Registers, 1578–1737, Northamptonshire Record Office 240P/1 [FHL #6, 128,350; DGS #101,392,543].

12. **THOMAS FRANKLIN** (*Thomas*[A], *Henry*[B], *Thomas*[C], *Robert*[D]) was baptized at Ecton, Northamptonshire, 11 March 1637, son of Thomas[A] and Jane (White) Franklin. He was buried there 6 January 1702.

He married **ELEANOR/HELEN** . She died at Ecton 14 March 1711.[159] She was buried there two days later.

Thomas ran a school at Ecton for a time until his work as a scrivener became so plentiful he focused solely on that. His brother Benjam described him as:

> a black thin man of very mean appearance, but of great understanding and quick app'hension, very passionate, soon reconciled, & Just in his dealings, Highly for the church of Eng. Yet wanted a cordial love for its ministers and toward his end had almost turn'd dissenter.[160]

Josiah later wrote to his son Benjamin that when Thomas died he left an estate "worth fifteen hundred pounds."[161]

Child of Thomas and Eleanor/Helen (—?—) Franklin:

19   i.   MARY FRANKLIN, bp. at Ecton 24 October 1673; d. at Wellingborough, Northamptonshire, 25 December 1758; m. RICHARD FISHER.

---

[159] Labaree, *Papers of Benjamin Franklin*, 1:li [see note 24]. No source is given for the information.

[160] Franklin, "Short Account" 5 [see Appendix B].

[161] "To Benjamin Franklin from Josiah Franklin, 26 May 1739," Founders Online, National Archives, accessed September 29, 2019, https://founders.archives. gov/documents/Franklin/01-02-02-0048. [Original source: *The Papers of Benjamin Franklin*, vol. 2, January 1, 1735, through December 31, 1744, ed. Leonard W. Labaree. New Haven: Yale University Press, 1961, pp. 229–232.]

13. **JOHN FRANKLIN** (*Thomas*[A], *Henry*[B], *Thomas*[C], *Robert*[D]) was born at Ecton, Northamptonshire, 20 February 1643, son of Thomas[A] and Jane (White) Franklin.[162] He was buried at Banbury, Oxfordshire, 9 June 1691.[163]

John married at Fawsley, Northamptonshire, 23 June 1681 **ANNE JEFFES**.[164] She was baptized at Banbury April 1662, daughter of John Jeffes. She died there May 1696.[165]

John served an apprenticeship to learn the trade of a dyer. His brother Benjamin said that "While he lived in the city he was like a father to me." He dated many women before finally marrying Ann Jeffes when he was thirty-eight years old.[166] He was very successful in business at Banbury, making important connections and helping his family members. His youngest brother Josiah[1] Franklin apprenticed with him to learn the trade of a dyer.

He died of an infection shortly before his youngest daughter was born. He planned on emigrating to New England at the time of his death.

Children of John and Anne (Jeffes) Franklin, born at Banbury:

20   i.   THOMAS FRANKLIN, b. 15 September 1681 or 1682;[167] d. at Birmingham, Warwickshire, ca. 1753.

---

[162] Franklin, "Short Account" 2 [see Appendix B].

[163] All references in the summary to baptisms and burials at Banbury from Church of England, Banbury St. Mary, Oxfordshire, Parish Registers, 1723–1801, p. 180. Oxfordshire History Centre PAR21/1/R1/4. "Oxfordshire, England, Church of England Baptism, Marriages, and Burials, 1538-1812" database online at www.ancestry.com. (Lehi, UT, USA: Ancestry.com Operations, Inc., 2016).

[164] Church of England, Fawsley St. Mary the Virgin, Northamptonshire, Parish Registers, Baptisms 1583–1731, Marriages 1587–1731, Burials 1591–1731. Northamptonshire Record Office 125P/1 [FHL Fiche #6,127,462; DGS #100,624,431].

[165] Church of England. Peculiar Court, Banbury, Oxfordshire, Original Wills, Administration Bonds, and Inventories, (surname E) 1557–1675 and (surname F) 1683–1799. Will and Administration of John Franklin [FHL #173,596; DGS #8,472,405].

[166] Franklin, "Short Account" 6 [see Appendix B].

[167] All references in the summary to births of John's children from Franklin, "Short Account" 5–7 [see Appendix B]. For Thomas see also Church of England. Peculiar Court, Banbury, Oxfordshire, Original Wills, Administration

ii. HANNAH FRANKLIN, bp. 26 November 1683; d. bet. 1717
and 1759.[168]

21 iii. ANNE FRANKLIN, bp. 3 February 1684/5; d. ca. 1771; m.
HENRY FARROW.

iv. MARY FRANKLIN, bp. 3 April 1687; d. bet. 1717 and 1759.

v. JANE FRANKLIN, b. say 1689 (ages of siblings); d.s.p. by
1758; m. aft. 1717 ROBERT PAGE.

vi. ELEANOR FRANKLIN, b. soon after 6 June 1691; d. bet.
1717 and 1759.

14. **JOSEPH FRANKLIN** (*Thomas*[A], *Henry*[B], *Thomas*[C], *Robert*[D]) was
born 10 October 1646, son of Thomas[A] and Jane (White) Franklin.[169] He died at Knodishall, Suffolk, 30 November 1683.[170]

Joseph married, probably at Knodishall **SARAH SAWYER**. She
married there second 27 May 1687 Robert Blakemore.[171]

Child of Joseph and Sarah (Sawyre) Blakemore:

i. JOSEPH FRANKLIN, bp. at Knodishall 7 May 1682;[172] d. at
Blythburgh, Suffolk, ca. 1703.[173]

Bonds, and Inventories, (surname E) 1557–1675 and (surname F) 1683–1799.
Will and Administration of John Franklin [FHL #173,596; DGS #8,472,405].

[168] Hannah, Mary, and Eleanor were all referred to in the present tense (i.e., still
living) when Benjamin Franklin the Elder wrote his "Short Account." Ann (Franklin) Farrow in a letter to her cousin Benjamin Franklin 8 January 1759 said "I
Should have joy without measure to see you I having Neither Brother nor Sisters
alive only a Daughter." ("To Benjamin Franklin from Anne Farrow, 8 January
1759," Founders Online, National Archives, accessed September 29, 2019,
https://founders.archives.gov/ documents/Franklin/01-08-02-0063. [Original
source: The Papers of Benjamin Franklin, vol. 8, April 1, 1758, through December
31, 1759, ed. Leonard W. Labaree. New Haven and London: Yale University Press,
1965, pp. 223–224.]).

[169] Franklin, "Short Account" 2 [see Appendix B].

[170] Franklin, "Short Account" 7 [see Appendix B].

[171] Winn, Arthur T. *The Register of the Parish Church of Knodishall, Co. Suffolk,
1566–1705* (London: Bemrose & Sons, Ltd., 1909) 66 (hereafter Winn,
Knodishall Church).

[172] Winn, *Knodishall Church*, 45 [note 171]. Entries in the seventeenth century appear to not be strictly chronological, with some years appearing in multiple
places. There is another entry in a different area that may be a duplicate entry
for this baptism: "Josuff Frenklon the sone of Josuff Frenklon And An Sawer

15. **BENJAMIN[1] FRANKLIN** (*Thomas*[A], *Henry*[B], *Thomas*[C]) was born at Ecton, Northamptonshire, 20 March 1650, son of Thomas[A] and Jane (White) Franklin.[174] He died at Boston, Suffolk County, Massachusetts, 17 March 1727.[175]

Benjamin married 23 November 1683 **HANNAH WELLES**.[176] She was baptized at Banbury, Oxfordshire , 5 December 1662, daughter of Samuel and Ruth (Johnson) Wells. She died at Westminster, Middlesex, 4 November 1705.[177]

Benjamin was a dyer at Ecton and at London. Unfortunately, he was not as good at business as his brothers. His brother John set him up with Hannah Welles, daughter of a Puritan minister at Banbury. The only record of their marriage to be found was in Benjamin's "Short Account." They had ten children, all but two, Samuel and Hannah, died in childhood. Hannah died at 21 years old. His daughter Elizabeth may also have lived to adulthood, but he information is contradictory.

After twenty-two years of marriage, Hannah died at Westminster 4 November 1705. She was forty-three years old. Benjamin said that at her death "I lost the delight of my mine Eyes, the desire of my heart, and the comfort of my Life."[178]

He landed at Boston 10 October 1715, coming to join his son Samuel who had emigrated earlier. He did not, however, live with his son. Instead he chose to live with his brother Josiah's family. Two years after he arrived, he sat down to write his "Short account of the Family of Thomas Franklin of Ecton in Northamptonshire." A decade later, on 27 March 1727, he died there and was buried near his brother's family in the Granary Burying Ground.

Children of Benjamin[1] and Hannah (Welles) Franklin:

---

his was Babtized the First Day of May in the yeare of 1682." (p. 41). These two entries, and the marriage record for Sarah Franklin are the only records in the parish for someone named Franklin up to 1705.

[173] Franklin, "Short Account" 7 [see Appendix B].

[174] Franklin, "Short Account" 2 [see Appendix B].

[175] Obituary of Benjamin Franklin. *New-England Weekly Journal* (Boston, Massachusetts) No. 50, March 27, 1727, p. 2.

[176] Franklin, "Short Account" 8 [see Appendix B].

[177] Franklin, "Short Account" 8 [see Appendix B].

[178] Franklin, "Short Account" 8 [see Appendix B].

i.   SAMUEL[2] FRANKLIN, b. at Goodman's Fields, Middlesex, England, 15 October 1684;[179] m. (1) at Boston, Suffolk County, Massachusetts, 13 August 1719 HANNAH KELLINECK.

ii. BENJAMIN FRANKLIN, b. Southwark [Christ Church Parish], Surrey, 6 August 1686; d. 22 Apr 1687.

iii. JANE FRANKLIN, b. Southwark [Christ Church Parish], Surrey, 14 September 1687; d. young.

iv. HANNAH FRANKLIN, b. Southwark [Christ Church Parish], Surrey, 13 November 1689; d. 31 December 1710.

v.   THOMAS FRANKLIN, b. Southwark [Christ Church Parish], Surrey, 31 August 1692; d. 2 March 1694.

vi. ELIZABETH FRANKLIN, b. Southwark [Christ Church Parish], Surrey, 27 October 1694; d. after 1717.

vii. MARY FRANKLIN, b. Southwark [Christ Church Parish], Surrey, 23 April 1696; d. 27 August 1696.

viii. JOHN FRANKLIN, b. at Westminster [St. Ann's Parish], Middlesex; d. young.

ix. JOSEPH FRANKLIN, b. at Westminster [St. Ann's Parish], Middlesex, London, 27 January 1700; d. young.

x.   JOSIAH FRANKLIN, b. at Westminster [St. Ann's Parish], Middlesex, London, 3 January 1703; d. 10 January 1703.

16. **HANNAH FRANKLIN** (*Thomas*[A], *Henry*[B], *Thomas*[C]) was born at Ecton, Northamptonshire, 29 October 1654, daughter of Thomas[A] and Jane (White) Franklin.[180] She died 24 June 1712.[181]

Hannah married 29 December 1684 at Great Billing, Northamptonshire, **JOHN MORRIS**.[182] He was a citizen of London and a dyer at the time of their marriage. He died 17 June 1695.[183]

---

[179] All references in the summary for births and deaths of Benjamin and Hannah's children from Franklin, "Short Account" 8–9 [see Appendix B].

[180] Franklin, "Short Account" 2 [see Appendix B].

[181] Franklin, "Short Account" 10 [see Appendix B].

[182] Church of England, St. Andrews Great Billing Parish Registers, Baptisms from 1662 to 1811 (wanting years 1736 to 1746), Marriages from 1664 to 1762, Burials from 1662 to 1810, Northamptonshire Record Office, 31P/1 [FHL Fiche #6,126,700; DGS#101,392,526]. Records are not paginated, but are in alphabetical order.

[183] Franklin, "Short Account" 10 [see Appendix B].

Children of John and Hannah (Franklin) Morris:

    i. ELEANOR MORRIS, prob. bur. at Westbury, Buckingham-
        shire, 2 July 1768.[184]

    ii. JANE MORRIS.

    iii. HANNAH MORRIS.

17. **JOSIAH**[1] **FRANKLIN** (*Thomas*[A]) was born at Ecton, Northamptonshire, 25 December 1657 son of Thomas[A] and Jane (White)
Franklin.[185] He was baptized there at St. Mary Magdelene three
days later.[186] He died at Boston, Suffolk County, Massachusetts, 16
January 1744/5.[187]

He married first **ANNE CHILD**, probably at Ecton about 1676
(birth of first child). She was baptized there 21 January 1654, daughter
of Robert and Debora (—?—) Child. She died at Boston 9 July
1689.[188]

He married second at Boston 25 November 1689 **ABIAH
FOLGER**.[189] She was born at Nantucket, Nantucket County, Mas-
sachusetts, 15 August 1667, daughter of Peter and Mary (Morrell)
Folger.[190] She died at Boston 8 May 1752.[191]

---

[184] Church of England, Westbury St. Augustine, Buckinghamshire, Parish
Registers, 1558–1812. Buckinghamshire Record Office PR223/1/1 [FHL
#1,999,918; DGS #7,909,425].

[185] Franklin, "Short Account" 2 [see Appendix B].

[186] All references in the summary to baptisms, marriages, and burials at Ecton from Church of England Parish Register, St. Mary Magdelene, Ecton, Northamptonshire, Baptisms and Burials 1638–1754, Marriages 1638–1753. Northamptonshire Record Office 114P/203 [FHL Fiche #6,127,382; DGS #100,430,949]
Books are unpaginated; records are in chronological order, grouped by record type.

[187] *The Boston Weekly News-Letter* (Boston, Massachusetts), January 17, 1745, p. 2.

[188] "Ann wife of Josiah Francklin| Aged abo^t 34 Years Died July | y 9
1689" Gravestone of Anne (Child) Franklin, Granary Burying Ground, Boston,
Massachusetts.

[189] Holbrook, *Boston Vital Records*, "Boston Marriages 1689–1720" from the
section "Marriages entered from Anno 1689 to 1695" unpaginated; records are
grouped by the first letter of the surname of the groom. It looks to be a copy
made in the eighteenth century [see note 7].

[190] *Vital Records of Nantucket, Massachusetts, to the Year 1850* (Boston: New
England Historic Genealogical Society, 1925), 1:465, citing the William C. Folger records at the Nantucket Historical Association.

After completing his apprenticeship in London, Josiah joined his father and brother in Banbury. No record of his first marriage to Anne Child has yet been found. She, too, was from Ecton (see "Anne[1] Child, wife of Josiah Franklin" on p. 193). At the age of twenty-six, Josiah took his young family away from the English Midlands and sailed for a new life in the Puritan town of Boston in the Massachusetts Bay Colony.

He attempted to continue the trade of a silk dyer, but there was simply not enough demand for his products in Boston. A talented, intellilgent, and resourceful man, he made a few different attempts before settling on becoming a tallow-chandler.

The three children, Elizabeth, Samuel, and Hannah, were soon joined by two more, Josiah and Ann, who were born in 1685 and 1686/7. A year later, Anne gave birth to another son, Joseph, who lived for less than a week. On 30 June 1689, Anne gave birth to another son, also named Joseph. There must have been complications from the birth, as she died nine days later. The newborn child himself outlived his mother by only a week, and died on 15 July.

With four young children aged 4 to 12, Josiah did not remain a widower long. In November, he married Abiah Folger of Martha's Vineyard. A decade younger than Josiah, she bore him ten more children over the next twenty-two years.

Josiah and Abiah were happily married for more than 55 years. He had seventeen children, and forty-four grandchildren. In fact, the vast majority of the descendants of his grandfather Henry[B] Franklin are Josiah's progeny. Josiah and his family are treated more fully in Volume 3 of *Benjamin Franklin's Family*.

Children of Josiah[1] and Anne (Child) Franklin:

      i. ELIZABETH[2] FRANKLIN, b. at Ecton 2 March 1677[/8];[192] bp. there 10 March 1677/8;[193] d. at Boston 25 August

---

[191] Jordan, *Franklin Genealogist* [see note 9].

[192] Franklin, "Short Account," 11 [see Appendix B]. Franklin says that she was born at Banbury, but it is far more likely that she was born at Ecton.

[193] Jordan, *Franklin Genealogist*, 4 [see note 9]. Franklin List in same gives birth date of 2 March 1677/8.

1759; m. (1) there 8 January 1707 JOSEPH BERRY; m. (2) there 19 March 1721 RICHARD DOUSE.

ii. SAMUEL FRANKLIN, b. at Banbury 16 May 1681;[194] bp. there 20 May 1681; d. at Boston 31 March 1719/20; m. at Boston 16 May 1705 ELIZABETH TYNG.

iii. HANNAH FRANKLIN, b. at Banbury 25 May 1683; bp. there 2 June 1683; d. at Boston 3 April 1723; m. (1) JOSEPH EDDY; m. (2) at Boston 22 June 1710 THOMAS COLE.

iv. JOSIAH FRANKLIN, b. at Boston 23 August 1685;[195] bp. 29 September 1685;[196] d. by 1717;[197] went to sea, returned after nine years, shipped out again and was never heard from again.

v. ANNE FRANKLIN, b. at Boston 5 January 1686[/7[;[198] bp. 9 January 1686[/7]; d. at Ipswich, Essex County, Massachusetts, 15 June 1729; m. at Boston 10 June 1712 WILLIAM HARRIS.

vi. JOSEPH FRANKLIN, b. at Boston 5 January 1687/8;[199] d. there 11 January 1687/8.[200]

vii. JOSEPH FRANKLIN, b. at Boston 30 June 1689;[201] bp. 30 June 1689;[202] d. there 15 July 1689.[203]

---

[194] All references in the summary to baptisms at Banbury from Church of England, Banbury St. Mary, Oxfordshire, Parish Registers, 1723–1801, p. 180. Oxfordshire History Centre PAR21/1/R1/4. "Oxfordshire, England, Church of England Baptism, Marriages, and Burials, 1538-1812" database online at www.ancestry.com. (Lehi, UT, USA: Ancestry.com Operations, Inc., 2016).

[195] Holbrook, *Boston VRs* "Births 1635–1744" unpaginated; records are grouped by years, then mostly by the first letter of the surname. This is a later transcription. The location of the originals is unknown [see note 7].

[196] "Boston, Massachusetts, Church Records" [database online at *www.AmericanAncestors.org.*] Originally published as Robert J. Dunkle and Ann S. Lainhart, *The Records of the Churches of Boston and the First Church, Second Parish, and Third Parish of Roxbury, Including Baptisms, Marriages, Deaths, Admissions, and Dismissals* (CD-ROM database, Boston: New England Historic Genealogical Society, 2001) "Records of the Old South Church in Boston," 101 (hereafter *Boston Churches*).

[197] Franklin, "Short Account," 11 [see Appendix B]

[198] Holbrook, *Boston VRs*, "Births 1635–1744," [see note 7].

[199] Holbrook, *Boston VRs*, "Births 1635–1744," [see note 7].

[200] Jordan, Franklin List [see note 9].

[201] Holbrook, *Boston VRs*, "Births 1635–1744" [see note 7].

[202] *Boston Churches*, "Records of the Old South Church in Boston," p. 115 [see note 196].

[203] Jordan, Franklin List [see note 9].

Children of Josiah[1] and Abiah (Folger) Franklin, born at Boston and baptized there at the Old South Church:

viii.   JOHN FRANKLIN, b. 7 December 1690;[204] bp. 7 December 1690; d. at Boston 20 January 1756; m. (1) MARY GOOCH; m. (2) ELIZABETH (GOOCH) HUBBART.

ix.   PETER FRANKLIN, b. 22 November 1692;[205] d. at Philadelphia, Philadelphia County, Pennsylvania, 1 July 1766; m. at Boston 2 September 1714 MARY HARMAN.

x.   MARY FRANKLIN, b. 26 September 1694;[206] bp. 30 September 1694; d. at Boston 1731; m. there 3 April 1716 ROBERT HOMES.

xi.   JAMES FRANKLIN, b. 4 February 1696;[207] bp. 7 February 1696; d. at Newport, Newport County, Rhode Island, 4 February 1735; m. at Boston 4 May 1723 ANN SMITH.

xii.   SARAH FRANKLIN, b. 9 July 1699;[208] bp. 16 July 1699; d. at Boston 23 May 1731; m. there 23 May 1722 JAMES DAVENPORT.

xiii.   EBENEZER FRANKLIN, b. 20 September 1701;[209] bp. 21 September 1701; d. at Boston 5 February 1703, drowned in a tub of suds.[210]

xiv.   THOMAS FRANKLIN, b. 7 December 1703;[211] bp. 12 December 1703;[212] d. at Boston 17 August 1706.[213]

xv.   BENJAMIN FRANKLIN, b. 6 January 1706;[214] bp. 6 January 1706; d. at Philadelphia, Philadelphia County, Pennsylvania, 17 April 1790; m. at Philadelphia 1 September 1730, DEBORAH (READ) ROGERS.

---

[204] Holbrook, *Boston VRs*, "Births 1635–1744" [see note 7].

[205] Holbrook, *Boston VRs*, "Births 1635–1744" [see note 7].

[206] Holbrook, *Boston VRs*, "Births 1635–1744" [see note 7].

[207] Holbrook, *Boston VRs*, "Births 1635–1744" [see note 7].

[208] Holbrook, *Boston VRs*, "Births 1635–1744" [see note 7].

[209] Holbrook, *Boston VRs*, "Births 1635–1744" [see note 7].

[210] "Ebenezer Franklin of the South Church male-infant of 16 months old, was drown'd in a Tub of Suds, Feb[r] 5 1702/3." M. Halsey Thomas, ed., *The Diary of Samuel Sewall, 1674–1729* (New York: Farrar, Strauss, and Giroux, 1973), 1:482. Also, Jordan, *Franklin Genealogist*, Franklin List [see note 9].

[211] Holbrook, *Boston VRs*, "Births 1635–1744" [see note 7].

[212] *Boston Churches*, "Records of the Old South Church in Boston," p. 148 [see note 196].

[213] Jordan, Franklin Franklin List [see note 9].

[214] Holbrook, *Boston VRs*, "Births 1635–1744" [see note 7].

xvi. LYDIA FRANKLIN, b. 8 August 1708;[215] d. probably at Newport, 1758; m. at Boston 1731 ROBERT SCOTT.

xvii. JANE FRANKLIN, b. 27 March 1712;[216] d. at Boston May
1794; m. there 27 July 1727 EDWARD MECOM.

18. SAMUEL RIDE (*Esther Franklin, Henry*[B], *Thomas*[C]) was the only
child of Robert and Esther/Hesther (Franklin) Ride. He worked
as a farmer and a gentleman's servant before moving to London
after the Great Fire of 1666 to help rebuild the city. All we know
of Samuel comes from Benjamin Franklin the Elder's "Short Account." He did not record the name of Samuel's wife or daughter,
and there is insufficient information to identify the daughter in
London.

Child of Samuel Franklin, mother unknown:

i. —?— (daughter), married a butcher at Clare Market, Westminster.

19. MARY FRANKLIN (*Thomas, Thomas*[A], *Henry*[B], *Thomas*[C]) was born
at Ecton, Northamptonshire, 24 October 1673, daughter of
Thomas and Eleanor/Helen (—?—) Franklin. She died 25 December 1758.[217] She was buried at All Hallows Parish, Wellingborough, Northamptonshire, 30 December 1758.[218]

Mary married **RICHARD FISHER** of Wellingborough, Northamptonshire. He died there 12 December 1758.[219] He was buried there 16
December 1758.

---

[215] Holbrook, *Boston VRs*, "Births 1635–1744" [see note 7].

[216] Holbrook, *Boston VRs*, "Births 1635–1744" [see note 7].

[217] Labaree, *Papers of Benjamin Franklin*, 1:li [see note 24].

[218] All references in the summary to baptisms, marriages, and burials at
Wellingborough from Church of England, Wellingborough All Hallows,
Northamptonshire, Parish Register, Baptisms and Burials 1702–1774, Marriages
1702–1754. Northamptonshire Record Office 350P/647 [FHL Fiche
#6,129,278; DGS #100,430,944].

[219] Labaree, *Papers of Benjamin Franklin*, 1:li [see note 24].

As an only child, Mary was her father Thomas' heir. She came into the Franklin property at Ecton, but eventually sold it out of the family, as she and her husband had no need for it. They had no children, and Richard was successful in his own right. In his will Richard left bequests to several nieces, and the majority of the estate went to Mary and to his nephew, Rev. William Fisher. [220]

When Benjamin Franklin and his son William toured Northamptonshire and Warwickshire in 1758, they were able to spend some time with Mary and Richard. Although they were first cousins, Mary was thirty years older than Benjamin. She was 85 years old when they visited, and she was able to tell him a number of stories about the family. The timing was auspicious, as the Fishers died within two weeks of each other that December.

Child of Richard and Mary (Franklin) Fisher:

   i. **ELEANOR FISHER**, d. ca. 1728.[221]

20. **THOMAS FRANKLIN** (*John, Thomas*[A], *Henry*[B], *Thomas*[C]) was born at Banbury 15 September 1681 or 82, son of John and Ann (Jeffs) Franklin.[222] He died possibly at Birmingham, Warwickshire, ca. 1752.[223] Thomas' wife is unknown.

Like his father John, Thomas was a dyer. He is occasionally confused with his son Thomas.

Children of Thomas Franklin:

   i. BENJAMIN FRANKLIN, res. at Blenheim Palace in 1743–1744.

---

[220] Church of England, Archdeaconry of Northampton Court; Original Wills, Administrations, Inventories, 1758; Will of Richard Fisher of Wellingborough, 18 December 1758 [FHL Film #187,746; DGS #8,473,627].

[221] Labaree, *Papers of Benjamin Franklin*, 1:li [see note 24].

[222] Franklin, "Short Account" 5–7 [see Appendix B]. For Thomas see also Church of England. Peculiar Court, Banbury, Oxfordshire, Original Wills, Administration Bonds, and Inventories, (surname E) 1557–1675 and (surname F) 1683–1799. Will and Administration of John Franklin [FHL #173,596; DGS #8,472,405].

[223] Labaree, *Papers of Benjamin Franklin*, 1:li [see note 24]. No source for the information is given.

22 ii. THOMAS FRANKLIN, b. ca. 1715 (age 87 at death); bur. at Lutterworth 20 January 1803; m. (1) ANN —?—; m. (2) MARY —?—; m. (3) SARAH —?—.

iii. JOHN FRANKLIN, bur. at Lutterworth 7 October 1729.

21. **ANNE FRANKLIN** (*John, Thomas*[A]*, Henry*[B]*, Thomas*[C]) was baptized at Banbury, Oxfordshire, 3 February 1684/5, daughter of John and Ann (Jeffs) Franklin.[224] She likely died by the summer of 1767 when Benjamin Franklin wrote to his cousin Samuel in Boston, listing Anne's daughter Hannah as among the living relatives in England, but does not mention Anne.[225]

Anne married by 1724 **HENRY FARROW**. He died before 1759.

Anne was a lacemaker at Hartwell, Northamptonshire England. Later she kept a school at Castlethorpe, near Stony Stratford, Buckinghamshire, England.[226]

Child of Henry and Anne (Franklin) Farrow:

23 i. **HANNAH FARROW**, b. 21 July 1724;[227] bp. at Castlethorpe, 9 August 1724; bur. at Westbury 9 January 1787; m. there 4 June 1754 **THOMAS WALKER**.

22. **THOMAS FRANKLIN** (*Thomas, John, Thomas*[A]*, Henry*[B]*, Thomas*[C]), son of Thomas Franklin, was born about 1715. He was buried at Lutterworth, Leicestershire, 20 January 1803 at the age of 87.

He married first **SARAH** —?—. She was buried at Lutterworth 20 April 1748.

He married second **MARY** —?—. She was buried there 31 August 1765.

---

[224] Gibson, *Banbury Register*, 45.

[225] "From Benjamin Franklin to Samuel Franklin, 17 July 1767," Founders Online, National Archives, accessed September 29, 2019, https://founders.archives. gov/documents/Franklin/01-14-02-0127. [Original source: *The Papers of Benjamin Franklin*, vol. 14, January 1 through December 31, 1767, ed. Leonard W. Labaree. New Haven and London: Yale University Press, 1970, pp. 215–216.]

[226] Labaree, *Papers of Benjamin Franklin*, 1:lii [see note 24].

[227] Labaree, *Papers of Benjamin Franklin*, 1:lii [see note 24].

The timing of his childrens' burials leaves it difficult to determine which wife was the mother of the two middle children. There are no baptisms for them at Lutterworth, which adds to the challenge.

Thomas followed the traditional occupation in his family of being a dyer. He visited Benjamin Franklin in London during the latter's sojourn there. After Mary's death, he brought his daughter Sarah to London to stay with Benjamin and his landlady, Mrs. Margaret (—?—) Stevenson. He took care of her, educated her, and ensured she had a good man for a husband.

Child of Thomas and Sarah (—?—) Franklin:

> i. JOHN FRANKLIN, bp. at Lutterworth 12 June 1747; bur. there 4 February 1747.

Children of Thomas Franklin, mother uncertain:

> ii. JOHN FRANKLIN, bur. at Lutterworth 25 April 1749.
> iii. ANN FRANKLIN, bur. at Lutterworth 31 April 1758.

Child of Thomas and Mary (—?—) Franklin:

> 24 iv. SARAH FRANKLIN, b. ca. 1753; d. 22 October 1781; m. ca. 1773 JAMES PEARCE.

23. **HANNAH FARROW** (*Anne Franklin, John, Thomas*[A], *Henry*[B], *Thomas*[C]) was born, probably at Castlethorpe, Buckinghamshire, 21 July 1724, daughter of Henry and Anne (Franklin) Farrow.[228] She was baptised there 9 August 1724.[229] She was buried at Westbury 9 January 1787.[230]

---

[228] Labaree, *Papers of Benjamin Franklin*, lii [see note 24].

[229] All references in the summary to baptisms, marriages, and burials at Castlethorpe from Church of England, Castlethorpe Church of St. Simon and St. Jude, Buckinghamshire, Bishop's Transcripts, 1600–1837. Buckinghamshire Record Office D/A/T/34, 210/2 [FHL #1,999,133; DGS #4,010,424].

[230] All references in the summary to baptisms and burials at Westbury from Church of England, Westbury St. Augustine, Buckinghamshire, Parish Registers, 1558–1812. Buckinghamshire Record Office PR223/1/1 [FHL #1,999,918; DGS #7,909,425].

She married at Castlethorpe 4 June 1754 **THOMAS WALKER.** His origins are unknown.

They resided at Castlethorpe, Buckinghamshire, and Westbury, Northamptonshire. They were quite poor, and Benjamin Franklin was quite supportive of them in many ways after his 1758 tour. There was come conflict between them when either Hanna or her husband did something untoward. The specifics are not known, but their correspondence continued afterwards.[231]

Benjamin later set her son Henry up with an indentured position, so the disagreement was likely not too serious. His great-nephews Josiah Williams and Jonathan Williams, Jr., had spent some time visiting him in London. Benjamin arranged for Henry to go home with them. Unfortunately, Josiah died young, and Jonathan had a falling out with Henry. But he arranged another position for him, and all seemed well after that.[232]

Children of Thomas and Hannah (Farrow) Walker:

    i.   JOHN WALKER, b. 4 March 1755.

    ii. HENRY WALKER, b. 29 November 1756.

   iii. THOMAS WALKER, bp. 26 December 1759 at Westbury.

   iv. BENJAMIN FRANKLIN WALKER, bp. 4 May 1762 at Westbury; bur. there 9 March 1763.

    v. WILLIAM FRANKLIN WALKER, bp. 13 May 1764 at Westbury; bur. there 20 November 1764.

   VI. WILLIAM FRANKLIN WALKER, bp. 13 May 1765 at Westbury; bur. there 16 November 1765.

---

[231] "To Benjamin Franklin from Hannah Walker, 16 June 1768," Founders Online, National Archives, accessed September 29, 2019, https://founders.archives.gov/documents/Franklin/01-15-02-0083. [Original source: *The Papers of Benjamin Franklin*, vol. 15, January 1 through December 31, 1768, ed. William B. Willcox. New Haven and London: Yale University Press, 1972, pp. 142–144.]

[232] "To Benjamin Franklin from Jonathan Williams, Jr., 13 October 1772," Founders Online, National Archives, accessed September 29, 2019, https://founders.archives.gov/documents/Franklin/01-19-02-0226. [Original source: *The Papers of Benjamin Franklin*, vol. 19, January 1 through December 31, 1772, ed. William B. Willcox. New Haven and London: Yale University Press, New Haven and London, 1975, pp. 337–338.]

25. **SARAH FRANKLIN**, (*Thomas, Thomas, John, Thomas, Henry, Thomas, Robert*) was baptized at Lutterworth, Leicestershire, 5 June 1752, son of Thomas and Mary (—?—) Franklin. She died 22 October 1781.

She married at Ewell, Surrey, 17 April 1773 **JAMES PEARCE**. He died sometime after 1784, possibly at Annapolis, Maryland.

After Sarah's mother died in 1765, her father brought her to London to stay for a time with his cousin Benjamin Franklin. He was not as successful as other members of the family, and wanted better things for her. Benjamin took care of her, and eventually made sure that she married a good man with prospects. He was a witness when when she married James Pearce just before her twenty-first birthday.

Sarah and James had four children in their eight years of marrige before she died. James went to America in 1783. He left his son with Sarah's father, but there is no record of what happened to his daughters. James wrote to his father-in-law a year later from Annapolis, Maryland, but it was the last communication they received from him.

In 1791 Thomas Franklin was 76 years old and in charge of his 13-year-old grandson. An acquaintance of his wrote to George Washington in America to try to get financial assistance for him (Benjamin Franklin died in 1790). The response from Washington's secretary was that the gentleman should get in touch with Benjamin's grandson, William Temple Franklin, who was recently gone to London.[233]

No record could be found of James Pearce at Annapolis. Nor could any record be found for any of the children after the Macaulay letter.

Children of James and Sarah (Franklin) Pearce, baptised at Richmond, Surrey:

    i. MARGARET PEARCE, bp. 17 April 1775.

---

[233] Mark A. Mastromarino, editor, and Jack D. Warren, Jr., assistant editor, *Papers of George Washington, Presidential Series (24 September 1788–3 March 1797)*, Volume 8 (22 March 1791–22 September 1791) (Charlottesville: University of Virginia Press, 1999) 497–99 (hereafter Mastromarino, *Papers of George Washington*).

ii. MARY PEARCE, bp. Richmond, 25 January 1777.

iii. THOMAS JAMES PEARCE, bp. 10 November 1778; res. at Lutterworth 1791.

iii. FRANCES PEARCE, bp. Richmond, 19 August 1780.

PART II

OTHER EARLY FRANKLINS OF NORTHAMPTONSHIRE

CHAPTER 11
FRANKLINS OF DALLINGTON

Dallington is a small village approximately seven miles west of Ecton, bordering on the northwestern edge of the city of Northampton. In the sixteenth and early-seventeenth centuries, it was the home to a single family of Franklins. The following records were found in the parish registers of Dallington St. Giles:[234]

Baptisms
Anne Franklin the daughter of Thomas Franklin was baptized the third day of July the same year [1588]
John Franklyn the Sonne of Thomas Franklyn was baptized the xxi[th] [21] day of Aprill in the Same yeare [1591]
Jonathan Franklin the Sonne of John Franklin and Sarah his wife was baptized the 14 day of Maie [1615]
John Franklin the Sonne of John Franklin and Sarah his wife was baptized the 3 day of Aougust. [1616]

Marriages
Thomas Franklyn and Alice Richardson were marryed the xiv[th] [14] of November A Dom 1585
John Franklin and Sarah Warner were Married the 14 day of Mar [1614]
William Marten and Sara Franklin were marryed the iij [3] of November [1632]

Burials
Ann Franklyn the Daughter of Thomas Franklyn was buryed the xix[th] [19] Day of July in the Same yeare [1588]
Agnes Franklyn was buryed the vii[th] [7] Day of Aprill in the Same yeare [1596]
John Franklyn was buryed the xxix[th] [29] Daye of June in the Same yeare [1597]

---

[234] Church of England, Dallington St. Giles, Northamptonshire, Parish Registers, 1577–1694; Northampton Record Office 95P/2 [FHL Fiche #6,127,185; DGS #100,342,799].

John Franklin [xxxxxxx] was buried the 28 day of Februarie
[1615]

Jonathan Franklin and John Franklin Sonnes of John Franklin
and Sara his wife the tenth of Auguste [1621]

John Frankling the Sonne of Thomas Frankling was buryed
viij of May [1631]

Elizabeth Frankling was buryed the xxiiii day of November
[1631]

Sarah Frankling the dafter of Sara Frankling was burryed the
vii [7] of Aprill [1632]

The family was fairly successful, and a number of members of
the family left wills that help clarify the various family groupings.

Will of Henry Franklyng, probated 11 May 1550[235]

[page 1]
In the name off god Ame[n] th^e xv day off September in the in
the 3 yere off or souvand lorde Edward th^e sext by the grace off
god kyng of England France and Ireland defender off th^e fayth
and no[xx]orth off this [xx]mese off inglande and Also off Ireland prsone gede I Henry Franklynge of th^e prshe off dalington
in the countie off North[hampton] and of the Dyoc of pet-
borou being hole of mynde wyth memorye but seke in my body
make th^{is} my testament: in man^r and forme folowyng Ffyrst I
bequeth my soule to god Allmyghtye and my body to be buried
in the church of dalyngton as forgyng th^e dysposytyon of All my
and catells movable and im movable I comyt and geve [illegible]
John Franklyng my sone whome I make my full executor paying
my debts before wyll[ia]m bayes whome I doe make and

[page 2]
of this mye last wyll and also before Rychard Jones John Latlaye
and thomas Attenburye Dy^r of Duston wytnesses to all and
syngulare the prmysses

---

235 Church of England, Archdeaconry Court of Northampton, Wills &
Administrations, Register Copy Wills, Will of Henry Franklyng of Dallington,
vol. K, fol. 175 [FHL Film #187,580; DGS #8,047,443].

John Franklyn of Dallington, probated July 1592[236]

In the name of god Amen the 4 day of June in the year of o[r] lord god 1592 I John Franklyn the eld[r] of Dallington in the countie of North[hamp]ton husbandman doman being sicke in body but of pfecte minde and memorie god be thanked Doe ordayne and make my Last Will and Testament in man[r] and forme following / First I comit my sole to Almightie god and my bodye to be buried in the churchyard of Dallington aforesd It[e]m I will that my land shall remaine betwixt my wife and Thomas my sonn until the decease of Agnes my wife and then I will that: Thomas my sonn shall have the whole land and in the meane time I will my catiall shall be pd betwixt them both: It[e]m I will that Thomas my sonn shall have the hovell tymbe[r] by the streakj and the rye house tymber the falt [xxxx] w[th] the falt ane Axre Owyfalt and a greate cheste It[e]m I give unto Thomas my sonn my best goode carte After the decease of Agnes my wife / And I will also th[t] after hir decease Nicholas Franklin and John Franklyn my sonnes shall share the nexte best carte It[e] I will and bequeathe th[t] after my wyffe decease John my sonn shall clame the of a closse yarde land one yeare and wthold my sonn   the [xx]oppe [xx] a half yarde lamland [xxx] yeare It[e]m I give unto 4 of my sonnes children every one a sheepe. It[em] I give [xxxx] [xxxx] my son [illegible] vjd pence apeece. It[e]m I give to everye one of ^my^ godchildren xj[d] It[e]m I give unto W[ch] hir [xxx] for my tithes bequeathed I give and bequeathe to Agnes my wife whome I make my sole sole executrix of this my last Will and Testa[mt] she paying my debtsL in witnes where of Robt Richards Thomas Batton John Franklyn the younger and James Batton with [xxxx]

[236] Church of England, Archdeaconry of Northampton Court, Register Copy Wills, vol. Y, fol. 40, Will of John Franklyn of Dallington, 1592 [FHL Film #187,590; DGS #8,047,459].

Nicholas Franklinge of Harleston, probated 7 November 1598[237]

In the name of God Amen The xviij daye of October I Nicholas Franklinge of Harelston in the Countie of North[ampton] beinge sicke in body but whole in minde doe ordaine and make this my last will and Testament in manner and forme foollowinge. That is to saye firste I com[mi]t my soule into the hands of Allmightie god and my body to be buried in the Church of Hareltston · Item I give unto my sonne Thos Franklinge threescore and one pounds and x^d and the best chest withe chamber to bee paide unto him at xxjth yeares of age Item I give unto my daughter Elizabeth Frankling lxj£ xx^s a great red coffer the best longe table cloath the best fowell, the best christening sheete a payre of the best pillow bears and a payre of the best sheets to bee payde to her at xviijth yeares of age Item I give to Willm Starman my [illegible short word crossed out] man one lambe to bee payd at midsomers next and I give unto him my best coate also · Item I give to Joan Chafer my maide one strike of millcorne, one perke of wheat and one sheepe to bee payd to her at the day of her marrage. · Item I give to Joane Ingream my maide one lambe to bee payde to hir at midsomer next Item I give vj£ viij^d to bee given to the most needye in Harelston at the discretion of myne executors Item I give iiij^d to every one of my godchildren · Item my will is that my brother Thomas Franklinge shall keepe my daughter Elizabeth and have the role of her stocke untill she come to xviij^t yeares of age pvided that if it please god that she dieth before she receiveth hir stocke or die unmarried after the the recevinge of her stocke then I give x£ of of her stocke to John Franklinge my brother Thomas his sonne and the rest of hir stocke I give to my sonne Thomas for the mendinge of his stock pvided that if my brother Thomas shall depart this lyfe before the payinge of my daughter Elizabeth his stocke that then my brother John shalle keepe my daughter Elizabeth and have the rolde of hir stocke untill she come to xviij^t yeares of age Item my will is that my brother John Franklinge shall keepe my sonne Thomas at scole until he can reade and write legablie and keepinge him shall have the role of

[237] Church of England, Archdeaconry of Northampton Court, Register Copy Wills, vol. W, fol. 77, Will of Nicholas Franklinge of Dallington, 1598 [FHL Film #187,588; DGS #8,047,477].

his stocke untill he cometh to one and twentie years of age pvided that if it please god that he dieth before he receiveth his stocke or die unmaried after hee hath received his stocke, then I give xx£ of his stock equally to my brother to John Franklinge his children and the rest of my sonne Thomas his stocke I give to my daughter Elizabeth for the mendinge of her stocke, pvided also that if my brother John shall depte this lyfe before the payinge of my sonne Thomas his stocke that then my brother Thomas shall keep my sonne Thomas and have the role of his stocke untill hee come to xxj^t yeares of age pvided also y^t if borth my children died before the receiving of their stocks that then my brother Thomas shall paye and give of my daughters stock xl^s to Nichas Phillp xl^d to George Richardson xl^d to Christopher Baffin x^s to Nicholas Starman xl^s to Margreat Ashborne all these being my godchildren and the rest of my daughters stocke I give to John Franklinge my brother Thomas his sonne also my will is that my sonne Thomas his stocke shall comme equally amongst my brother John his children allwaies pvided if it please god y^t my children die both, which thinge if it please god to bringe to passe my will is also th x^s shalbe given to the poore in either towne where the dwell. Item I give xij^d to to m^r Gregory because I knowe not whether I have forgotten any tithings or not · Item I give xij^d to willm Browne · all the rest of my goodes I give to my brother Thomas Franklinge and to my brother John Franklinge which I make myne exectors of this my last will and Testament and I give them full power and authorie to deale in my livinge our farme which I hold in Harelston for the better performinge of the legacies contained in this my sayd last will and Testament prvided y^t they shall paye all my debts ·In the p^{r}sence of sd willm Browne willm Larke Richard Carver

John Franklin of Dallington, probated 5 November 1615[238]

In the name of god Amen, the Firste daie of January one thousand six hundred and Fifteen I John Franklin holder of Dallington in the county of Northampton husbandman being weake of

---

[238] Church of England, Archdeaconry of Northampton Court, Original Wills, Series 2, vol. 2, no. 81, Will of John Franklin of Dallington, 1615 [FHL Film #187,613; DGS #8,517,841].

body but of pfect memory the lord be raised therefore, doe make and ordaine this my last will and testament in mann^r and forme following (vizt)

Imprimie I give and bequeath my soule to almighty god my maker hoping through tht morills death and passion of his dearly beloved sonne Jesus Christ my redeem^r and by none other meanes to be saved;

Secondlie I give and bequeath until Nathaniel Phips my grandchilde Five pouonds of lawfull money of England to be paid him when and at such time as he shall accomplish the age of Twenty and one yeares

Thirdlie I give and bequeath unto my granchilde Phebe Phips Five pouonds of lawfull money of England to be paid her within one month next after she shalle marrie or when she shall accomplishe the age of Twenty and one yeares

Fourthlie I give and bequeath to unot my grandchilde hanna Phips Five pouonds of like money to be paid her w^thin one moneth next after she shaalbe married or when she shall accomplish the age of twenty and one yeares.

Fifthly I give and bequeath unto my grandchilde John Phips two ewes:

Sixthly I give and bequeath unto ^my^ well beloved wife Elizabeth Franklin all the residue of ^my^ goods rabbell and Chattells herein before not bequeathed whom I make and ordaine sole executrix of this my last will and testament. In witness whereof I the said John Franklin have hereunto set my hand [illegible] published it for my last will in the prdet [?] of Robt Boise.

Robert
Boise

Thomas Franklin   Phillip Cooper   John Franklin
his marke   his marke

Will of Thomas Franklyn of Dallington, probated 4 January 1623[239]

In the name of God Amen the xxvj[th] day of Aprill 1622 ·/ I Thomas Franklin of Dallington in the Countie of Northton husbandman being of good and pfect memorie the Lord by thanked therefore yet knowing all men must dye though the tyme be most [xxx]ordained doe make and ordayne this my last Will and Testament in mann[r] and forme following viz Imprimis I commit my soule into the hands of almightie god saying throught the meritts death and passion of his sonne and my Saviour Jesus Christ and by none other meanes to be saved and my body to the earth and to be buried in the churchyard of Dallington when it shall please god to call me out of this transitorie lyfe and my worldly goods w[ch] it hath pleased god to lend me I disposse and bequeath them in man[r] and forme following viz Item I give to my wyfe Alice Franklin all my corne and grayne in and about my barnes and hovell half a yard land w[th] all comodities and appurten[a]ncs thereunto belonging to be equally devided out of the three yard lands and a half more in the tenure of comacon of me the said Thomas and my sonne John the rie barne to lay her corne and stuffe in the turffe hovell and the hovell in the Conyard to lay her cattle in the buttery the boulting house and the Chamber and the butery for her habitation during her Lease noeew have of the same And my will is my said sonne John shall according to good and pfect husbndry dresse and till the said half yard lande for the said Alice his mother, and bringe and carry some the corne grayne and all other comodities from tyme to tyme growing and increasing upon the same cleerely w[th]out any consideracon or other recompense she the said Alice sending foode for the same, and also manure and compost and making all things reaty to the carte durign the contynuance of my said Lease And paying the Lords rent apportionallly vizt the fiste parte of the ~~Lease~~ Rente referred in the said Lease, And when the said lease is ended my will is that the said Alice my wyfe shall have the said land and premisses above bequeathed during her said lyfe paying the

---

[239] Church of England, Archdeaconry of Northampton Court, Register Copy Wills, vol. AV, fol. 143, Will of Thomas Franklyn of Dallington, 1623 [FHL Film #187,585; DGS #8,947,421].

Lords rent and other payments ratablely and exportionnally as
in said sonne John or his assigns doth And he the said John or
his assigne to plane[?] till dresse and bring some the Corne adnd
grayne and the comodities as aforesaid during her said lyfe, Item
I give to the said Alice my wyfe three m[xx]h beasts and one
heifer to be taken out of my bine at my departure neither of the
best nor worst sorte but to be indifferently taken

[page 2]
and shalbe one [illegible]be likewise chosen [illegible] said the
second best [illegible] and [illegible] a little brasse panne the
least [illegible] and skillet half my panter a lattin char and the the
[sic] and the biggest latine candlestick the great cheste two bedds
in the parlor two pailes three tubbs little chest one old rafer[?] a
woodden chaire the table and forme in the buttery a little forme
in the chamber three stooles the reste of the boultingten and
mill during her lyfe the lesser spitt two drink barrelles (the close
next John Richardson in the brooke land and the little grasse
yard all the linene and woollen in the said Coffers and Chests
above menconed and bedding on the said bedds And my will is
their Ca[xxx]e shall have [xxx]te in co[m]mon in the whole yard
together not offeding one an other. Item I give unto my said my
stone salt seller all mine and her apparell and all other lynnens
and wollens in the plow one hogg and one pigg and the farmost
hayfield. Item I give to the pore of Dallington that are most
needy vj⁵ viij⁴: or soe much corne as chall amount thereunto at
the discretion of myne executor and to all our servants Twelve
pence appeece ·/ Item all the rest of my goods Cattells and
Chattells herein not before bequeathed my debts and funeralls
discharged, I give an bequeath to my said sonne John whome I
make sole executor of this my last will and Testamᵗ and I doe
intreat my loving frinds and kinsmen Francis Batton and John
Phips to be overseers of the same And doe publishe it for my
last will in the [xx]dre of the said John Phipps the marke of Sara
Frankline.

The surviving sacramental records of Dallington St. Giles date
back only to 1577. The first record of the family is the will of
Henry Franklyng written 15 September 1549 and probated 11 May
1550. He names son John his sole heir and executor.

John Franklyn the elder wrote his will 4 June 1592. The will is extremely difficult to read in parts due to fading. He names his wife Agnes, and sons Thomas, Nicholas, and John. One of the witnesses was John Franklin the younger. Thomas shares the estate with the widow, with Nicholas and John splitting her half after her decease, indicating the Thomas is likely the eldest son.

The first parish records of the family are for the marriage of Thomas Franklyn and Alice Richardson 14 November 1585. They had two children baptised there: Anne, who died in infancy in 1588, and John in 1591.

NICHOLAS FRANKLIN

The 1598 will of Nicholas Franklin of Harlestone is quite detailed, and names a number of family members. Nicholas had two children, both of whom were minors. His brother John was to take care of son Thomas until he turned 21 and brother Thomas was to keep daughter Elizabeth until she turned 18. The will also mentions brother Thomas's son John, and brother John's son Thomas.

There are three records for Nicholas and his family at Harlestone St. Andrew:[240]

Thomas Franklyn the sone of nicholas franklyn was Baptized the 12th of Septe[m]ber Ao Dm 1591

Agnes Franklin the wife of Nicholas franklin was buryed the 18th of June Ao Dm 1593

Nicholas Franklin was buried the 20th of october Anno Super [1598]

No baptism has been found for the daughter Elizabeth named in the will. Nicholas's father John left a legacy "unto 4 my sonnes children every one a sheepe." Nicholas's brother Thomas had one child, son John. Brother John had two children: Thomas and Agnes. Nicholas's son John was baptised in 1591. Thus it is likely

---

[240] Church of England, Harlestone St. Andrew, Northamptonshire, Parish Registers, Baptisms 1570–1709, Marriages 1570–1711, Burials 1574–1615 Northampton Record Office 153P/1, [FHL Fiche #6,127,669; DGS #100,342,745].

that Elizabeth was born after sometime after John wrote his will in June 1592. Nicholas' wife Agnes was buried 18 June 1593.

JOHN FRANKLIN

John Franklin, the second of the three brothers to die, was buried at Dallington 28 February 1615. Although Nicholas's will mentioned that his brother John had a son Thomas, no mention was made of the son in John's will. He left bequests to his grand-children Nathaniel, Phebe, Hannah, and John Phipps. The parish registers of Northampton All Saints provide additional information about the children and their parents:[241]

> Robertus Phippes dt Dallington et Agnes Franklyn dt cadem parochia nupti fuirunt ventisimo septimo dit [May 1587]
> Phebe filia Roberti Phipes dt Dallington baptizata xxvij° [November 1593
> Nathaniel filius Robert Phipes dt Dallington baptizat fuit xvj dit [December 1599]

No record of baptism was found for Hannah or John Phipps, but these records are clearly for John's daughter and grandchildren.

THOMAS FRANKLIN

The first record for the family in the Dallington parish regis-ters was the marriage of the third brother, Thomas, and Alice Richardson on 14 November 1585. Two children of the couple were baptised there: Anne in 1588 and John in 1591. Baptised on 3 July 1588, baby Anne was buried on 19 July, just two weeks later. was the last of the three sons to die.

There is no burial for record for him at Dallington, but his will, written there 26 April 1622 was probated 4 January 1623. He left his estate to his wife Alice and son John. The will was wit-nessed by Sara Franklin.

John Franklin married Sarah Warner at Dallington 14 March 1614. They had two sons baptised at Dallington: Jonathan in 1615

---

[241] Church of England, Northampton All Saints, Northamptonshire, Parish Registers, 1559–1722 Northampton Record Office 223P/1, [FHL Fiche #6,128,174; DGS #100,430,869].

and John in 1616. The boys were both buried there in 1621. John was buried 8 May 1631. Sarah, daughter of Sarah Franklin was buried 7 April 1632. Although there is no baptismal record for her, she is clearly a daughter of John who had died the year before. William Marten and Sara Franklin married 3 November 1632.

After John's widow remarried in 1632, the Franklin surname disappears from Dallington records. There is no evidence to connect them to the family of Benjamin Franklin.

GENEALOGICAL SUMMARY

1. HENRY FRANKLIN was residing at Dallington, Northampton-shire, when he wrote his will in 1550.[242] No wife is mentioned in the will, indicating she likely predeceased him.

Child of Henry Franklin:

2   i.   JOHN FRANKLIN, bur. at Dallington 23 June 1592;[243] m. Agnes —?—.

2. JOHN FRANKLIN (*Henry*) was buried at Dallington 23 June 1592. He was a son of Henry Franklin who died there in 1550.

John married AGNES —?—, likely before the start of the parish registers in 1577. She was buried at Dallington 7 April 1596.

His will, probate in July 1592, splits the majority of his estate between his wife Agnes and son Thomas. Sons Nicholas and John were to split Agnes's share after her death.[244]

---

[242] Church of England, Archdeaconry Court of Northampton, Wills & Administrations, Register Copy Wills, Will of Henry Franklyng of Dallington, vol. K, fol. 175 [FHL Film #187,580; DGS #8,047,443].

[243] All references in the summary to baptisms, marriages, and burials in Dallington from Church of England, Dallington St. Giles, Northamptonshire, Parish Registers, 1577–1694 Northampton Record Office 95P/2, [FHL Fiche #6,127,185; DGS #100,342,799].

[244] Church of England, Archdeaconry of Northampton Court, Register Copy Wills, vol. Y, fol. 40, Will of John Franklyn of Dallington, 1592 [FHL Film #187,590; DGS #8,047,459].

Children of John and Agnes (—?—) Franklin:

3   i. THOMAS FRANKLIN, m. at Dallington 15 November 1585
        ALICE RICHARDSON.
4   ii. NICHOLAS FRANKLIN, bur. at Harlestone, Northamptonshire30
        October 1598; m. AGNES —?—.
5   iii. JOHN FRANKLIN, bur. at Dallington 28 February 1615; m.
        ELIZABETH —?—.

3. **THOMAS FRANKLIN** (*John, Henry*) He died between 31 April 1622, the date of his will, and 4 January 1623, when it was entered into probate.[245]

He married at Dallington 14 November 1585 **ALICE RICHARDSON.**

In his will, Thomas divided his estate between his wife Alice and son John. He required John to perform labor around the farm to support Alice.[246]

Children of Thomas and Alice (Richardson) Franklin, baptized at Dallington:

    i.   ANN FRANKLIN, bp. 3 July 1588; bur. at Dallington 19 July
         1588.
    iv. JOHN FRANKLIN, bp. 21 April 1591; bur. at Dallington 8 May
         1631; m. there 14 March 1614 SARAH WARNER.

3. **NICHOLAS FRANKLIN** (*John, Henry*) was buried at the village of Harlestone, Norhamptonshire, 20 October 1598.[247] He married **AGNES —?—.** She was buried there 18 November 1593.

---

[245] Church of England, Archdeaconry of Northampton Court, Register Copy Wills, vol. AV, fol. 143, Will of Thomas Franklyn of Dallington, 1623 [FHL Film #187,595; DGS #8,047,421].

[246] Church of England, Archdeaconry of Northampton Court, Register Copy Wills, vol. AV, fol. 143, Will of Thomas Franklin of Dallington, 1623 [FHL Film #187,585; DGS #8,947,421].

[247] All references in the summary to baptisms and burials at Harlestone from Church of England, Harlestone St. Andrew, Northamptonshire, Parish Registers,

In his will Nicholas left his children in the care of his brothers, Thomas and John.[248]

Children of Nicholas and Agnes (—?—) Franklin:

    i. THOMAS FRANKLIN, bp. 12 September 1591.

    ii. ELIZABETH FRANKLIN, b. after June 1592.

5. **JOHN FRANKLIN** (*John, Henry*) was buried at Dallington 28 February 1615. He married **ELIZABETH** —?—.

In his will, John left legacies to his grandchildren Nathaniel, Phebe, Hannah, and John Phipps. The remainder of the estate went to his wife Elizabeth.[249]

Children of John and Elizabeth (—?—) Franklin:

    i. THOMAS FRANKLIN

7 ii. AGNES FRANKLIN, m. at Northampton All Saints 27 May 1587 ROBERT PHIPPS, both of Dallington.

6. **JOHN FRANKLIN** (*Thomas, John, Henry*) was baptized at Dallington 21 July 1591, son of Thomas and Alice (Richardson) Franklin. He was buried there 8 May 1631.

John married at Dallington 14 March 1614 **SARAH WARNER**. She married there second 3 November 1632 William Marten.

Children of John and Sarah (Warner) Franklin:

    i. JONATHAN FRANKLIN, bp. at Dallington 14 March 1615; bur. there 10 August 1621.

Baptisms 1570–1709, Marriages 1570–1711, Burials 1574–1615; Northampton Record Office 153P/1 [FHL Fiche #6,127,669; DGS #100,342,745].

[248] Church of England, Archdeaconry of Northampton Court, Register Copy Wills, vol. W, fol. 77, Will of Nicholas Franklinge of Dallington, 1598 [FHL Film #187,588; DGS #8,047,477].

[249] Church of England, Archdeaconry of Northampton Court, Original Wills, Series 2, vol. 2, no. 81, Will of John Franklin of Dallington, 1615 [FHL Film #187,613; DGS #8,517,841].

ii. JOHN FRANKLIN, bp. at Dallington 3 November 1616; bur. there 10 August 1621.

iii. SARAH FRANKLIN, bur. at Dallington 7 April 1632.

7. **AGNES FRANKLIN** (*John, John, Henry*), daughter of John and Elizabeth (—?—) married in the parish of Northampton All Saints, Northamptonshire, 27 May 1587 **ROBERT PHIPPS**.[250]

Their children are named in the 1615 will of her father, John Franklin.[251] He is likely the kinsman John Phipps who was named an overseer and witnessed the will of his mother's uncle Thomas Franklin above.[252]

Children of Robert and Agnes (Franklin) Phipps):

i.   NATHANIEL PHIPPS.

ii. PHEBE PHIPPS.

iii. HANNAH PHIPPS.

iv. JOHN PHIPPS.

---

[250] Church of England, Northampton All Saints, Northamptonshire, Parish Registers, 1559–1722; Northampton Record Office 223P/1 [FHL Fiche #6,128,174; DGS #100,430,869].

[251] Church of England, Archdeaconry of Northampton Court, Original Wills, Series 2, vol. 2, no. 81, Will of John Franklin of Dallington, 1615 [FHL Film #187,613; DGS #8,517,841].

[252] Church of England, Archdeaconry of Northampton Court, Register Copy Wills, vol. AV, fol. 143, Will of John Franklin of Dallington, 1615 [FHL Film #187,585; DGS #8,947,421].

CHAPTER 12

FRANKLINS OF LITTLE BOWDEN

There appears to be a small cluster of Franklins in the parish of Little Bowden at the turn of the seventeenth century. Located about four miles west of Desborough, it sits on the border with Leicestershire. In fact, the bordering parish of Great Bowden is located across the border in Leicestershire. In two different wills, John Franklin is named as the father of men in Little Bowden (also called Bowden Parva).

Unfortunately, none of the original records, and only a few bishop's transcripts survive for the Church of England parish in Little Bowden for the period prior to 1663. The wills of the two brothers at least partially reconstruct the family.

Will of Richard Franklin, probated 24 February 1581[253]

[page 1]
In the name of god Amen The fourth Daie of the month of November in the Yeare of o^r Lord god 1581 I Richard Franklyn of Bowden Pva in the Countie of Northton Husbandman be-inge of good and pfect remembrance Laude and prayse be to god doe make & ordaine my Last will and Testament in maner and forme Following First

[page 2]
First I geve and donnytt my Soule into thands of Almightie god my maker and redeemer and my bodie to be buried in the churchyard of Little Bowden aforesaid It[e]m I give to the poore of the said pish xij^d to be Devided amongst them It[e]m

---

253 Church of England, Archdeaconry Court of Northampton, Wills & Administrations, Register Copy Wills, vol. V, fol. 81–2 Will of Richard Franklin of Little Bowden, 1581 [FHL Film #187,587; DGS #8,228,227].

I will that my father John Franklyn and my mother his wiffe shall dwell in my house and and give them all such easments remedies and Lysenge as they have had heretofore during their natural liffes, provided always that my said father and mother doe use my wiffe and my children as kyndlie and Frendlie as they have done heretofore in Lending unto my Wiffe all Such chattell and goods as they have consented to lend unto me in my Liffe tyme / It[e]m I give unto my sonne Richard Franklyn one sheepe and xx£ Sterlinge / It[e]m I give unto my Sonne Will[ia]m Franklyn one shepe and xx£ Sterlinge / Ite[]m I give unto my Sonne Thoms Franklyn one shepe and xx£ Sterlinge / It[e]m I give unto my Daughter Anne Franklyn one shepe and xx£ Sterlinge / Item I give unto my Daughter Grace Franklyn one shepe and xx£ Sterlinge It[e]m I geve all the rest of my goods and chattelle moveabls and Unmoveabls unto my wiffe and children and I make my wiffe Jane Franklyn my sole executrix of this my Last will and Testat witnesses Willm Pope gent; Robt Dent pson; Thomᵃs Simmone; and Thomas Chapman.

Will of Leonard Franklin, probated 27 March 1586[254]

[page 1]
In the Name of God Amen the ninth Day of November in thᵉ yeare of our Lord 1586 I Leonard Francklin of Bowden Pva in the County of Northton husbandman being sicke in body but in goode and pfict memory praise be to god therefore Do make Constitute and ordaine this my pute Last Will and Testament in manner and forme hereafter following first I bequeath and recommend my Soule into the merciefull hands of god trusting thoroughe his goodness and his sonnes merritte to be received into the blessed Company of his blessed angels And saints And my body to be buried in the Churchyard of Bowden aforesaid Item I give to the Church of Bowden afforesed ijˢ xjᵈ It[e]m I give towarde the reparing of the highway xijᵈ It[e]m I give to every of the Children of my late brother Richard Franklyn Deceased namely to Richard Willia[m] Thom[a]s Agnes and Grace

---

254 Church of England, Archdeaconry Court of Northampton, Wills & Administrations, Register Copy Wills, vol. V, fol. 273, Will of Leonard Franklin of Little Bowden, 1586 [FHL Film #187,587; DGS #8,228,227].

x[ld] and xj pence a peece to be delivered at their Severall ages of xxj yeares Provided th[t] if it shall happen any of them to Depte this mortall life before th[e] said age that then their said share or shares aforesaid shall remaine to the rest survivinge to be equally Devided amongest them. It[e]m I give to my brother John Franklyn x[ld] to be paid unto him within one yeare next after my decease. It[e]m I give to Leonard Dix x[s] and one sheepe to be paid unto him at the age of xx yeares It[e]m I give unto Alice Knight ij sheepe Item I give unto Alice Smith ij sheepe Item I bequeath to every of my godchildren xj[d] All the rest of my goods Chattell and Chattell whatsoever both moveable and immoveable not before given and bequeathed I Do give and bequeath to my naturall father John Franklin of Bowden aforesaid whom I make my full and sole executor of this my present last will and testament to pay and pforme all my debts and legacies to see my body honestly co[m]mitted to the burial and to discose upon my funeral and other waies as he shall so Cause to the glory of god and his name Discharge herein And I ordaine overseers hereof Willm Pope gent Richard Lot of Bowden aforesaid to them for their paines herein to be taken I give iij[s] iiij[d]. In witness whereof

[page 2]
whereof I have Sett hereunto my hand the Daye and Yeare first above written In presence of these witnesses Willm Pope Clement Pope Richard Daie and Richard Smith ·/·/·/·/·//·

It is possible that this family originated in Leicestershire. Their presence in a location so close to Desborough at the same time that Benjamin Franklin's ancestors were there cannot be discounted, but there is nothing so far to indicate a connection between the two families.

GENEALOGICAL SUMMARY

1. **JOHN FRANKLIN** resided at Little Bowden (Bowden Parva), Northamptonshire. While he left no will, two of his sons mentioned him in theirs. His wife's name is unknown.

Children of John Franklin:

  2 i. RICHARD FRANKLIN, d. at Little Bowden by February 1581; m.
         JANE —?—.

    ii. LEONARD FRANKLIN, d. at Little Bowden by March 1586, ei-
         ther unmarried or widowed with no surviving children, as
         none are mentioned in his will.

   iii. JOHN FRANKLIN.

2. **RICHARD FRANKLIN** (*John*) died at Little Bowden, Northamptonshire, by February 1581 when his will was entered into
probate. His wife's name is unknown. His will mentions his
father, wife, and children by name, but only references his
mother without naming her. The presumption is that John
Franklin's wife in 1581 was the mother of his children.[255] Richard married **JANE** —?—, who survived him.

Children of Richard Franklin:

    i. RICHARD FRANKLIN.
   ii. WILLIAM FRANKLIN.
  iii. THOMAS FRANKLIN.
  iv. ANNE/AGNES FRANKLIN.
   v. GRACE FRANKLIN.

---

[255] Church of England, Archdeaconry Court of Northampton, Wills &
Administrations, Register Copy Wills, vol. V, fol. 81–2 Will of Richard Franklin of Little Bowden, 1581 [FHL Film #187,587; DGS #8,228,227].

CHAPTER 13

FRANKLINS OF TITCHMARSH

The village of Titchmarsh in eastern Northamptonshire lies about twenty miles northeast of Ecton, on the border of Huntingdonshire. Records there reveal two Franklin families in the seventeenth century. Parish registers of Titchmarsh St. Mary the Virgin have a limited number of records:[256]

Baptisms
Susanna filia Nichalaj Franckli baptizata fuit Septembus 3° [1626]
Feb. 25 [1634/5] Margrita fil Joh[ann]is Franklin
[Feb] 26 [1636] Anna fil. Joh[ann]is Franklin
Jan. 27 [1638] Eliz. filia Joh[ann]es Francklin
[faded out]ana Franklin Filia Johannes [faded] [1640]

Marriages
Nicholaus Francklin Gratiana Williamson uxorem duxit Octobris vigesimo die [1625]
Samuel Whitney uxorem duxit Annaa Franklyn Julÿ 3°./ [1662]
April 23 [1663] April 23 Joh[ann]es Ayre & Margareta Franklyn
Janÿ 27° [1670] Johannes Meadows & Elizabeth Franklin
Octob.10. [1671] Thomas Franklin & Sarah George
Novemb:17. [1674] Johannes Beeby & Alicia Franklyn

---

[256] Church of England, Titchmarsh St. Mary the Virgin, Parish Registers, Baptisms 1544–1651, Marriages 1556–1646, and Burials, 1543–1646; Northamptonshire Record Office 328P/1 [FHL Fiche#6,129,102; DGS #100,624,492]. Baptisms and Burials 1653–1715, Marriages 1654–1715; Northamptonshire Record Office 328P/2 [FHL Microfiche #6,129,103; DGS #100,430,861]. Unpaginated, records in chronological order

Burials

     Susanna fila Nichola Francklin sepulta fuit Septembris 29° [1634]
     April 24 [1674] Joh[ann]es Franklin
     Alicia Franklyn: Dec:30 [1690]
     Thomas Franklyn Aug 26 [1704]

Although there are two families, neither of the heads of household left wills. The only pertinent will is one left by Thomas Franklin, son of John Franklin, but it is very informative.

Will of Thomas Franklin of Titchmarsh, probated 2 September 1704[257]

     In the Name of God Amen I thomas Franklin of Titchmarsh in the County of Northton yeoman Doe this sixteenth day of August in the Third year of the Reigne of our sovereigne Lady Ann by the Grace of God Queen of England &c And in the year of our Lord God one thousand seven hundred and Four make constitute & Appoint the p^rsent Writing to be my last Will & Testament in manner & Form Following First I comitt my body to the Earth to be buryed at the Discrse^ttcon of my Executrix hereinafter named with Christian buryall And As for the Worldly Estate it hath pleased God in mery to bestow upon me I give bequeath As Followethh First I give & bequeath to ^Sarah^ my deare & Loveing Wife all my goods chattells moneys & creditte^s It. I give and bequeath to my said Loveing Wife for and during the terme of her naturall life All that my House and Homestead and allso all my Arrable Land Ley meadow pasture & inclosed ground scittuate Lying & being in the Parrish bounds & p^ermite of Titchmarsh aforesaid Together with all the rights members com[m]ons profitts hereditaments & Apurtenances to the same belonging And from and after the decease of my said wife I give and bequeath my said House and homestead Arrable Land Ley meadow pasture & inclossed ground & all rights members com[m]ons profitts hereditaments & Appurtenances to the same belonging unto my nephew Franklin

[257] Church of England, Consistory Court of Peterborough, Wills & Administrations, Original Wills, vol. Z, no.17, Will of Thomas Franklin of Titchmarsh, 1704 [FHL Film #174,864; DGS #8,285,975].

Chapman of Glatton in the County of Huntingdon whiture &
to his heirs & Asignes for ever To have and to hold to my said
nephew Franklin Chapman & to his heirs & assignes forever
upon condition that the said Franklin Chapman & his heirs shall
good Well & Truly Pay the Legacys & sums of money to the
psons thereinafter named Expressed & declared And my said
house & homestead Arrable Land Ley meadow pasture & In-
clossed ground & all comons profitts rights members hereditaments & Appurtenances to the same belonging in the hands of
my said nephew Franklin Chapman & of the heirs shall stand
chargeable And are hereby Charged with and made subject &
Lyable to Pay to the Persons thereinafter named the sums of
money & Legacyes as is to them herein after given & bequeathed expressed or declard (That is to Say) to my sister the
wife of John Peeby of Tichmarsh aforesaid whiture the Legacy
or sum: of Ten pounds of good & Lawfull money of England
And to my nephew & neeces Henry Alice & Rebecca three
Children of my Sister Jane Houson of Barnwell in the said
County of Northton the Sum: of Five pounds apeece And to
my nephews & neece Abraham Nathaniel Josia & Mary Four
Children of my Sister Margarett Aires of Kettering in the said
county of northton the sum: of Five pounds Apeece And to my
Nephews Samuell John Joseph Thomas & James children of my
sister Whitney of Olney in the County of Buckingham the sum:
of Five pounds apeece And to my neece Martha Meadows
Daughter of my sister Elizabeth Meadows the sum: of Five
pounds And to my neece Sara Mariner wife of William Mariner
of Thrapston in the County of Northton & to her two children
Sarah & William five pounds Apeece And to the Five Children
of my neece Elizabeth Bellamy of Ringstead in the said county
of Northton Twenty shillings each And to the three children of
my Cozen Thomas Franklin of Everton Two shillins six pound
each And the seven Children of my Cozen Nicholas Franklin of
Harold in the County of Bedford the sum: of Two shillings six
ound each to be payed them Six months after my said wifes decease And I doe hereby make vide & doe revoke all former

Wills by me made And doe Constitute nominate & Appoint Sarah my said wife sole Executrix of this my lasat Will & testament In Wittnes whereof I the said Thomas Franklin have
hereunto sett my hand & seals & have published & declared this
p^esent Writeing to be my last Wil & testament the day & year
first above Written

Thomas Franklin

Sealed And Delivered Published &
Dclared by the said Thomas
Franklin to be his last Will and
Testament in the p^esence of
John Barnes
John Formedows
Edm: Bramston

The Titchmarsh parish registers show two family groups.
Nicholas Franklin married Gratiana Williamson 20 October 1625.
They have one daughter at Titchmarsh who was baptised and bur-
ied in September 1626. Then they disappear from the parish.

The other family is that of John Franklin. Four of his children
were baptised there: Margaret in 1634/5, Anne in 1636, Elizabeth
in 1638, and another daughter in 1640. That record is too faded to
read the name. No further identifiab;e Marriage records show
three women marrying at Titchmarsh: Margarita to John Ayres in
1663, Anne to Samuel Whitney in 1662, and Elizabeth to John
Meadows in 1670. Thomas Franklin's will names his sisters Margaret Aires of Kettering, sister Whitney of Olney, Buckinghamshire,
and sister Elizabeth Meadows. Not only does this tie in Thomas as
a son of John, three other sisters are identified in the will: the
mother of his nephew Franklin Chapman, the wife of John "Peeby"
and Jane Houson of Barnwell. Titchmarsh parish registers show a
marriage between John "Beeby" and Alicia Franklin in 1674. The
Chapman and Houson marriages must have taken place elsewhere.

The burial of Alicia Franklin on 30 December 1690 is not spe-
cifically tied to the family, but they appear to be the only Franklins
in the parish at the time. With a daughter of John also named Alicia, the burial is probably for the wife of John Franklin, who himself left no will.

It is possible that the two families are related. Thomas also left small cash legacy to his "Cozen Nicholas Franklin of Harold in the County of Bedford." There is nothing to indicate that they are related to the family of Benjamin Franklin.

GENEALOGICAL SUMMARIES

1. NICHOLAS FRANKLIN married at Titchmarsh, Northamptonshire, 20 October 1625 GRATIANA WILLIAMSON.[258]

Child of Nicholas and Gratiana (Williamson) Franklin:

 i. SUSANNA FRANKLIN, bp. 3 September 1626; bur. at Titchmarsh 29 September 1634.

1. JOHN FRANKLIN was buried at Titchmarsh, Northamptonshire, 24 April 1674. He was likely married to ALICIA —?—, who was buried there 30 December 1690.

Children of John Franklin:

 i. —?— FRANKLIN (daughter) m. —?— CHAPMAN. *Child*: Franklin Chapman. Res. 1704 Glatton, Huntingdonshire.
 ii. JANE FRANKLIN, m. —?— HOUSON. *Children*: Henry Houson, Alice Houson, and Rebecca Houson. Res. 1704 Barnwell, Northamptonshire.
 iv. MARGARET FRANKLIN, bp. 27 February 1634/5; m. at Titchmarsh 23 April 1663 JOHN AYRES. *Children*: Abraham Ayres,

---

[258] All references to Titchmarsh baptisms, marriages, and burials are from Church of England, Titchmarsh St. Mary the Virgin, Parish Registers, Baptisms 1544–1651, Marriages 1556–1646, and Burials, 1543–1646; Northamptonshire Record Office 328P/1 [FHL Fiche#6,129,102; DGS #100,624,492]. Baptisms and Burials 1653–1715, Marriages 1654–1715; Northamptonshire Record Office 328P/2 [FHL Microfiche #6,129,103; DGS #100,430,861]. Unpaginated, records in chronological order.

Nathaniel Ayres, Josia Ayres, and Mary Ayres. Res. 1704
Kettering, Northamptonshire.

iii.   ANNE FRANKLIN, bp. 28 February 1636; m. at Titchmarsh 3
       July 1662 SAMUEL WHITNEY. *Children:* Samuel Whitney,
       John Whitney, Joseph Whitney, Thomas Whitney, Joane
       Whitney. Res. 1704 Olney, Buckinghamshire.

v.   ELIZABETH FRANKLIN, m. at Titchmarsh 27 June 1670 JOHN
       MEADOWS. *Child:* Martha Meadows.

vi.   THOMAS FRANKLIN, bur. 26 August 1704; m. at Titchmarsh 10
       October 1671 SARAH GEORGE.

vii. ALICIA FRANKLIN, m. at Titchmarsh 17 November 1673 JOHN
       BEEBY.

CHAPTER 14

FRANKLINS OF BUGBROOKE

There are two records for individuals named Franklin in the parish registers of Bugbrooke St. Michael and All Angels. The first is a burial and the second is a marriage: [259]

William Franklin was Buryed the: 21 · day of March [1641]

Bernard Franklin and Mary Houghton of Gayton Novembr 11th
    by Lic [1697]

In addition to the parish registers, there is a single Franklin will from the village of Bugbrooke, that of William Franklin.

Will of William Franklin, dated 9 March 1641 [260]

The ninth Day of March Anno Dom 1641

In the name of god Amen; I William Franklin of Bugbroke in the County of Northton yeoman; Doe make this my Last will and testament in maner and forme following, first I give and Bequeath my soule into the hands of Almighty god my Creator and redeemer And my Body to be buried in the Parish Church or Churchyard of Bugbroke in decent and orderly maner; and my will is that my goods shalbe thus dispersed; I give and be-queath unto Oliver Wallopp the su[m]me of five pounds to bee

---

[259] Church of England, Bugbrooke St. Michael and All Angels, Parish Registers, 1657–1705; Northamptonshire Record Office 53P/2 [FHL Microfiche #6,126,894; DGS #101,380,915]. Unpaginated, records in chronological order.

[260] Church of England, Archdeaconry Court of Northampton, Wills & Administrations, Series 2 1630–1642, vol. L, no.191, Will of William Franklin of Bugbrooke, 1641 [FHL Film #187,606; DGS #8,047,431].

paid within three months after my desease. I give unto Mrs Audrie Midlton the su[m]me of tenn shillings to bee paid within six months after my Desease, I give unto Tamasin White the sume of tenn Shillings to be paid within six months after my Desease I give unto Francis Midlton the su[m]me of ten shillings to bee paid within six months after my Desease; I give unto Alice holmes the su[m]me of tenn shillings to be paid within six months after my Desease: I give unto Sarah holmes the su[m]me of tenn shillings to be paid within six months after my Desease: I give unto Ann Peasnole the su[m]me of ten shillings to be paid within six months after my desease, I give unto Mary Jones the Daughter of John Jones the sume of tenn shillings to be paid within six months after my Desease, I give unto Elisabeth the Daughter of John Oliver the su[m]me of ten shillings to be paid within six months after my Desease, I give unto Elisabeth Asheby the Daughter of Steven Asheby the sume of tenn shillings to be paid within six months after my desease, I give unto Ann [crossout] Davy the Daughter of Edward Davy the su[m]me of [crossout] tenn shillings to be paid within six months after my Desease, I give unto Hanna holmes the su[m]me of two shillings and six pence to be paid within six months afer my Desease; I give unto John Saxby the su[m]me of twelve pence, I give unto old mary Carlisle twelve pence; I give unto Elisabeth England [crossout] the su[m]me of twelve pence, I give unto the poore people of Bugbroke the sume of twenty shillings to be paid within six months after my Desease, I give tenn shillings for a funeral sermon at my Buriall I give unto m^r Oliver Wallopp twenty shillings to Buy twenty paires of Gloves to bee given at my funeral; I give unto Richard Curtis foure shilli[torn] for his foure Children; I give unto Richard Curtis six shillings eight pence to provide a C[torn] for my Body to be Buryed in; All the [crossout] residue of my goods unbequeathed I give [torn] Joane Lovell of Sumerton in the County of Oxford; my [torn]turall mother; and [torn] Humphrey Franklin my natural Brother of Sumer[torn] [torn]shire, who I m[torn] [torn]xecutors; I make John Davy and John Jones my [torn] [torn]verseers of this [torn] [torn]ill and Testament and I give them three shilling[torn] [torn] peice.

No wife or children are named in the will. It shows that William was a natural son of Joane Lovell and he had a natural brother named Humphrey Franklin. The term natural indicates that William and Humphrey may have been born out of wedlock. Another possibility is that their parents were married and Joane married a man named Lovell after the death of their father.

Both Joane and Humphrey were residing in Somerton, Oxfordshire, when William made his will. Whether they removed there from Northamptonshire, or William removed from there (or elsewhere) to Bugbrooke, there is no evidence to show that William is in any way connected to the family of Benjamin Franklin. Likewise, no connection can be found to link Leonard Franklin to either William Franklin of Bugbrooke, or to the family of Benjamin Franklin.

The marriage of Bernard Franklin and Mary Houghton of Gayton took place fifty-six years later. One child of the couple was found at Upton St. Michael, near Northamptonshiire:

Bernard Frankie the son of Bernard Frankie and Mary his wife was baptized Nov:8th 1698.[261]

This is the only Bernard Franklin found to date. there is currently no evidence to tie him to Benjamin Franklin's family.

---

[261] Church of England, Upton St. Michael, Northamptonshire, Parish Registers, 1594–1779; Northamptonshire Record Office 332P/1 [FHL Fiche #6,129,157; DGS #100,431,063].

CHAPTER 15
UNPLACED FRANKLINS

In addition to those mentioned previously, the Franklins named in the following pre-1700 marriage records in Northmptonshire cannot be placed in either Benjamin Franklin's family or any of the other identified family groups. As commerical websites continue to index Northamptonshire records, most of which were not previously abstracted, this list will likely grow.

Decemb[r] 6 [1584] Philip Stuarte & Joane franklyn joyned in matrymony [Stoke-Bruerne St. Mary the Virgin].[262]

[1601] November Henry Franklin and Alice Riggbie were marryed the xth [10] Daye [Northampton St. Giles].[263]

July 1619 Lawrence Franklyn et Ursula Adkyns nupt fuer xiiij [14] die [Northampton All Saint].[264]

Williā Rogers and Joan Franklin weare maried June 29° 1625 [Harpole All Saints] .[265]

George Thonger & ~~Fransis~~ Francis Francklin were married. Nov:18th [1666] [Brackley St. Peter][266]

---

[262] Church of England, Stoke-Bruerne St. Mary the Virgin, Northamptonshire, Parish Registers, Baptisms and Burials, 1560–1775, Marriages 1560–1754; Northamptonshire Record Office 303P/11 [FHL Fiche #6,128,956; DGS # 100,431,011].

[263] Church of England, Northampton St. Giles, Northamptonshire, Parish Registers, Baptisms, Marriages, and Burials, 1559–1748; Northamptonshire Record Office 233P/7 [FHL Microfiche #6,128,286]. Unpaginated, in chronological order grouped by record type.

[264] Church of England, Northampton All Saints, Northamptonshire, Parish Registers, Baptisms, Marriages, and Burials 1559–1722; Northamptonshire Record Office 223P/1 [FHL Fiche #6,128,174] [DGS # 100,344,951]. Unpaginated, in chronological order grouped by record type.

[265] Church of England, Harpole All Saints, Northamptonshire, Parish Registers, 1539–1654; Northamptonshire Record Office 154P/1 [FHL Fiche #6,127,678; DGS #101,392,496]. Unpaginated, in chronological order.

[266] Church of England, Brackley St. Peter, Northamptonshire, Parish Registers, vol. II: Baptisms and Marriages, 1637–1687, Burials, 1636–1687; North

William Brice & Elizabeth Franklin Jan:22. [1676] [Paulerspury St. James the Great].[267]

Thomas Woollams and Anne Franklin were married the 3th of May 1696. [Brackley St. Peter].[268]

The "Northamptonshire Marriages" database on Find My Past shows three additional marriages:

Frances Francklin married at Syresham 11 February 1695 Michael Osborn

John Francklin married at Syresham 4 August 1695 Anne Cook

William Francklin married at Syresham 3 January 1697 Elizabeth Bull.

What is curious about these entries is that the copies of the original church rcords at the Northamptonshire Archives are missing the years 1689–1736. The microtext copies were taken from the originals at the archives. The website does not provide any information about how the database was created or where the information came from.

---

amptonshire Record Office 42P/2 [FHL Microfiche #6,126,767]. Unpaginated, in chronological order grouped by record type.

[267] Church of England, Paulerspury St. James the Great, Northamptonshire, Parish Registers, Baptisms, Marriages, and Burials, 1671–1742; Northamptonshire Record Office 255P/3 [FHL Microfiche #6,126,527; DGS #100,624,327]. Unpaginated, in chronological order.

[268] Church of England, Brackley St. Peter, Northamptonshire, Parish Registers, vol. III: Baptisms, Marriages, and Burials 1687–1702; Northamptonshire Record Office 42P/3 [FHL Microfiche #6,126,768; DGS #100,342,660]. Unpaginated, in chronological order grouped by record type.

Part III

THE LADIES

CHAPTER 16

ANNE[1] CHILD, WIFE OF JOSIAH FRANKLIN

The Child family has a long history in Ecton. Anne's ancestry can be traced back to James Child, who had several children baptized there in the 1560s. It appears that several family members were married elsewhere than Ecton. Parish registers show the following records for individuals named Child/Childs/etc.[269]

Baptisms

Alice the Daughter of James Childes was baptised the xviii[th] [18] of Julye Anno Predicte [1563]

William the sonne of James Childe was christened the last of May Anno Predict [1565]

James the sonne of James Childe was christened the ii[th] [2] of April Anno Dom 1568.

Francis the sonne of James Childe was christened the [ink blot][th] of November Anno Predit [1591]

Thomas the sonne of James Childe was christened the xi[th] [11] of March Anno Predic [1593/4]

James the sonne of James Childe was christened the vii[th] [7] of Decemb[r] Anno PDic [1595]

Francis the sonne of James Childes was christened the xii[th] [12] of February Anno Dom 1597[/8]

Richard the sone of James Child was christened the xxi[th] [21] of March Anno Dom 1599[/1600]

Anne the Daughter of Jeames Childe was christened the xxiith [22] of January: Anno Dom Pect [1601[/2]

John the sonne of James Child was christened the xxii[th] [22] daye of January Anno Dom Pect [1607][/08]

---

[269] Church of England Parish Register, Ecton St. Mary Magdelene, Northamptonshire, 1559 to 1637; Northamptonshire Record Office 114P/202 [FHL Fiche #6,127,381]. 1638 to 1754; Northamptonshire Record Office 114P/203 [FHL Fiche #6,127,382; DGS #100,430,949]. Unpaginated, records in chronological order.

Elizabeth the Daughter of James Childe was christened the xxix[th] [29] day of January Anno Dom Pdit [1608/9]

Arthur the sonne of James Childe was christened the xxi[th] [21] Day of December Anno Dom Pdct [1610]

Mary Childe Daughter unto James Childe was christened the thirty one of January Anno Predict [1611/2]

Sara Childes Daughter unto James Childes was christened May th[e] 2: Anno Predict [1615]

Michaell sonne to James Childe and Katherine his wife the fourteenth of September 1618

John Child the sonn of James Child and Catherine his wife was baptized the Eleventh Day of June 1620

Thomas the sonne of Catherine Child was baptised the 20th of Januar An predi [1625].

Ann the daughter of Francis Childe and Eme his wife was baptized the first day of th[e] month of June. [1628]

Mary the daughter of Francis Childe and Eme his wife baptized the xxi [31] day of th[e] month of May. [1631]

Sarah the daughter of Francis Child and Eme his wife was baptised the xxix [29] day of the month of March [1633]

Mary the Daughter of Arthur Child baptised Febr. 8 1641

1647 June 27 Sara daughter of Arthur Child and Alice his wife

Anne the Daughter of Robert Child and Debora his wife was borne the first day of January and baptized the 2ith [21] of January [1654]

James the Sonne of John Childe and Mary his wife was borne the 29 as I take it of Aprill being Tuesday and baptized the 4 of May [1656]

[1658] Febr. 27. Debora daughter of Robert Child and Debora his wife:

[1660.] Sept. 16. Rebecca daughter of Rob[t] Child and Debora his wife.

[1662.] Decemb 12 Mary daughter of Rob[t] Child and Debora his wife.

January 3. James son of Robert Child and Debora his wife [1663/4]

Januar 21. John son of Robert Child and of Debora his wife [1665/6]

Dec. 21. Thomas son of Robert Child and of Debora his wife: [1667]

[1669] Nov. 28. Francis son of Robert Child and of Debora his wife

[1672] Oct. 27 Robert son of Robert Child and Debora his wife

[1680] Octobe 9. Arthur son of John Child and of Elizabeth his wife.

[1684/5] Janu:6. John Son of John Child the younger and of Elizabeth his wife

[1685] April 10. Thomas son of Rebecca Child spinster.

Marriages

Robert Child and Alise Maxie married Februarie 5 [1622]

Burials

William the sonne of James Child was buryed the xxi[th] of August Anno Pdit [1574]

Francis the sonne of James Childe was buryed the xxviii[th] [28] of June Anno Pdct [1594]

Alice Childe was buryed the xiii[th] [13] of Aprill Anno Dom Pdit [1595]

John Childes the sonne of James Childes was buryed the xxii[th] [22] daye of January : Anno Dom Pdct [1607][/8]

James Childe husbandman was buried the 10th of October [1621]

Sarah Childe the daughter of Katherin Childe was buried Septem[b] 7 [1630]

[1631] Ann Childe Spinster was buried October xi [11].

[1649] May 29 Thomas Child an elderly man

Arthur Childe was [Bur]yed the 15th Day of December: 1657:

[1668] Apr.7. Anne Child daughter of Francis Child

[1671] Novemb. 11. Francis son of Robert Child

[1672][/3] Febr.24. Robert Child (son of Francis Child) a married man.

1675. May 27. Francis Child yeom an aged man

1680 March 29. Mary wife of John Childe Husbandman

1685 April 13. Thomas bastard Infant of Rebecca Child Affid. Before Mr. Nicols R$_x$[d] April 17th

[1688] Febru:25 James Child a young Man. Affid. Before Mr. Wood. R[d] March 3[d]

[1692.] Nov: 28 John Childe Sen[r] an ancient Husbandman. Affid: before Mr. Walker. Rd Dec:3[d]

[1705][/6] Febr.24th. Deborah Childs an ancient poor Widow. Affid: before Mr. Whaley. R[d]. March i[st] [1]

Four wills for people named Child in Northamptonshire relate to the family. Three are direct line ancestors: James[D], James[C], and Francis[B]. The fourth is for Anne Child, sister of Francis.

Will of James Child of Ecton, probated 28 April 1586[270]

[page 1]
In the Name of God Amen the foure and twentieth Day of Aprill in the yeare of our lord god one thousand five hundred foure score & fower I James Child of Ecton of the county of Northampton Yeoman being sicke in body but of goode & pfect remembrance thankes be unto almighty god do make & ordayne this my last will & testament in maner & forme fol-lowinge Vz first I commend my soule unto the hands of al-mighty god my savio[r] and redeemer Jesus Christ by whose most glorious mortte death & passion my full trust & confidence is to saved & my body to be buryed in the church yard of Ecton Itm I give & bequeath to the people of Ecton thirteene shillings & foure pence Itm I give & bequeathe to the poore people of litle Houghton in the sayd county of Northton six shillinge and eight pence. Itm I give & bequeathe to James Child my sonne the summe of twenty pounds of lawfull money of England to be paid ~~to hir by my executo[r]s~~ him within one yeare next after my decease. Itm I give & bequeath to my daughter Audrye twenty pounds of lawfull money of England to be paid to hir by my exector[s] within one month after my decease Itm I give & bequeath to Alice my daughter twenty pounds of like lawfull money to be payd to hir when she shall attayne and come to the age of xviij yeares or at the Day

[270] Church of England, Archdeaconry of Northampton Court, Register Copy of Wills, vol. V, fol. 110, Will of James Child of Ecton, 1585 [FHL Film #187,587; DGS #8,228,227].

[page 2]

Day of hir marriage Which shall first happen Itm whereas my
sonne in law George Sherman doth owe unto me the the [*sic*]
summe of six pounds thirteen shillings and fower pence I do
give & bequeath to the said George 6ld xiijs foure pence of the
said summe & the other twenty shillings I give & bequeath unto
Anne Sherman daughter of the said George Itm my will &
mynde is that Jane my wyfe & James Child my sonne shall have
& occupye after my decease Joyntly together the farme wherein
I now dwell in Ecton above said wth all and singulr thapper-
tenannce & all my goodes & cattell that shalbe there
remayninge after my debts and legacyes payd during the continuance of the yeares that I gave therein and also my land wth the
appurtenannces in litell Houghton abovesaid during the lease of
of ye said Jane my wyfe Provided always and my will and mynd
is that yf it shall happen the said Jane to marry & take a husband after my deceasse that hten she shall immediately after hir
marriage no further dealing or occupynge of the said farme with
thappurtenannces in Ecton but shalle lave the same wholly to
the said James my sonne & then my will is that after hir such
marriage she shall have & enioy during hir naturall lyfe all my
lande tente & hereditants wth halfe of all the goods & cattell that
shalbe at the said day of hir marriage in the occupation of the
said   my wyfe & James my sonne Itm I do make constitute & ordayne Jane my wyfe & James Child my sonne executors of this my last will & testamet I do appoynt my welbeloved
frende George Bayne & Robt Hensman to be supvisors thereof
& do give to eyther of them for their panes to be taken therein
In witnes whereof I the said James Child have hereunto sett my
name the day & yeare abovesaid in the pns of witnesses George
Baine Robt Hensman John Morris Richard Lacke who tht the
said James Child being of pfect mynd & memory after he had
made his testaste & last will did give & bequeath by words only
to Audrie his daughter iijld vid and beside hir legacy given & bequeathed by his testamente abovesaid And also to Alice his
daughter [smeared]iijld vid and beside he legacye given by hir
sayd father deceased to be payd to the sayd Alice accordinge to
his sayd testament and last will further the said testator did for-
give his sonne in law George Sherman fourtie shillings vid & beside the debts wch are specified & declared in his testate ·/·/· · ·

Will of James Chillde of Ecton, probated 25 September 1623[271]

In the name of God, Amen I james Chillde of Ecton in the county of Northampton yeoman being sicke in body but of good & pfect memorye, doe make & ordayne this my last will & testament in manner & forme followinge revokinge hereby all former willes by me made whatsoever, First I bequeathe my sole unto Allmighty God my maker & redeemer & my bodye to the earth from where I tooke it And as concerning all my lands tenements hereditaments goods cattells & chattells I give & bequeath the said in manner & forme followinge (that is to say) First I give & bequeath unto my welbeloved wyfe Katherine Chyllde the use & proffitte of the moitye of one halfe of all my messuage or tenement wth thapptenence in Ecton wherein I doe nowe inhabitt & dwell & of the moitye or one halfe of one yardland & an half yardlande ^with the appertence^ (wch I prchasd of Mr George Catesbye Esquire) four & during the naturall lyfe of the said Katherine my wyfe & af[ter] [torn] hir death & deceasse I give & bequeathe the other moitye or half of all & singul[ar] [torn] the sayd premisses unto my sayd sonne Thomas Chyllde & to his heirs & assignes forever Itm I give unto James Chyllde my sonne the somme of fyve pounds of lawfull english money to be payd within one yeare after my deceasse & fyve pounds more of lyke money wthin two years after my deceasse Itm I give unto Francis Chyllde my sonne the somme of tenne pounds of lyke money fyve pounds thereof wthin three years after my deceasse & the other fyve pounds thereof wthin foure years after my deceasse Itm I give unto my Daughter Agnes Chyllde the somme of foure pounds of lyke money the one halfe thereof to be payd wthin fyve years after my deceasse & the other fyve pounds theeof to be payd wthin six years after my deceasse. Itm I give unto my sonne Richard Chyllde [folded and illegible] foure pounds of lyke money thereof to by payd wthin eight years after my deceasse Itm I give unto my sayd sonne Francs Chyllde

---

[271] Church of England, Archdeaconry of Northampton Court, Second Series, Original Wills, vol. O, no. 109, Will of James Chillde of Ecton, 1623 [FHL Film #187,586; DGS #8,098,669].

free passage & liberty of ingresse & egresse in by to from &
through my yarde & richarde to his nowe dwellinge house duringe
his [xxxxx] & [xxx]ieying thereof onley [smudge] manner of r[ink
smear]ge & carriage w^th[smudge]y manner of [l/r]eadinge whatsoever wth teame or team[es] carte or cartes & [ink smear and crease]
onely for the managinge & guydinge thereof any thinge before
[xxxxx]ed to the contrary in anywise notw^thstandinge. Itm I give
unto my three sonnes Arthure Chyllde Michaell Chyllde & John
Chyllde each of them the somme of fyve pounds of lyke money to
by payd to each of them at each of their sev^rall adge of one &
twenty years Itm I give & bequeath unto my three daughters Elizabeth Chyllde Mary Chyllde & Sara Chyllde each of them the
somme of fyve pounds of lyke money to be payd unto each of
them at each of their sev^rall adges of eighteene years. Item I give
& bequeathe unto myne executo^rs hereafter named one yeardland
& halfe yardlandes wth thapptenancs in Ecton aforesayd wi^ch I
pchased of Mr Henry Goodman to this prsents & ppose That they
or the survivour of them ^ech one of them with the consente of
mye executors herein hereafter named^ shall sell the same & w^th
the money thereof arysinge pay & satisfy all my debts wch I doe
and [xxxxx] indebted to buy pson or psons whatsoever & the
overplus thereof if any be fowarde the payments of [illegible word
crossed out] all legacies herein by me before given. All the rest of
my goods cattells & chattells whatsoever unbequeathed my dedbts
legacies & funeral expense Dischardged I give & bequeath the
same unto my sayd well beloved wyfe Katherine Chyllde & unto
my sayd sonne Thomas Chyllde whom I doe make my [xx]ynte
executors of this my last will & testament & I make overseers of
the same my welbeloved brothers William Morris of Billinge
Magna & John Morris of Ecton aforesayd ^& William Brytain &
George Lot of Ecton aforesayd^ Dsyringe ^them^ to see this my
will pfourmed in all paynts & I give them for their paynes therin
[page has a crease which obscures the next three words]. In witt-
ness whereof I the sayd James Chyllde have phereunto set myny
hande & seals the day & yeare first above written . /

The marke of James Chyllde

Readd sealed pulished & declared [torn] be the last will & testa-
ment of [torn]e the sayd Jame Chyllde in the Presence of Francs
Muscote William Corbye
Anthony Barker

prvided that if my sonne Thomas die wth oute issue, the land before mentions I doe give & bequeathe unto my sonne Richard &
his heires for ever: this pviso was marke in the [torn]resence of
William Parker Sen. Mychaell Jones Anthony Barker and William
Corbye

Will of Anne Child of Ecton, probated 22 October 1631[272]

The 9th day of october in the yeare of our Lord god on ~~thosand~~
thousand six hundred thirtie and on

In the name of god Amen I Ann Childs of Ecton in the Countie of North^ton Beinge sicke in bodie but of good and pfet
memorye at the making hereof thanks be given to god doe
make & ordaine this my last will and Testament in maner and
forme following revoking hereby all Former willes by me made
whatsoever first I ~~bqueth~~ bequeath my soult to Almyghty god
my maker and redeemer and my body to the Earth from whenc
I seek and as touching my earthly goods wherewith god hath
blessed me I give and bequeth the same in maner and forme
following that is to say First I give to Arthur Childes ten shilings
It[em] I give my mother my greine wastcote and russet petticote
and A ruffe band Itē I give Marie Childs my best hat and two
gloves hands Itē I give Anise Childs a payre of sheets the on
having a whit seaming dowane the wideste and the other a black
[xxx] towell and a Hencloth It[em] I give to Anise Christopher-
ingten[?] two of my woolen plean bands and two of my warger
coiffes It[em] I give to my sister Em Childs fower
[crossout]workclothes and two apernes It[em] I give to Alice
Kent my best aperne and all the rest of my goods whatsoever

---

[272] Church of England, Archdeaconry of Northampton Court, Second Series, Original Wills, vol. K, no. 14, Will of Anne Childe of Ecton, 1531 [FHL
Film #187,605; DGS #8,047,430].

my debtes legacies and funerall expenses discharged I tive and
bequeath the same to my S Brother Richard Childes which I
doe make Executore of this my last will and testament

Annis Childs

Held and declared to be my last will   hir marke
and testament in the presence of

John Hensman
Nathan Prisse
Thomas Franklin

Will of Francis Child, probated 17 June 1675[273]

In the Name of God Amen. I Francis Child of Ecton in the
Countie of Northampton yeoman, being aged & weak in body,
but of perfect understanding & memory, do make this my last
Will & Testament in maner following. First I com[m]end my
soule into the hands of Almighty God trusting to be saved only
through the morits of our Lord Jesus Chrits, And my body I
leave to be buryed at the discretion of my Executour. Also I
bequeath to my daughter in law Debora Child one shilling. & to
Joshua James John Thomas Robert Anne Debora & Rebecca
children of my said daughter in law to each of them one shilling. to my grandchild Mary King one shilling. & to my grandchildren Sara Goosie Mary Goosie & Elizabeth Goosie to each
of the one shilling. And to the intent that my son John may be
the better enabled to pay my debts & to continue in the occupation of the land which I hold of Mr Catsby I give & bequeath to
him all my lands goods & chattels & make him sole Executour
of this my last Will and Testament. And I require him that according to his ability he show kindness to the widow & children
of my son Robert deceased as their need shall require, & their
virtuous carriage shall seem to deserve. & also that within three
dayes after my decease re make his Testament & renew it from
tiem to time as there shall be occasion, & that therein he bequeth such legacies to the said widow & her children, as upon

[273] Church of England, Archdeaconry of Northampton Court, Series 4,
Original Wills, vol. 8, no. 48, Will of Francis Child of Ecton, 1675 [FHL Film
#187,642; DGS #8,047,495].

due consideration of his own ability & of their necessity & virtuous carriage shall seem to him reasonable & convenient. In witness whereof & have set my hand & seale march 26.1675·

Signed & sealed by the testator in p^r^sence of John Palmer of Ecton — Francis Chillde

Unfortunately, there are some gaps in the parish registers that occur at key times for the Child family. The largest occurs from 1585 to 1591. Fortunately, there is enough information in the surviving records to be confident in the paternal lineage of Anne Child, the first wife of Josiah Franklin.

Anne was baptized at Ecton 21 January 1654, daughter of Robert Child and his wife Debora. She was the first of their nine children recorded there. There is no record of the marriage of Robert and Debora at Ecton. Unfortunately, few marriages were recorded there during the middle part of the seventeenth century. In total, in the twenty-four years between 1641 and 1665, only seven marriages were recorded:

- 1641, one marriage
- 1642–1644, no marriages
- 1645, one marriage
- 1646–1653, no marriages
- 1654, one marriage
- 1655–1661, no marriages
- 1662–1665, one marriage each year

It is particularly interesting that baptisms and burials continued to be registered during this time. Only the marriages went unrecorded. While this period covers the Commonwealth era (1649–1660), it extends before and afterwards, so that alone is not the reason for the missing records.

Examination of baptismal records of Ecton shows no baptism for Debora between 1621 and 1640. It is likely that she and Robert married in another parish, probably around 1652 (given the baptism of Anne in January 1654).

There is no baptismal record for Robert at Ecton, either. He was buried at Ecton 24 February 1672/3. Unusually for an adult during this time, his burial record gives the name of his father. "Robert Child (son of Francis Child) a married man." Debora survived him by more than thirty years and never remarried. She was buried at Ecton 24 February 1705/6, "an ancient poor widow."

The baptisms of three other children of Francis and his wife Eme are recorded: Ann in 1628, Mary in 1631, and Sarah in 1633. The will of Francis Child names his sons Robert and John. He also names his daughter-in-law, Debora, and her children Joshua, James, John, Thomas, Robert, Anne, Debora, and Rebecca. He later refers to them as "the widow & children of my son Robert deceased." He also named grandchildren Mary King and Sarah, Mary, and Elizabeth Goosie.

Three children of Francis Child and his wife Eme were baptized at Ecton: Anne, 1628; Mary, 1631; and Sarah, 1633. There is no marriage record for the couple at Ecton, nor is there a baptism for a woman named Eme at Ecton between 1590 and 1615. Francis was about thirty-one years old at Anne's baptism. It is quite likely that they married in another parish, where Robert and John might have been baptized. The question is whether they were born to Eme, a previous wife, or were born out of wedlock.

Francis does not refer to his daughters in his will, either directly or indirectly as the mothers of his grandchildren. His major concern seems to be Debora and her children. Anne, "daughter of Francis Child" was buried in 1668. No record of marriage could be found for Sarah Child and a man named King. The name of granddaughter Mary King is too common to identify her with a father's name.

John Goosey of Wold and Mary Child of Ecton married at Abington 25 March 1663.[274] The parish registers of Old (formerly Wold), Northamptonshire, provide more details:[275]

---

[274] Church of England, Abington St. Peter and St. Paul, Northamptonshire, Parish Registers, Baptisms and Burials, 1637–1763, Marriages, 1637–1757; Northamptonshire Record Office 1P/1 [FHL #6,126,530; DGS #100,342,658].

[275] Church of England, Old (Wold) St. Andrews, Northamptonshire, Parish Registers, 1653–1694; Northamptonshire Record Office 246P/2 [FHL Fiche #6,128,436; DGS #100,31,056]. 1678–1790; Northamptonshire 246P/11

Sarah the Daughter of John Goosie and Mary his wife was baptized the 17th of May ——————— May 17th 1663

Mary the daughter of John Goosie and Mary his wife was baptized Octob. 2d [1664]

Elizabeth the daughter of John Goosie and Mary his wife was
baptized Novemb. 26 [1665]

Mary the wife of John Goosie buried Decemb. 24 [1665]

John Goosey was buried Sept 9th [1689]

The next question becomes "Who is the mother of Francis?"
No marriage records have been found for James. The 1626 will of
James Child shows that he had a large number of children. Francis
was baptized at Ecton 12 Februray 1597/8, son of James Child.
He was the fourth of six children born to James and his first wife:
Francis, bp. 1591, bur. 1594; Thomas, bp. 1593/4; James, bp.
1595; Francis, bp. 1597/8; Richard, bp. 1599/1600; and Anne, bp.
1601/2. There is then a five-year gap, and then seven children of
James Child and Katherine his wife were baptized at Ecton: John,
bp. 1607/8; Elizabeth, bp. 1608/9; Arthur, bp. 1610; Mary, bp.
1611/2; Sara, bp. 1615; Michael, bp. 1618; John, bp. 1620. The
large gap between groups and the 29-year gap between the 1591
baptism of James' first child and the 1620 baptism of the youngest
child of James and Katherine make it almost certain that he had
two wives.

James was buried at Ecton 10 October 1621. Four years later,
on 20 January 1625, "Thomas the sonne of Catherine Child was
baptised." This last child was likely born out of wedlock, as families did not wait that long to have their children baptized, especially in a small village like Ecton. That puts the difference between
the first and last child at thirty-four years—a highly unlikely sce-
nario for a single mother. It is far more probable that James was

---

[FHL Fiche #6,128,442; DGS #101,392,596] Unpaginated, records in chronological order.

married twice, with the first marriage taking place during that 1584–1591 gap in the records.

James was the youngest child and only surviving son of the earliest known ancestors, James Child and his wife Jane. There are baptismal records for three children of the couple at Ecton: Alice, bp. 1563; William, bp. 1565; and James, bp. 1568. There is no record for their daughter Audrey, nor is there a marriage record for the couple. Since the Ecton parish registers start in 1539, it is likely that they came from another parish.

Estimating that Audrey was born in 1561 (a couple of years prior to Alice), James and Jane probably married around 1561. Estimating age 25 at marriage (typical for men in this period), James was born say about 1536, prior to the start of parish registers.

In his will James left money to the poor of Little Houghton, and property he had there to his wife Jane and son James. Parish registers for Little Houghton St. Mary the Virgin parish registers begin in 1541. Only two records for anyone named Child can be found in the early years:[276]

> Marche xj Daye Elizabeth Child daughter of Will[iam] child and Jane his wife was baptized 1541

> August xxv Jane Child ~~daughter of~~ Willm of Willm Child buryed 1542

Although James had a son William, the name is far too common to be able to use onomastics as proof of a familial connection to the William of Little Houghton (also known as Houghton Parva). No will can be found in Northampton for a William in the proper period.

James also named a son-in-law in his will, George Sherman. The will identifies only two daughters: Audrey and Alice. Alice is not yet 18 and still unmarried, leaving Audrey as the wife of George Sherman. No record of the marriage has been located.

---

[276] Church of England, Little Houghton St. Mary the Virgin, Northamptonshire, Parish Registers, Baptisms, Marriages, and Burials, 1541–1648; Northamptonshire Record Office, 111P/1 [FHL Microfiche #6,127,352; DGS #100,624,328]. Upaginated, records in chronological order

GENEALOGICAL SUMMARY

1. **JAMES^D CHILD** was born say 1536 (estimated from probable marriage). He died at Ecton, Northamptonshire, by 1586 when his will was probated.[277] He married say about 1560 (ages of children) **JANE —?—**.

    Children of James^D and Jane (—?—) Child:

  2   i.   AUDREY CHILD, b. say 1561 (births of younger children) m. GEORGE SHERMAN.
        ii. ALICE CHILD, bp. 18 July 1563; bur. 13 April 1595, unmarried.
        iii. WILLIAM CHILD, bp. 31 May 1565; bur. at Ecton 21 August 1574.
  3   iv. JAMES CHILD, bp. 2 April 1568; bur. at Ecton 10 October 1621; m. (1) by 1591 —?—; m. (2) bet. 1602 and 1607 KATHERINE —?—.

2. **AUDREY CHILD** (*James^D*), was born say 1561 (births of younger siblings), daughter of James^D and Jane (—?—) Child. She married by 1586 **GEORGE SHERMAN**.

    Child of George and Audrey (Child) Sherman:

        i.   ANNE SHERMAN, born by 1586.

3. **JAMES^C CHILD** (*James^D*) was baptized at Ecton 2 April 1568, son of James Child. He was buried there 10 October 1621.

    The name of his first wife is unknown. They were likely married by November 1591 when their first child was baptized at Ec-

---

[277] All references to baptisms, marriages, and burials at Ecton are from Church of England Parish Register, Ecton St. Mary Magdelene, Northamptonshire, 1559 to 1637; Northamptonshire Record Office 114P/202, [FHL Fiche #6,127,381]. 1638 to 1754, Northamptonshire Record Office 114P/203 [FHL Fiche #6,127,382; DGS #100,430,949]. Unpaginated, records in chronological order.

ton. There is a gap in the Ecton registers from 1585 to 1591, which matches exactly the time when they would have married. She likely died between January 1601/2 (when her last child was baptized) and March 1606/7 (when James's first child with his second wife would have been conceived).

James married second by January 1607/8 **KATHERINE** —?—. There is no record of this marriage at Ecton.

They had seven children together. Four years after James' death, she baptized another child, a son born out of wedlock that could not belong to James.

Children of James[C] Child, mother uncertain, baptized at Ecton:

  i. FRANCIS CHILD, bp. November 1591; bur. at Ecton 28 June 1594.
  ii. THOMAS CHILD, bp. 11 March 1593/4.; bur. at Ecton 29 May 1649.
  iii. JAMES CHILD, bp. 7 December 1595.
4 iv. FRANCIS[B] CHILD, bp. 12 February 1597/8; bur. at Ecton 27 May 1675; m. EME —?—.
  v. RICHARD CHILD, bp. 21 March 1599/1600.
  vi. ANNE CHILD, bp. 22 January 1601/2; bur. at Ecton 11 October 1631, unmarried.

Children of James[C] and Katherine (—?—) Child, baptized at Ecton:

  vii. JOHN CHILD, 22 January 1607/8; bur. at Ecton 22 January 1607/8.
  viii. ELIZABETH CHILD, bp. 29 January 1608/9.
5 ix. ARTHUR CHILD, bp. 21 December 1610; bur. 10 December 1657; m. ALICE —?—.
  x. MARY CHILD, bp. 31 January 1611/2.
  xi. SARAH CHILD, bp. 2 May 1615; bur. at Ecton 7 September 1630.
  xii. MICHAEL CHILD, bp. 14 September 1618.
6 xiii. JOHN CHILD, bp. 11 June 1620. m. Mary —?—.

Child of Katherine (—?—) Child, father unknown:

  xiv. THOMAS CHILD, bp. 20 January 1625.

4. **FRANCIS**[B] **CHILD** (*James*[C–D]) was baptized at Ecton, Northamptonshire, 12 February 1597/8, son of James Child and his unknown first wife. He was buried there 27 May 1675.

He married by 1628 **EME** —?—. No burial record was found for her at Ecton. Since she is not mentioned in Francis' will, she likely predeceased him.

No record of baptism has yet been found for their first two children, both sons, in Northamptonshire.

Children of Francis[B] and Eme (—?—) Child:

7   i.   ROBERT[A] CHILD b. say 1624; bur. at Ecton 24 February 1672[/3]; m. ca. 1652 (based on baptism of first child in January 1654) DEBORA —?—.

    ii. JOHN CHILD, b. say 1626, liv. 1675.

    iii. ANN CHILD, bp. at Ecton 1 June 1628; bur. there 7 April 1668

8   iv. MARY CHILD, bp. at Ecton 31 May 1631; bur. at Wold (now Old), Northamptonshire, 24 December 1665; m. at Abington, Northamptonshire, 25 March 1663 JOHN GOOSIE.

9   v.   SARAH CHILD, bp. at Ecton 29 March 1633; m. —?— KING.

5. **ARTHUR CHILD** (*James*[C–D]) was baptized at Ecton, Northamptonshire, 21 December 1610, son of James[C] and **KATHERINE (—?—)** Child. He was buried there 10 December 1657.

He married, probably around 1640, **ALICE** —?—.

Children of Arthur and Alice (—?—) Child, baptised at Ecton:

    i.   MARY CHILD, bp. 8 February 1641.

    ii. SARA CHILD, bp. 27 June 1647.

6. **JOHN CHILD** (*James*[C–D]) was baptized at Ecton, Northamptonshire, 11 June 1620, son of James[C] and Katherine (—?—) Child. He was buried there 28 November 1692.

He married Mary —?—. She was buried at Ecton 29 March 1680.

Children of John and Mary (—?—) Child:

    i. JAMES CHILD, b. 29 April and bp. 4 May 1656.

7. **ROBERT[A] CHILD** (*Francis[B]*, *James[C–D]*) was born say 1624, son of Francis[B] and Eme (—?—) Child. He was buried at Ecton 24 February 1672[/3].

He married ca. 1652 (based on baptism of first child in January 1654) **DEBORA** —?—. She was buried at Ecton 24 February 1705/6.

Robert and Debora had eight children baptised at Ecton, the last born posthumously. The will of Robert's father Francis, probated in 1675, names his daughter-in-law Debora and each of the eight children, leaving each one shilling. After leaving the majority of his estate to his son John, he went on to say:

> And I require him that according to his ability he show kindness to the widow & children of my son Robert deceased as their need shall require, & their virtuous carriage shall seem to deserve. & also that within three dayes after my decease re make his Testament & renew it from tiem to time as there shall be occasion, & that therein he bequeth such legacies to the said widow & her children, as upon due consideration of his own ability & of their necessity & virtuous carriage shall seem to him reasonable & convenient. [278]

Francis was clearly very concerned about the family, who apparently had little money. Daughter Anne was 21 years old when her grandfather died, and likely married within a year of his death. The rest of the children were between three and seventeen years old.

"James Child A young Man." was buried at Ecton 25 February 1688. This is possibly Robert's son, who would have been twenty-four years old at the time. Daughter Rebecca had a child born out of wedlock in 1685. Other than that, there is no further record of

---

[278] Church of England, Archdeaconry of Northampton Court, Series 4, Original Wills, vol. 8, no. 48, Will of Francis Child of Ecton, 1675 [FHL Film #187,642; DGS #8,047,495].

the children at Ecton. "Deborah Childs an ancient poor Widow" was buried at Ecton 24 February 1705/6.

Children of Robert[A] and Debora (—?—) Child, baptised at Ecton:

     i.   ANNE[1] CHILD, bp. 21 January 1654; d. at Boston, Massachusetts, 9 July 1689; m. probably at Ecton ca. 1676 JOSIAH FRANKLIN.

     ii. DEBORA CHILD, bp. 27 February 1658.

10 iii. REBECCA CHILD bp. 16 September 1660.

     iv. JAMES CHILD, bp. 3 January 1663/4; poss. the James Child "young man" bur. at Ecton 25 February 1688.

     v.   JOHN CHILD, bp. 21 January 1665/6.

     vi. THOMAS CHILD, bp. 28 November 1669.

     vii. FRANCIS CHILD, bur. at Ecton 11 November 1671.

     viii. ROBERT CHILD, bp. 27 October 1672.

8. **MARY CHILD** (*Francis*[B], *James*[C–D]) was baptised at Ecton, Northamptonshire, 31 May 1631 daughter of Francis[B] and Eme —?—. She was buried at Wold (now Old), Northamptonshire, 24 December 1665.[279]

She married at Abington, Northamptonshire, 25 March 1663 **JOHN GOOSIE**.[280] He was buried at Wold 9 September 1689.

Mary bore three children in quick succession after marrying John. Sarah, Mary, and Elizabeth were born within two and a half years. The last child was baptised 26 November 1665. Mary may have died of complications from the birth, as she was buried less than a month later, on 24 December. Sarah, Mary, and Elizabeth

---

[279] All references in the summary to baptisms and burials at Wold are from Church of England, Old (Wold) St. Andrews, Northamptonshire, Parish Registers, 1653–1694; Northamptonshire Record Office 246P/2 [FHL Fiche #6,128,436; DGS #100,31,056]. 1678–1790; Northamptonshire 246P/11 [FHL Fiche #6,128,442; DGS #101,392,596] Unpaginated, records in chronological order.

[280] Church of England, Abington St. Peter and St. Paul, Northamptonshire, Parish Registers, Baptisms and Burials, 1637–1763, Marriages, 1637–1757; Northamptonshire Record Office 1P/1 [FHL #6,126,530; DGS #100,342,658].

Gousie were named in the will of their grandfather Francis[B] Child, with each receiving one shilling.[281]

Children of John and Mary (Child) Goosie, baptised at Wold:

   i. SARAH GOOSIE, bp. 17 May 1663.
   ii. MARY GOOSIE, bp. 2 October 1664.
   iii. ELIZABETH GOOSIE, bp. 26 November 1665.

9. **SARAH CHILD** (*Francis[B], James[C–D]*) was baptised at Ecton, Northamptonshire, 29 March 1633, daughter of Francis[B] and Eme (—?—) Child. Likely died by 1673. She married —?— **KING**.

They had one daughter, Mary, mentioned in the will of Sarah's father, Francis[B] Child. He left her a bequest of one shilling. There was no mention of Sarah in the will, indicating that like her sisters, she likely predeceased her father.[282] No record of Sarah's marriage can be found, and her husband's given name is unknown.

Child of —?— and Sarah (Child) King:

   i. MARY KING, b. by 1673.

10. **REBECCA CHILD** (*Robert[A], Francis[B], James[C–D]*) was baptised at Ecton 16 September 1660, daughter of Robert[A] and Debora (—?—) Child.

She had a child born out of wedlock in 1685 that died only a few days later. The father is unknown. There is no further record of her at Ecton after the birth and death of her son.

---

[281] Church of England, Archdeaconry of Northampton Court, Series 4, Original Wills, vol. 8, no. 48, Will of Francis Child of Ecton, 1675 [FHL Film #187,642; DGS #8,047,495].

[282] Church of England, Archdeaconry of Northampton Court, Series 4, Original Wills, vol. 8, no. 48, Will of Francis Child of Ecton, 1675 [FHL Film #187,642; DGS #8,047,495].

Child of Rebecca Child, baptised and buried at Ecton:

    i. THOMAS CHILD, bp. 10 April 1685; bur. 13 April 1685, "bastard Infant of Rebecca Child" "

CHAPTER 17

JANE^A WHITE, WIFE OF THOMAS FRANKLIN

No record of marriage for Thomas^A Franklin and Jane White has been found. Most sources don't even provide names for her parents. Some state that her father was George White, but none provides a source for this information. Examination of original records from Northamptonshire, however, provides the necessary evidence to identify both of her parents, and one set of grandparents, as well as numerous other family members.

Most of what is known of Jane White's origins comes from Benjamin Franklin the Elder discussing his mother in his "Short Account." In one passage he reports that his father Thomas:

> married Jane white Neece to Coll: White of Nethrop near Banbury in oxfordshire, she had one brother who lived at Grundon two miles from Ecton and one sister who married m^r Ride in Warwickshire, and had by him one son Named Samuel Ride to whom he left about 60l per An: free land which he in a few years spent & sold and became a Gent. Servant and afterward a Labourer in building the city of London after that Great and Dreadful fire that burn^'d it on the 2, 3, and 4 of sep 1666, which did destroy 13300 houses, This Samuel

Ride had onley one daughter who married a butcher in Clarke Market, Westminster[283]

The village of Grendon lies on the eastern border of Earls Barton. Records from the Anglican parish church of Grendon St. Mary's show the following records for individuals named White: [284]

Baptisms

Rebecca White the Daughter of William White was baptized the xiv[th] [14th] day of September. 1607.

Elizabeth Whyte the Daughter of Willim Whyte was baptized the xxv[th] [25th] Day of November 1609.

John White the sonne ~~sonne~~ of Willm White was baptized the xxj[th] [21] Day of June.1612.

Bridget White the Daughter off Willm White was baptized the xxj[th] [21] day of October 1614.

Jane White the Daughter of Willm White was baptized the xxjth [21] Day of March 1616[/17].

Jane White the Daughter of George White and Priscilla his wife was baptized the xxx[th] [30] day of November.1617./

Ann White the Daughter of Willm White & Jane his wife was baptized the Day & yeare aforesaid. [xx[th] [20] day of March 1618].

Willm White the sonne of Willm White and Jane his wife was baptized the xx[th] [20] Day of Aprill.1623.

Marriages

Willm White and Jane Harrys were marryed the xxiv[th] [24] Day of October .1606.

---

[283] Franklin, "Short Account" 1–2 [see Appendix B].

[284] Church of England, Grendon St. Mary, Northamptonshire, Parish Registers, Baptisms, Marriages, and Burials, 1559–1695; Northamptonshire Record Office, 141P/1 [FHL Microfiche #6,127,571; DGS #100,430,932]. Unpaginated, in chronological order.

George White and Priscilla Warner widow were marryed the xv^th [15] Day of September 1607.

William Hutton & Elizabeth White weare marryed the three & twentyth of Aprill 1631.

Thomas Hull & Anne Whyte maryed the ninth of July 1640.

John Houghton & Jane Whyte marryed the same day 1640 [ninth of July].

Burials

Annys White widow was buryed the Day & year aforesaid. [xxvth [25] Day of December 1606].

Nicholas White sojourner under his sonn Willm White was buryed the fourth Day of April 1619.

George Whyte yeoman was buriyd the xxv^th [25] Day of February 1622.

Jane the wife of Williā Whyte was buryed the ~~eleventh~~ ^eighteenth^ day of February 1630.

John Whyte yeoman buryed the 18th of Decemb. [1642]

In addition to the parish registers, there are two wills of interest in Northamptonshire. These are for the brothers George and William White of Grendon.

Will of George White of Grendon, probated 5 March 1622[285]

In the Name of God Amen. The sixth day of Februarie Ao Dm 1622°. I George White of Grendon in the Countie of Northampton yeoman being sick in bodie but sound of minde and memorie (Thanks bee to god for it) doe make and ordaine this my Last Will and Testament in manner and forme following. Vizt. Imprimis I give and bequeath my soule into the hands of Almightie God my Creator trusting

[285] Church of England, Archdeaconry of Northampton Court, Register Copy Wills, vol. AV, fol. 83, Will of George White of Grendon, 1662 [FHL Film #187,595; DGS #8,047,421].

to bee saved by the death and assion of his sonne Jesus Christ my Savior and redeemer And my bodie to bee buried in the Churchyard of Grendon aforesaid, Item I give and bequeath unto my daughter Jane White all that my house werein I now dwell: with the Closes and Land. That is to say to enter on my Land at the age of one and Twentie yeares, and the house and close at the decease of ~~my~~ ^her^ mother. I give to my said daughter Jane the best Cuppard with the pewter hereto belongonge Also one brasse pott and one brasse panne. I give also to hir my great roll copper, with five paire of the best shootes and the little round table. Item I give to my said Daughter my biggest bible and one gold ringe And if it shall happen my said daughter shall die and without issue of her bodie lawfully begotten then my will is that my said house Closes and Land shall goe to my Cozen John White my brother William Whites sonne Also my will is that if my said daughter shall die and bee without issue, that then all the aforesaid moveables shall goe to my said brothers daughters equallie to be divided betwixt them. Item I give to my d[smudged] brother William White tenne pounds and my best Cloake. Item I give to my mother in law Elizabeth Bromley Fourtie shillings. Item I give to my brother Thomas Henrie fortie shillings Item I give to my brother in law Nathaniell Bromley fourtie shillings. Item I give to the rest of my wives brothers and sisters fourtie shillings that is to say xx^s to bee divided betwixt the three brothers, and the other Twentie shillings to bee equallit divided betweixt my wives two sisters Item I give to my wives Cosen John Dobbe my best suite of apparel Item I give to Mr Stevenson o^e[?] vicar — x^s. Item I give to the poore of Grendon xi^s–viii^d. Item my will is that the house and Close which I bought of Mr Worsten, and the house which is now in the tenure of John Brad, and the house which is now in the tenure of Richard Rawlyns should all be sould towarde the payment of my debts and Legacies Item I make and ordaine my wife Priscilla my sole executrix of this my Last Will and Testamente, and that she shall have my aforesaid house and Close, duringe hir natural life rutting no tymber on the ground, All the rest of my goods and Chattells unbequathed I do give unto my said wife. Lastlie I doe make my brother Willlm White and my brother Thomas Heirson Supvisours of this my Last Will and Testam^t In witttness thereof I have hereunto sett my hand and seale the day and yeare abover written. George White. Wittnes herewith Adam Stevenson vicar of Grendon. . . . .

Will of William White, probated 9 June 1666[286]

In the Name of God Amen The seaventeenth day of November in the seaventeenth yeare of the Raigne [torn] our Souvaigne Lord Charles the Second of England Scotland France & Ireland Koinge defender of the Fayth &c and in the year of our [torn] Christ 1665 I William White of Grendon in the Countie of Northton yeoman of good and pfect memory the Lord God be prays[torn] for it. But considering the casualties of this transitory life doe make and ordayne this my last will and testament First & p[torn] I bequeath my spiritt and soule into the hands of Almighty God my Creator assuredly trusting to be saved by the pretious death and resurrection of my Lord Savio^r Rdeemmer Jesus Christ and sovereine life everlaasting with the Saints & Sert of God [torn] day and time when all Flesh shall appear before the Throne of the Almighty. And as for my worldly estate which God hath lent [torn] bestowed upon mee (my Body being decently buried & my debts and funerall rites paid & discharged) I give and [words crossed out and illegible]^dispose of^ of as Follows that is to say Imprimus I give and bequeath unto the poore of Easton Mauditt where I was bornd Twentie shillings It I give [torn] the poor of Grendon where I know live Thirtie Shillings It I give unto all my Godchildren living in Grendon at th etime of my decease twelve pence to each of

---

286 Church of England, Archdeaconry of Northampton Court, Original Wills, Series 4, vol. 9, no. 4, Will of William White of Grendon, 1666 [FHL Film #187,643; DGS #8,047,402].

them It I give and bequeath unto my Elizabeth my now wife
all the Goods in the Chambers over the Hall and the parlour
and over the kitchen ^except graine [illegible]^ except onely
one great Chest in the Chamber over the parlour and one
other Chest at my Beds Foote [torn]Chamber over the Hall
and one other Coffer standing at my Beds side with all things
therein contayned, which saide Coffers or Chests as
afores[torn] I give unto my Executor hereafter named, It I
also give and bequeath unto the saide Elizabeth my wife all
the Goods in the Hall, Kitchen [torn] Dairie as Brass pewter
Cheespres Barrells Tubbs Forms and all other the utensills of
Housewifery in and belonging to the saide Roomes with her
Dairie and utensills belonging to the said Daireie, with the
poultrie in and belonging to the yards, as also in the new
house in the yarde of the M[torn] with other the woodn ware
there (Except one spatt usuall employed to put Mault into
with some shippwark & sides) Also my saide wife to have
[torn] young Cowes the one a young Black Cow the other a
young Browne Cow with going for them into a certaine
Close called Cotton Close at the Spar[torn] fall for one yeare
next after my decease, at such time and times as my exector^rs
Cowes shall goo or be but to grass in the saide Close, also my
wil[torn] that my Executor shall also after my decease give to
my saide wife Three strike of wheate three strike of mault
and three strikes of barley w[torn] all the ^fire^ wood in the
yarde (Except some Theyles over the Hovell where the
pumpe stands & some Rayles under the wood Hovell to
mend Cotton Close Itē also my will is that my wife shall have
and eioy the house and land at Deynton & Com[m]ons ther-
to belonging late pchased of John Chapman th[torn] and lying in the town & Fields of Deynton aforesaide, Itē I give
and bequeath unto my two Grandchildren Hannah White &
Jane Newsome [torn] daughters & Coheires of my son John
Wite (deceased) and Ales his wife the Bed and Beding in my
parlour with the Greenish coloured Hilling (and [torn] that
Hilling which udually lyes upon it) with the Great Cubbord
thre and table and frame with Four ioynd stooles and two

Couered low stool[torn] one spreene ^onely grean chairs^ and two Formes all belonging to the saide parlous, also I give the saide Grandchildren one Great Brass Pott, with the Furnace & dresser bord (which saide Furnace and dresser my will is shall remaine as standers to the saide House during my wifes st[torn] there) with the shutts for the windows and mivard Doores alsoe the Hovell ouer the pumpe with the pumpe, and the pales and posts in the Garden [torn]Yrchard, also the Hovells in the Farme yard with a long Table in the Farme House and one Farme and all the moveables in and about the saide F[arme] House and yarde that are knowne to be mine, Ite alsoe it is my will that my wife and my Executor hereafter named shall have six months time to take up remoue and carry away all such goos cattell and chattells as shall and are herein given and bequeathed by the aforesaid William Wh[ite] to them or eyther of them, Itē I give and bequeath to my Grandchild Willim Hutton Three Acres of Aerable land as the are sett out alreadie [torn] and annexed to this my will by a Terrar, with Foure willow Trees lyinge next the ground of the saide William Hutton neare Easton Bridg[torn] I give and begeath unto my three daughters Elizabeth Hutton Jane Houghton & Anne Hull all the residue of my land & lay ground in the Com[torn] Fields of Grendon aforesaid (being seaventeene Acres more or less) equally parted and divided between them three, as by a Terrar annexed to th[torn] will I the saide William Whyte have affixed and alreadie parted and devided the said [crossed out illegible] seaventeene Acres (more or less) into three equall pa[torn] relation being thereunto had will & may more plainely appeare (that is to say) one thirde part to Elizab: Hutton for her to have and eioy during her naturall life & after he death & decease to the use benefitt & behoofe of William Hutton her sonn & his [cossed out] Heires forever & for default of such heires [illegible] right heires of the saide Elizab. Hutton for evere Itē also it is my will that the saide William Hutton aforesaide shall out of the third part afore[illegible] pay unto White Hutton his Brother the some of Twentie pounds of lawfull money of England when he the sayde William Hutton shall enbo[illegible] upon the sayde land bequeathed unto his Mother & himselfe in manner & forme aforesayed & for default ot none paiment of yͤ saide Twentie poun[illegible] the saide White Hutton to have & enioy the land aforesaide for ever if he shall be then living Itē I give allow & bequeath unto Jane Houghton the next third parte as it is alreadie devided & annexed to this my will in a Terrar during her naturall life, & after her decease to her son[illegible] William Houghton & his Heirs forever & for default of such yffice to the Right Heires of the saide Jane for ever Itē I also give & bequeath the other third part as it s annexed in my^the saide^ terrar to Anne Hull & her husband Thomas Hull during their naturall lives & the longer lived of them two & afterwards to b[illegible] use benefitt & behoofe of Elizabeth Hull their Daughter & her heiresfor ever & for default of such uffice to the heires of the saide Ann Hull for ever And if it shall please God that my death & decease shalbe ^[xxxx]^ after the sixteenth day of Aprill in any yeare whatsoever that then it is my absolut will that none of my Daughters shall enfix upon any of their saide parts until the Twentie First day of March next following & then to enter onely upon [illegible]Followes & the rst of their parts according to the Custome of he Country Itē I give & bequeath unto al my Grandchildren that shall be borne and ^be^ alive at my death of Roberrt Elizab: & Anne five pounds to each of them (Except William Hutton & White Hutton who are by this my will excluded from having any Five pounts) that is to say to all those that shall be at the age of Twentie and ^one^ yeare at my death to be paide their severall Five pounds (except before excepted) within Nine Months next after my decease if the shallbe then living and therefi[illegible] of their saide & children that are not at the age of one & twentiy at my decease to have their severall Five pounds within six moneths a[fter] their severall ages of one & Twentie if they shall be then living, Itē I give unto Elizabeth Hull my Grandchilde Tenn pounds to be[illegible]

as aforesaide, And if it shall soe happen that any of my
Grandchildren shall depart this life before their saide Five
pounds shall by this my will be dne that then my will is that
their Five pounds who shall be soe dead, shall dye also &
remaine to my Executor hereafter named Itē I give unto my
wifes Mother Ellen Emerie of Yardley Twentie shillings, Itē I
give unto Sarah Emery my former maide Fortie shillings to
be paide them within three months after my decease Itē also
I give unto Elizabeth my now wife if it shall please God shee
[torn] by me neither left in childe by me before my death,
That then I the saide William Whyte do solelye & absolutely
give & bequeath the saide [torn] Close to my daughter Ann
Hull & her heires for ever paying out of the said Cotton
Close to Elizabeth Hutton the sum[m]e of Thirtie pou[torn]
within one yeare & a halfe after my decease & Thirtie pounds
more to Jane Houghton within two yeares after my decease if
they shall b[torn] [illegible]ieing Itē: alsoe I give unto Anne
Hull my Daughter Tenn pounds to be paide at Twelve
Months end next after my decease. Itē I give un[illegible]
John Hobbs my ancient servant Tenn shillings Itē all the rest
of my goods cattles & chattells whatsoever undisposed of &
not formerly bequ[eathed] give & bequeath absolutely unto
my beloved sonne in law Thomas Hull & doe hereby make &
ordayne him the saide Thomas Hull sole executor [torn] my
last will & Testament revokeing hereby all former wills before by me made & ordayned; In Wittnes whereof to this will
& Testament I the [torn] [illegible]ered by the saide William
Whyte

The Signe & Seale of
William Whyte

Thomas Aspinall
[illegible]ph Button

There is no burial record for William as there is a gap in the Grendon burial records, which were not recorded for the years 1665 through 1669. George and William each had a daughter named Jane. William's daughter was baptized 21 March 1616/17. George's daughter was baptized eight months later, on 30 November 1617. The prenuptual agreement for Thomas and Jane (White) Franklin identifies George as her father.

George's will names his daughter Jane, who would have been five years old when her father died in 1622. It also names his wife Priscilla, brother Thomas Henrie, brother-in-law Nathaniell Bromley, mother-in-law Elizabeth Bromley, cousin John Dobbe, and his daughter Jane as his primary heir.[287] George married widow Priscilla Warner at Grendon 15 September 1607. The only child of this marriage recorded there is their daughter Jane, who was baptized ten years later.

One of the trustees in the prenuptual agreement was Nathaniel "Brimley."[288] This is no doubt his brother-in-law, called Nathaniel "Bromley" in George's will. The will also names George's mother-in-law Elizabeth Bromley, but does not provide a location for either of them. The prenuptual agreement states that Nathaniel was residing at Olney, Buckinghamshire, at the time. No other records have yet been found of the family there or elsewhere.

The first record for the White family at Grendon is the marriage of William White and Jane Harris on 24 October 1606. All the subsequent records through 1630 for individuals named White are for members of the family save one. The widow Annys White who was buried 25 December 1606 cannot be tied to the family. The lack of earlier records indicates the family must have come from elsewhere.

---

[287] Church of England, Archdeaconry of Northampton Court, Register Copy Wills, vol. AV, fol. 83, Will of George White of Grendon, 1662 [FHL Film #187,595; DGS #8,047,421].

[288] See Thomas[A] Franklin and Jane White Feoffment in Trust, p. 28.

This is supported by the record for Nicholas White. He was buried there 4 April 1619 as a "sojourner under his sonn Willm White." He died while visiting his family, but was resident elsewhere. William's will provides the necessary information to trace the family back. His very first bequest states "Imprimus I give an bequeath unto the poore of Easton Mauditt where I was bornd Twentie shillings. . ."

THE WHITE FAMILY AT EASTON-MAUDIT

The village of Easton-Maudit lies in Northamptonshire on the eastern border of Grendon. The registers of Easton-Mauditt Saints Peter and Paul provide us with a great deal of information William and George, their parents, and additional family members:[289]

Baptisms

Agnes White daughter of Wm White baptised 20 of Jannarie [1549]

Helen White daughter of Wm White baptised 7 of August [1551]

John White sonne of Wm White & of Agnes his wife baptized 23 of November [1558]

Christopher White sonne of Nicholas and Joanne White baptised March [1577/8]

Joanne white daughter of Nicholas & Joanne White baptised 20 of June [1580]

George White sonne of Nicholas & Joanne White baptised 29 of June 1582

Wm White sonne of Nich & Joanne White baptised 23 of June [1585]

---

[289] Church of England, Easton-Maudit Sts. Peter and Paul, Northamptonshire, Parish Registers, Baptisms 1539–1812, Marriages 1539-1755, and Burials, 1561–1812; Northamptonshire Record Office, 111P/1 [FHL Microfiche #6,127,352; DGS #100,624,328]. Records in chronological order

Margerie White and Joanne White daughters of Nich. & Joanne White Baptised 29 of Maie [1588]

Anne White daughter of Nicholas and Alice White baptised 24 of June [1590]

Marriage

Nhich[ol]as White et Alicia Riding matrimo contrax 7o Die Augusti [1589]

Burials

Georgius White Fil W^{illi} White Sen seconda Die Decembre erat sepult [1570]

Joha[n] White fil Nichi et Johane White sepulta erat 2o Die Juini [1581]

Joha[na] White Nich[olas] White uxor sepulta 21o Die Maii [1588]

Margeria White Fil Nichi White sepult 23o Die Octob. [1588]

Anne White fil Nicho[las] White sepulta erat 23o Die July [1590]

W^{illa} White sepulta erat quoderno die novembris [1594]

Christophea White Fil Nich[olas] White sepult 14o die april [1595]

Agnes White Vid sepulta erat octano die Septembris [1595]

Alicia White uxor Nocholas White Agricola, sepulta erat Decimo Die Marcij 1604

Margeria White filia Nicholai White sepulta erat primo die Aprilis. 1605

Parish registers for Easton-Maudit start in 1539. There is no record of baptism for Nicholas there, nor is there a record of his first marriage to Joanne. This indicates that they came frojm elsewhere. Their first recorded child was Christopher baptized in 1578. This suggests that their marriage took place around

1577. It is possible that the marriage took place earlier other children were born in the same village where they were married.

The average age of a man at first marriage in this period is about 25, indicating a birth for Nicholas around 1552. There are three baptism at Easton-Maudit about that time:

Agnes, daughter of William, bp. 20 January 1549[/50]
Helen, daughter of William, bp. 7 August 1551
John, son of William and Agnes, bp. 23 November 1558

The birth of Nicholas would fit perfectly into the seven-year gap in the baptisms between Helen and John. Review of every entry in this period, however, reveals no record for anyone else named White. It is possible that William and Agnes went elsewhere for a few years and had additional children before returning to Easton-Maudit.

These are not the original records, however. The first pages of the volume show that the first three registers were rebound together in 1766. The note for the first original volume says:

The most <u>Ancient Register</u>, beginning at 1539 (when Registers were first appointed to be kept) & ending with 1599: When the whole was transcribed by a public scrivener, all in one fair hand.

Whenever something is transcribed from the original, there is always a chance of error being introduced. An entry may have been missed during copying. Or multiple entries may have been combined into a single entry. Unfortuntely, no will exists for either William or Agnes White to assist us in filling out the family, so we cannot be certain that Nicholas belongs to them.

Nicholas and Joanne had five children: Christopher, baptized March 1577/78; Joanne, baptized June 1580; George baptized June 1582; William, baptized June 1585; and Margerie and

Joanne, baptized May 1588. Nicholas's wife Joanne was buried 21 May 1588, leaving him with three young children. He married second at Easton-Mauditt 7 August 1589 "Alicia" Alice Riding. Their daughter Anne was born in 1590. No baptism has yet been found for daughter Margery, daughter of Nicholas, who was buried there 1 April 1605, but there is no doubt she was a daughter of Alicia. Joanne died just a few days before her daughter Margery in 1588. Alice died in March 1604. While it is possible that Nicholas married again elsewhere, it would be difficult for him to have done so and had another child who died, all within a year of Alice's death. Out of Nicholas's eight children, only George, William, and Joanne survived to adulthood and left descendants.

No record of either marriage or children was found for George at Easton-Mauditt. He was twenty-five years old when he married the widow Priscilla (Bromley) Warner at Grendon, which is the average age at first marriage for a man at that time. Even if he had married early and had two children prior to his marriage to Priscilla, those children would still have been minors when George died, and provisions would have been made for them in the will. Thus it is unlikely that George had any other children.

This contradicts the information from Benjamin the Elder that Jane had a sister and a brother. Benjamin wrote his "Short Account" at Boston in 1717. He was 67 years old and recounting stories from his youth, with only his younger brother Josiah available to talk about them. He was only 12 years old and Josiah but 5 when their mother died. It is not surprising that there are mistakes in the information.

There are two possibilities to explain the error. Benjamin stated that "My Mother had a brother White whom I never saw but once." This was likely before Jane's death, so he would have been a young boy when he saw his uncle. It is possible that this uncle was a half-brother from Priscilla's first marriage.

Another possibility is that the brother was not a brother, but her cousin, John White.

The sister of Jane who married a "Mr. Ride" that he wrote of is probably not Jane's sister. She is almost certainly Esther, the sister of Thomas^A Franklin who married Robert Ride.[290] Confusing with of the parents she was related to is not a surprise for younger children.

Benjamin Franklin the elder wrote that in addition to the children who lived, his parents

> had two sons more, Twins, born before benjam— but tis tho't they dyed unbaptized because their names are not found in the church Register at Ecton where we were all born & brought up.[291]

This trend seems to come from Jane White's family. Her grandparents, Nicholas^C and Joanne—?—, had twins Margery and Joanne. Her cousin Elizabeth (White) Hutton had twins Thomas and Jane. And her cousin Jane (White) Houghton had twins Thomas and Paul.

GENEALOGICAL SUMMARY

1. **NICHOLAS**^C **WHITE** was residing at Grendon temporarily with his son William when he died and was buried there 4 April 1619. No will has been found for him.

He married first **JOANNE** —?—. She was buried at Easton-Mauditt, Northamptonshire, 21 May 1588.a[292]

---

[290] See the section on Esther/Hesther Franklin in "Henry^B Franklin" above, p. 29].

[291] Franklin, "Short Account" 1 [see Appendix B].

[292] All references in the summary to baptisms, marriages, and burials at Easton-Maudit are from Church of England, Easton-Maudit Sts. Peter and Paul, Northamptonshire, Parish Registers, Baptisms 1539–1812, Marriages

He married there second 7 August 1589 "Alicia" Alice Riding. She was buried there 10 March 1604.

Children of Nicholas[C] and Joanne (—?—) White, baptised at Easton-Mauditt Saints Peter and Paul:

     i.   CHRISTOPHER WHITE, bp. 1578; bur. there 24 April 1590.
    ii.   JOANNE WHITE, bp. 20 June 1580; bur. there 2 June 1581.
2 iii.   GEORGE[B] WHITE, bp. 29 June 1582; bur. at Grendon 25 February 1622; m. at Grendon 15 September 1607 PRISCILLA (BRIMLEY/BROMLEY) WARNER.
3 iv.   WILLIAM WHITE, bp. 23 June 1585; bur. at Grendon m. (1) 24 October 1606 JANE HARRIS; m. (2) ELIZABETH EMERY.
    v.   MARGERY WHITE, bp. 29 May 1588; bur. 23 October 1588.
   vi.   JOANNE WHITE, bp. 29 May 1588.

Children of Nicholas[C] and Joanne (—?—) White:

  vii.   ANNE WHITE, bp. at Easton-Mauditt 24 June 1590; bur. 23 July 1590.
 viii.   MARGERY WHITE, bur. at Easton-Mauditt 1 April 1605.

2.   **GEORGE[B] WHITE,** (*Nicholas[C]*) was baptised at Easton-Mauditt Saints Peter and Paul, Northamptonshire, 29 June 1582, son of Nicholas and Joanne (—?—) White. He was buried at Grendon 25 February 1622.

George married at Grendon 15 September 1607 **PRISCILLA (BROMLEY) WARNER.** She was a daughter of Elizabeth (—?—) Brimley/Bromley.

1539-1755, and Burials, 1561–1812, Northamptonshire Record Office, 111P/1. [FHL Microfiche #6,127,352; DGS #100,624,328]. Records in chronological order.

Child of George^B and Priscilla (Bromley) (Warner) White:

    i.   JANE^C WHITE, bp. at Grendon 30 November 1617; bur. at Ecton, Northamptonshire, 30 October 1662; m. by 1637 THOMAS^A FRANKLIN.

3. **WILLIAM WHITE** (*Nicholas*^C) was baptised at Easton-Maudit Saints Peter and Paul, Northamptonshire, 23 June 1585, son of Nicholas and Joanne (—?—) White. He died at Grendon by 9 June 1666 when his will was probated.[293]

He married there 24 October 1606 **JANE HARRIS**.[294] She was buried there 18 November 1630.

He married second **ELIZABETH EMERY**, daughter of Ellen (—?—) Emery of Yardley Hastings, Northamptonshire.

Children of William and Jane (Harris) White, baptised at Grendon St. Mary:

    i.   REBECCA WHITE, bp. 14 September 1607; prob. d.s.p. by 1665 (date of father's will).

4 ii. ELIZABETH WHITE, bp. 25 November 1609; m. at Grendon 23 April 1631 WILLIAM HUTTON.

5 iii. JOHN WHITE, bp. 21 June 1612; bur. at Grendon 18 December 1642; m. ALES —?—.

    iv. BRIDGET WHITE, bp. 21 October 1614; prob. d.s.p. by 1665 (date of father's will).

---

[293] Church of England, Archdeaconry of Northampton Court, Original Wills, Series 4, vol. 9, no. 4, Will of William White of Grendon, 1666 [FHL Film #187,643; DGS #8,047,402].

[294] All records in the summary refering to Grendon baptisms, marriages, and burials, from Church of England, Grendon St. Mary, Northamptonshire, Parish Registers, Baptisms, Marriages, and Burials, 1559–1695; Northamptonshire Record Office, 141P/1 [FHL Microfiche #6,127,571; DGS #100,430,932]. Unpaginated, in chronological order.

6	v.	JANE WHITE, bp. 21 March 1616[/17]; m. at Grendon 9 July 1640 JOHN HOUGHTON.
7	vi.	ANNE WHITE, bp. 20 March 1618[19]; m. at Grendon 9 July 1640 THOMAS HULL.
	vii.	WILLIAM WHITE, bp. 20 Day April 1623; prob. d.s.p. by 1665 (date of father's will).

4. **ELIZABETH WHITE** (William, Nicholas[C]) was baptised at Grendon St. Mary, Northamptonshire, 25 November 1609, daughter of William and Jane (Harris) White.

She married at Grendon 23 April 1631 **WILLIAM HUTTON**. He was buried there 18 September 1653.

Children of William and Elizabeth (White) Hutton, baptised at Grendon St. Mary

	i.	WILLIAM HUTTON, bp. 10 June 1632.
	ii.	THOMAS HUTTON, bp. 28 October 1633.
	iii.	JANE HUTTON, bp. 28 October 1633.
	iv.	ELIZABETH HUTTON, bp. 7 December 1634.
	v.	ROBERT HUTTON, bp. 21 June 1636.
	vi.	AMY HUTTON, bp. 4 May 1637.
	vii.	JANE HUTTON, bp. 9 May 1641.
	viii.	WHITE HUTTON, bp. 2 February 1642.
	ix.	REBECCA HUTTON, bp. 28 March 1647.
	vii.	SAMUEL HUTTON, bp. 25 March 1649.

5. **JOHN WHITE** (William, Nicholas[C]) was baptised at Grendon St. Mary, Northamptonshire, 21 June 1612, son of William and Jane (Harris) White. He was buried there 18 December 1642.

John married **ALES —?—**, who survived him.

Children of John and Ales (—?—) White:

    i.   HANNAH WHITE

   ii. JANE WHITE, m. by 1665 —?— NEWSOME.

6. **JANE WHITE** (William, Nicholas[C]) was baptised at Grendon St. Mary, Northamptonshire, 21 March 1616[/17], daughter of William and Jane (Harris) White. She was buried there 19 March 1691.

She married there 9 July 1640 **JOHN HOUGHTON**.

Children of John and Jane (White) Houghton, baptised at Grendon St. Mary:

      i.   JOHN HOUGHTON, bp. 12 September 1641; bur. at Grendon 3 September 1648.

    ii. THOMAS HOUGHTON, bp. 12 March 1647[/8].

   iii. PAUL HOUGHTON, bp. 12 March 1647[/8]; poss. bur. at Grendon 27 September 1691.

   iv. MARTHA HOUGHTON, bp. 13 January 1649.

    v. ELIZABETH HOUGHTON, bp. 6 April 1651.

   vi. SAMUEL HOUGHTON, bp. 9 April 1654.

  vii. JOSEPH HOUGHTON, bp. 30 December 1655.

7. **ANNE WHITE** (William, Nicholas[C]) was baptised at Grendon St. Mary, Northamptonshire, 20 March 1618[/19], daughter of William and Jane (Harris) White.

She married at Grendon 9 July 1640 **THOMAS HULL**.

Children of Thomas and Anne (White) Hull, baptised at Grendon St. Mary:

    i.   ELIZABETH HULL, bp. 10 October 1652.

CHAPTER 18

AGNES[B] JONES, WIFE OF HENRY FRANKLIN

Agnes, wife of Henry[B] Franklin, has been variously reported as having the surname Joanes/Jones or James. While the James family is present in Ecton later on, sixteenth-century records are limited to the Jones family. Examination of the original parish registers shows the name is clearly spelled as Jones, Joanes, or other slight variations thereof, not as James.

The parish registers at Ecton start in the year 1559, and the Jones family appears in them right from the beginning. Only one baptism was recorded in 1559, and that at the end of the year. The seventh baptism to appear in the records is that of Alyce, daughter of William Jones. The following records for individuals named Jones (or spelling variants) are found in the parish registers:[295]

Baptisms

Alyce Jones, the daughter of Wm Jones was bapt, the Fyrste of
  Septe [1560]

Rychard the Son of Roger Jones, was baptysed, the xix^th [19]
  daye Februarye [1561]

Mychell, the Son of Wyllyā Jones Sen was bapt the xij^th [12] of
  Febru · [1562]

Maryan, the Daught of Wm Jones Sen was bapt, the xxj^th [21] of
  December [1565]

---

[295] Church of England Parish Register, Ecton St. Mary Magdelene Northamptonshire, 1559 to 1584, 1592 to 1598; Northamptonshire Record Office 114P/201 [FHL Fiche #6,127,380; DGS #101,392,523]. Baptisms, Marriages, and Burials, 1559–1637; Northamptonshire Record Office 114P/ 202 [FHL Fiche #6,127,381]. Books are unpaginated; records are in chronological order, grouped by record type.

Marget, the Daughter of Wm Johnes was bapt, the xvij · [17] of the same [Sept 1568]

Ellyn the Daughter of W^{l.} Jones was bapt, the xxjth [21] of the same [Aprill 1570]

John, the Son of Wyllyā Jones. Senr. was bapt. the. xth [10] of June An° pd [1571]

Isabell, the Daughter of Wm Jones Junr. was bapt. the. xth. [10] of October · AP. [1572]

Agnes, the daughte^r of. Wm Jones Senr. was bapt. the. xxijth [22] Noveb [1573]

Roger, the Son of Wm Jones Junr was bapt. the. xxijth. [26] July [1575]

Thom^s the Sonne of W^{l.} Jones Junr was bapt the xxvijth [22] of March Ao pd [1578]

Marye the Daughter of Wm Jones Junr. was bapt the xxjth [21] December. Ao pd· [1580]

Elizabeth Joanes the Daughter of Willm Joanes the yonger was christened the xxvjth of Ano Dom 1592.

Memoram

A special note was found amongst the baptism records:

1598

Richard Jones

Memoram that Elizabeth the late wife of William Joanes jn^r Doeth Saye That Richard her Sonne was iv [4] yeares old [xxx] wthin: 24 Dayes of s^t which[xxxx] last past

Marriages

Wyllyam Jones, and Elizabeth Keape were marr. The xviijth [18] of June [1569].

John Bledsoe and Hellen Joanes were married the xvijth [17] of October Anno Pdict [1593]

Richard Fassaker and Isabell Joanes were marryed the vth [5] of Octobe Anno Dom 1594

Henrye Frankline & Annis Joanes were marryed the xxxth [30] of October Anno pdict [1595]

Burials

Ales Jones the daughter of Roger Jones was drowned the xxjth of the sam monythe [November 1560]

John[e] Jones, the son[e] of W[m] Jones Jun[r] was bur. the xth [10]
    daye of June An[e] pd [1571]

Margaret the wife of William Jones was buryed the xx[th] [20] of
    January Anno pdicto [1593]

William Jones was buried the 23th of November A[o] Pdict [1615]

There is only one will for someone named Jones at Ecton in this
early period, that of Roger Jones.

Roger Jones Will, probated 9 May 1586[296]

[page 1]
In the Name of God Amen th[e] xxvij[th] of January and in the
yeare of our lord god one thousand five hundreth foure score
and six op I Roger Jones of Ecton in th[e] county of Northampton husbandman being sicke in body but of good will & Testament in maner & forme as followeth first I bequeathe my soule
to Almighty god and my body to be buryed in the church yard
of Ecton Item I give unto the poore people of Ecton xij[d] Item I
give unto Richard Jones my younger soonne teenn pounds to
be payd unto him in maner & forme followinge th[t] is to say th[t]
day twelve month after my depture three pounde five shillinge
eight pence The same day twelve month after three pounds five
shillds and eight pence And that same Day twelve month after
three pounds six shillings and eight pence more untill the
summe of tenn pounds by fully satisfyed and payd Itm I will my
sonne Richard shall have a post or baffle a bed a bedstead a
coverlett a blanket and foure paire of sheetes foure pewter dish-
es two great and two small ones Itm I give unto my wyfe Alice
three quarters of corne to be payed unto hir yearly so long as
she lyve the one halfe to be rye and the other halfe to be barley
I will also my wyfe to have two mylce kyne and xv sheepe to be
kept yearely at the charges of my sonne W[m] both winter

---

296 Church of England, Archdeaconry of Northampton Court, Register
Copy of Wills, vol. V, fol. 209, Will of Roger Jones of Ecton, 1586 [FHL Film
#187,603; DGS #7,904,798]. Also, Register Copy Wills, vol. AE, pt. 2, fol. 26
[FHL Film #187,587; DGS #8,228,227].

[page 2]

winter & summer I will also my wyfe shall have hir bord & washinge at the charges of also of my sonne Will[ia]m I will also my wyfe to have hir chamber to hir selfe with free egresse and regresse thereunto without any loss or contradiction Itm I give & bequeath unto every one of my sonne Will[ia]m his children one sheepe a peece Itm I will y^t my soonne Williā Jones shall have the leases of my farme fully & wholly unto him selfe after my decease all the rest of my goods unbequeathed I give unto my sonne Williā Jones. My debtsa and legacy ot being payed and pformed making ye sayd Williā Jones my soonne my full & sole executour of this my last will & Testament In witnes whereof to this my last will I have setto my signet in the presence of Williā Jones and Williā Tomson whom I do make also my overseers of this my will giving unto each of them xx^d Witnesses Williā Jones Willi[a]m Tomson John Garrett ·/·/·

There is one clear father with three children in the parish registers and will: Roger Jones and his son William, daughter Ales (d. 1560), and son Richard (bp. 1561). There are a dozen more children born to men named William Jones:

- William Jones children Alice (bp. 1560), Margaret (bp. 1568), and Ellen (bp. 1570).
- William Jones, Senior, children Michael (bp. 1562), Margery (bp. 1565), John (bp. 1571, bur. 1571), and Agnes (bp. 1573).
- William Jones, Junior, children Isabel (bp. 1572), Roger (bp. 1575), Thomas (bp. 1578), and Mary (bp. 1580).
- William Jones the Younger child Elizabeth (bp. 1592).

William, senior, is clearly the father of Agnes who married Henry[B] Franklin. Sorting out the remaining fathers is a bit more challenging. In this period the terms junior and senior did not neccessarily indicate relationship. When multiple individuals with the same name lived in the village, the eldest would be called senior or the elder and the youngest would be junior or the younger.

Others would be called the third, fourth, etc. When one person in the chain died or moved away, everyone beneath him moved up a position, i.e., junior becomes senior, the third becomes junior, etc. Examination of the records indicates as many as seven different men may have lived at Ecton in the second half of the sixteenth century. Presented in strict chronological order, they are:

1560, William
1562, Senior
1565, Senior
1568, William
1570, William
1571, Senior
1572, Junior
1573, Senior
1575, Junior
1578, Junior
1580, Junior
1592, Younger

William Junior, and William the Younger are likely not a single individual. There is a twelve-year gap between the last child of William Junior, and the only child of William the Younger. Such a large gap indicates at least the possibility of two separate individuals. It is also possible that William Junior's wife died, and the 1592 baptism is the product of a second marriage to a younger woman. There is insufficient evidence to determine whether it is one or two individuals.

William Senior in the births of John in 1571 and Agnes in 1573 are likely a single individual. This William is different from William Junior. The overlapping births of children to Senior and Junior indicate two different men.

The earlier births show that there was likely one man named William in 1560. But by 1562 and through 1565 the use of senior indicates that there is another William in the village. By 1568, one has likely died or moved away, as births in 1568 and 1570 name William without the use of junior or senior. So, they could be three different men. But the timing of these births is such that they also might belong to a single individual. This would require the following timeline:

- 1560 Alice, daughter of William
- another William appears; becomes Senior
- 1562 Michael, son of Senior
- 1565 Margery, daughter of Senior
- other William dies/relocates; Senior becomes William
- 1568 Margaret, daughter of William
- 1570 Ellen, daughter of William
- another William appears; becomes Senior again
- 1571 John, son of Senior
- 1573 Agnes, daughter of Senior

Such a timing of children every 1–3 years is average for the period. Michael Jones was a very successful individual, and he had close ties to the Franklin family. He was a witness to the will of James Child (father of Josiah Franklin's first wife Ann Child). He partnered with Henry Franklin to purchase land, and he appears as a witness for Thomas[A] Franklin in the feoffment in trust the latter signed at the time of his marriage to Jane White.[297]

While these points lend credence to the theory that Michael is Agnes's brother and the births belong to a single individual, they are still insufficient to be completely certain of their relationship. They could be full siblings, half-siblings, cousins, or no relationat all. In the genealogical summary, the five older children are listed as possibly children of the same father.

The marriage of William Jones and Elizabeth Keape in 1569 is most likely for Junior. The date fits perfectly with the births of his children, and the namesake daughter Isabel (a version of Elizabeth). This would leave the Margaret who was buried in 1592 as the wife of William, Senior.

The will of Roger Jones names two children: sons Richard and William. There is no baptism at Ecton for William, and he is the major heir. This points to him as the eldest son, with a birth prior

---

[297] See the full indenture transcription on page 114.

to the start of parish registers at Ecton. It is also possible that he was born elsewhere and Roger moved to the village close to the time his daughter Alice died.

The next question is whether the Elizabeth, wife of William Jones, whose memorandum appears in 1598 is Elizabeth Keap, wife of William Junior. While this is possible, it would require the existence of a son Richard whose baptism was not recorded at Ecton. As mentioned previously, it is also possible that William Junior, married twice, and this may be his second wife. but this still leaves us with the problem of the missing baptism of Richard. While it is possible the baptism went unrecorded, it is at least equally likely that this Elizabeth is a different woman. She could be the wife of Roger's son Richard, with a marriage and children recorded elsewhere. The use of the name Richard as a son of Elizabeth indicates a possible link to the family of Roger Jones.

GENEALOGICAL SUMMARIES

Franklin Line

1. **WILLIAM**^C **JONES** married **MARGARET** —?— by 1560. They resided at Ecton during the second half of the sixteenth century, where he was called William Jones, Senior. He is possibly the William Jones who was buried at Ecton 23 November 1615.[298] Margaret was buried at Ecton 20 January 1592.

---

[298] All references in the summaries to baptisms, marriages, and burials at Ecton are from Church of England Parish Register, St. Mary Magdelene, Ecton, Northamptonshire, 1559 to 1584, 1592 to 1598; Northamptonshire Record Office 114P/201 [FHL Fiche #6,127,380; DGS #101,392,523]. Baptisms, Marriages, and Burials, 1559–1637; Northamptonshire Record Office 114P/ 202 [FHL Fiche #6,127,381]. Books are unpaginated; records are in chronological order, grouped by record type.

Children of William[C] and Margaret (—?—) Jones, baptized at St. Mary Magdelene, Ecton:

   i.   ALICE JONES (poss.), bp. 4 September 1560.
   ii. MICHAEL JONES (poss.), bp. 12 February 1562.
  iii. MARYAN JONES (poss.), bp. 21 December 1565.
  iv. MARGARET JONES (poss.), bp. 17 April 1568.
   v. ELLEN JONES (poss.), bp. 21 April 1570; m. at Ecton 13 October 1593 JOHN BLEDSOE.
  vi. JOHN JONES, bp. 10 June 1571
 viii. AGNES[B] JONES, bp. 22 November 1573; m. at Ecton 30 October 1595 HENRY FRANKLIN.

Other Lines

1. **ROGER JONES** married by 1561 **ALICE** —?—. He died at Ecton by 9 May 1656 when his will was probated.[299] No relationship has been established between Roger and William[C] Jones.

Children of Roger and Alice (—?—) Jones, baptized at Ecton:

     i. ALES JONES, drowned 21 November 1560.
2   ii. WILLIAM JONES, m. at Ecton 15 June 1569 ELIZABETH KEAP.
    iii. RICHARD JONES, bp. 19 February 1561.

2. **WILLIAM JONES** married at Ecton 15 June 1569 **ELIZABETH KEAP**. He is possibly the William Jones who was buried at Ecton 23 November 1615. He was known as William, Junior.

Children of William and Elizabeth (Keap) Jones, baptized at Ecton:

   i. ISABEL JONES, bp. 11 October 1572, m. there 5 October 1594 RICHARD FASSATER.
  ii. ROGER JONES, bp. 21 July 1575.

---

[299] Church of England, Archdeaconry of Northampton Court, Register Copy of Wills, vol. V, fol. 209, Will of Roger Jones of Ecton, 1586 [FHL Film #187,603; DGS #7,904,798]. Also, Register Copy Wills, vol. AE, pt. 2, fol. 26 [FHL Film #187,587; DGS #8,228,227].

iii. THOMAS JONES, bp. 28 March 1578.
iv. MARY JONES, bp. 21 December 1580.

1. **WILLIAM JONES**, known as William the Younger, resided at Ecton in 1592.

Child of William and —?— Jones, baptized at Ecton:

   i. ELIZABETH JONES, bp. 22 February 1592.[300]

---

[300] Church of England Parish Register, Ecton, St. Mary Magdelene, Northamptonshire, Parish Registers, 1559 to 1584, 1592 to 1598; Northamptonshire Record Office 114P/201 [FHL Fiche #6,127,380; DGS #101,392,523]. Book is unpaginated; records are in chronological order, grouped by record type.

CHAPTER 19

MARGERY[C] MEADOWS, WIFE OF THOMAS FRANKLIN

Only two records for someone named Meadows (or any spelling variant) can be found in the parish registers for Earls Barton in the sixteenth century:[301]

> xi day of Novembr Thomas Franklin Single and Margerie Meadowes Single were married [1560]

> Nuptial Parte evant inter Robtm Henson de Hygham Ferrers and margaretam meadowes quinto dit decembries 1590 34 ·Regni Elizabeth

The second record occured thirty years after the first. No connection can be found between the two women. There is a generation between them, and no other mention of anyone named Meadows in the parish. Margaret likely came from another parish.

Northamptonshire probate records likewise reveal a dearth of information on any individuals with the surname in the sixteenth and early-seventeenth centuries, with fewer than a dozen wills over the course of a century, and none from Earls Barton:

John Meadow, Northampton, 1515
Thomas Medowes, Oakham, 1567
Richard Medowes, Kettering, 1581

---

[301] Church of England, Earls Barton All Saints, Northamptonshire, Parish Registers, Baptisms, 1558–1724, Marriages 1559–1728, Burials 1558–1725; Northamptonshire Record Office 110P/11. Register is not paginated but records appear in chronological order.

Isabell Meadowes, Warkton, 1598
Avery Meadowes, Kettering, 1599
Emme Meadows, Cranford St. John, 1600
Thomas Meadowes, Geddington, 1607
Henry Meadowes, Carlton, 1612
Roland Meddowes, Oakham, Rutland, 1612
Thomas Meadowes, Warkton, 1619

The will of John Meadow is a generation too early to be of assistance. Any child of someone who died around 1515 would be too old to bear children in the 1560s and 70s. Other early wills have no mention of Margery. The wills and a summery of the bequests thy contain are listed below.

Thomas Medowes of Oakham, 21 December 1566:[302]
- Agnes Medowes my wiffe
- Jane my daughter [no surname given]
- William Meadowes my sonne
- Robert Medowes being my eldest sonne

Richard Medowes of Kettering, 12 March 1580:[303]
- my sonne M[?]
- Elizabeth my wiffe
- my sonne Edward
- my daughter Agnes [no surname given]
- my sonne John
- Thomas Medowes [no relationship given]

---

[302] Church of England, Archdeaconry of Northampton Court, First Series, Register Copy Wills, vol. S, folio 8, verso, Will of Thomas Medowes of Oakham, 1567 [FHL Film #187,586; DGS #8,098,669].

[303] Church of England, Archdeaconry of Northampton Court, First Series, Register Copy Wills, vol. V, folio 58, recto, Will of Richard Medowes of Kettering, 1581, [FHL Film #187,587; DGS #8,228,227].

Isabell Meadowes of Warkton, 21 December 1598:[304]

- Richard Meadowes my cozen
- my daughter Elizabeth Pell
- my sonne Thomas Meadowes

Avery Meadowes of Kettering, 18 August 1599 (noncupative):[305]

- "to Katherine his wife to bring up his children"

Emme Meadowes of Cranford St. John, spinster, 26 July 1600[306]

- John Pell, my sisters sonne
- Elizabeth Pell my sisters daughter
- Isabell Tweltricke my sisters daughter
- Thomas Bendee, son of John Bendee (no relationship given)
- Thomas Meadowes my brother and Agnes Bendee my sister and Alice Tweltricke my sister.

Thomas Meadowes of Geddington, 22 March 1607[307]

- Bridget my wyfe
- Thomas Bland and William Bland (no relationship given)
- Marye my daughter [no surname given]

---

[304] Church of England, Archdeaconry of Northampton Court, First Series, Register Copy Wills, vol. W, folio 82, recto, Will of Isabell Meadowes of Warkton, 1598 [FHL Film #187,588; DGS #8,047,477].

[305] Church of England, Archdeaconry of Northampton Court, First Series, Register Copy Wills, vol. W, folio 144, recto, Will of Avery Meadowes of Kettering, 1599 [FHL Film #187,588; DGS #8,047,477].

[306] Church of England, Archdeaconry of Northampton Court, First Series, Register Copy Wills, vol. W, folio 198, recto, Will of Emme Meadows of Cranford St. John, 1600 [FHL Film #187,588; DGS #8,047,477].

[307] Church of England, Diocese of Peterborough, Consistory Court, Original Wills, vol. B, no. 70, Will of Thomas Meadows of Geddington [FHL #174,843; DGS #8,285,942].

- Elizabeth Jackson [no relationship given]
- John White the younger and Mary White his sister [no relationship given]
- my brother William [no surname given]

Henry Meadowes of Carlton, 20 April 1612[308]

- my daughter Agnes [no surname given]
- my daughter Bridget Meadowes
- my daughter Katherine Meadowes
- Margaret Meadowes my wife
- William Meadowes my sonne

Roland Meddowes of Oakham, Rutland, 26 June 1612[309]

- Elizabeth Meddowes my daughter
- Alice Meddowes my daughter
- my sonne Roland Meddowes
- my sonne John Meddowes
- Agnes Meddowes my wife
- my sonne Will[ia]m Meddowes

Thomas Meadowes of Warkton, 11 December 1619 [310]

- my daughter Dorothie [no surname given]
- my daughter Elizabeth [no surname given]

---

[308] Church of England, Diocese of Peterborough, Consistory Court, Original Wills, vol. B, no. 344, Will of Henry Meadows of Carlton [FHL #174,843; DGS #8,285,942].

[309] Church of England, Diocese of Peterborough, Consistory Court, Original Wills, vol. A, no. 142, Will of Roland Meadowes of Oakham [FHL #174,842; DGS #8,046,860].

[310] Church of England, Archdeaconry of Northampton Court, Second Series, Original Wills, vol. M, No. 175, Will of Thomas Meadows of Warkton, 1619 [FHL Film #187,607; DGS #8,085,017].

- my brother Burges & George How & William Cane [no relationships given for last two]
- my sonne Joseph
- John my eldest sonne

There are no clues at all in the probate records of Northamptonshire for the origin of Margery Meadows. Given the few records for anyone of the surname at the time, it is quite possible that she came from another county.

Appendix A:
Benjamin[2] Franklin's First Autobiography

Benjamin Franklin's first autobiography was written on a trip he made from London in 1771. He wrote it in a matter of days. The format was as a letter to his son William. This was before their falling out, which occured a few years later. This excerpt is from the beginning, where Benjamin wrote about his family.[311]

Twyford, at the Bishop of St. Asaph's, 1771

Dear Son: I have ever had pleasure in obtaining any little ancecdotes of my ancestors. You may remember the inquiries I made among the remains of my relations when you were with me in England, and the journey I undertook for that purpose. Imagining it may be equally agreeable to you to know the circumstances of my life, many of which you are yet unacquainted with, and expecting the enjoyment of a week's uninterrupted leisure in my present country retirement, I sit down to write them for you. To which I have besides some other inducements. Having emerged from the poverty and obscurity in which I was born and bred, to a state of affluence and some degree of reputation in the worked, and having gone so far through life with a considerable share of felicity, the conducing means I made us of, which the blessing of God so well succeeded, my posterity may like to know, as they may find some of them suitable to their own situations, and therefore fit to be imitated. . .

The notes of one of my uncles (who had the same kind of curiosity in collecting family anecdotes) once put into my hands, furnished me with several particulars relating to our ancestors.

311 Van Doren, *Autobiographical Writings*, 220–227 (see note 1).

From these notes I learned that the family had lived in the same village, Ecton, in Northamptonshire, for three hundred years, and how much longer he knew not (perhaps from the time when the name of Franklin, that before was the name of an order of people, was assumed by them as a surname when others took surnames all over the kingdom), on a freehold of about thirty acres, aided by the smith's business, which had continues in the family till his time, the eldest son being always bred to that business; a custom which he and my father followed as to their eldest sons. When I searched the registers at Ecton, I found an account of their births, marriages and burials from the year 1555 only, there being no registers kept in that parish at any time preceding. By that register I perceived that I was the youngest son of the youngest son for five generations back. My grandfather Thomas, who was born in 1598, lived at Ecton until he grew too old to follow business longer, when he went to live with his son John, a dyer at Banbury, in Oxfordshire, with whom my father served an apprenticeship. There my grandfather died and lies buried. We saw his gravestone in 1758. His eldest son Thomas lived in the house at Ecton, and left it with the land to his only child, a daughter, who, with her husband, one Fisher, of Wellingborough, sold it to Mr. Isten, now lord of the manor there. My grandfather had four sons that grew up, viz.: Thomas, John, Benjamin, and Josiah. I will give you what account i can of them, at this distance from my papers, and if these are not lost in my absence, you will among them find many more particulars.

Thomas was bred a smith under his father; but being ingenious, and encouraged in learning (as all my brothers were) by an Esquire Palmer, then the principal gentleman in that parish, he qualified himself for the business of scrivener; became a considerable man in the county; and much taken notice of and patronized by the then Lord Halifax. He died in 1702, January 6, old style, just four years to a day before I was born. The account we received of his life and character from some old people at Ecton, I remember, struck you as something extraordinary, from its similarity to what you knew of mine. "Had he died on the same day," you said, "one might have supposed a transmigration."

John was bred a dyer, I believe, of woollens. Benjamin was bred a silk dyer, serving an apprenticeship at London. He was an ingenious man. I remember him well, for when I was a boy he came over to my father in Boston and lived in the house with us some years. He lived to a great age. His grandson, Samuel Franklin, now lives in Boston. He left behind him two quarto voalums, MS., of his own poetry, consisting of little occasional pieces addressed to his friends and relations. He had formed a short-hand of his own, which he taught me, but, never practising it, I have now forgot it. I was named after this uncle, there being a particular affection between him and my father. He was very pious, a great attender of sermons of the best preachers, which he took down in his short-hand, and had with him many volumes of them. He was also much of a politician; too much, perhaps, for his station. There fell lately into my hands, in London, a collection he made of all the principal pamphlets relating to public affairs, from 1641 to 1717; many of the volumes are wanting as appears by the numbering, but there still remain eight volumes in folio, and twenty-four in quarto and octavo. A dealer in old books met with them, and knowing me by my sometimes buying of him, he brought them to me. It seems my uncle must have left them here when he went to America, which was above fifty years since. There are many of his notes in the margins.

This obscure family of ours was early in the Reformation, and continued Protestants through the reign of Queen Mary, when there were sometimes in danger of trouble on account of their zeal against popery. They had got an English Bible, and to conceal and secure it, fastened open with tapes under and within the cover of a joint stool. when my great-great grandfather read it to hs family, he turned up the joint stool upon his knees, turnign over the leaves then under the tapes. One of the children stood at the door to give notice if he was the apparitor coming, who was an officer of the spiritual court. In that case the stool was turned down again upon its feet, when the Bible remained concealed under it as before. This anecdote I had from my uncle Benjamin. The family continued all of the Church of England till about the end of Charles the Second's reign, when some of the ministers that had been outed for non-conformity holding conventicles in Northamptonshire, Benjamin and Josiah adhered to them, and so continued all their lives: the rest of the family remained with the Episcopal Church.

Josiah, my father, married young, and carried his wife with three children into New England, about 1682. The conventicles having been forbidden by law, and frequently disturbed, induced some considerable men of his acquaintance to remove to that country, and he was prevailed with to accompany them thither, where they expected to enjoy their mode of religion with freedom. By the same wife he had four children more born ehre, and by a second wife ten more, in all seventeen. . .

Appendix B:
Benjamin[1] Franklin the Elder's
"Short Account"

Benjamin[1] Franklin, the Elder, compiled this account at his brother Josiah's home in Boston in June 1717, when he was 67 years old.[312] He had earlier immigrated to Boston to live with his son Samuel and join his brother Josiah. As is to be expected of an older person writing decades after events took place with only his younger brother to talk with, not all the details are accurate. But it provides an excellent look at Benjamin Franklin's family. The manuscript is currently at the Beinecke Rare Book and Manuscript Library at the Yale University Library.

[page 1]
    A short account of the Family of Thomas Franklin of Ecton in Northamptonshire. 21 June 1717.

I have a dark Idea of the Grnfather of Tho. Franklin my Father, that his name was Henery, that he was an Atturney and lived at Houghton two Miles from Northampton, and that he had an Estate there of about Eighty pounds a year free land. In his dayes the Gent. of that town were for having their land Inclosed, but this Gent. being of honest principles, knowing the Laws in force against it, and that it would be a great wrong to the poor, opposed their designe & stood in deffence of the poor Inhabitants and soe spent his Estate and did himselfe nor them any good therby for Might overcame Right. Having thus spent his Estate his son

---

312 Benjamin Franklin, "A short account of the family of Thomas Franklin of Ecton in Northamptonshire" 21 June 1717, Uncat MS Vault Franklin, Benjamin Franklin Collection. Beinecke Rare Book and Manuscript Library, Yale University, New Haven, Connecticut.

was put to a blacksmith and setled at Ecton but whether the atturney had any other child I know not and therfore I proseed to
speak of   Franklin who lived at Ecton 4 miles east-
ward of Northampton and practiced the trade of a blacksmith
there. The character which I have heard rep^{E}sents him as a
reserv'd, unsociable m[an]. He lived in his own freehold and there
he dyed, He had only one son Named Thomas which he bro't up
to his own trade and upon his Father's demise He was possessed
of his free hold at Ecton aforesaid It being in vallue about 18 or
20 £ pr an:

Thomas Franklin (the son of   Franklin — above)
was born at Ecton in Northamptonshire on the 8 day of Oct: in
the year 1598. After his fathers decease He married Jane White
Neece to Coll: White of Nethrop near Banbury in oxford

[page 2]
oxford-shire, she had one brother who lived at Grundon two
miles from Ecton and one sister who married Mr Ride in Warwickshire and had by him one son named Samuel Ride to whome
he left about 60 £ per An: free land which he in a few years spent
& sold. and became a Gent. servant and afterward a labourer in
building the city of London after that Great and Dreadful fire that
burnt it on the 2, 3, and 4 of sept 1666. which did destroy 13300
houses, This samuel Ride had only one daughter who married a
butcher in Clare Market, Westminster

Thomas Franklin had by his Wife Jane White Nine children
whose names follow

Thomas born	9 Mar. 1637
Samuel born	5 Nov. 1641
John born . .	20 Feb. 1643 dyed 7 June 1695
Joseph born	10 Oct 1646
Benjamin	20 Mar. 1650
Hannah . .	29 Oct 1654
Josiah born	25 Dec. 1657

They had two sons more, Twins, born before benjam— but tis tho't they dyed unbaptized because their names are not found in the church Register at Ecton where we were all born & brought up.

I remember nothing of my mothers father nor my fathers father but what you have above. of my Father it sd he was naturaly of a chearfull temper, pleasant conversation, Just in his dealings, My Mother had a brother White whom I never saw but once.

[page 3]

his dealings, as to his hade an Exelent workman, a man of understanding in the best things, a constant Attender on ordinances, and family dutys, and a great observer of the works of providence. His son Josiah resembles him most both as to his person (save in his feet) and his Naturall disposition · while he was young he made a clock which went well for many years in my remembrance, he alsoe practised for diversion the trade of a Turner, a gun-smith, a surgeron, a scrivener, and wrote as prety a hand as ever I saw. He was a historian and had some skill in Astronomy and chymistry which made him acceptable company to Mr John Palmer the Arch-deacon of Northampton

He left off all business borth as to his trade, and farm, sev^{r}all years before he dyed put it into his son Thomas's hand, and went to his son John at banbury in oxfordshire where he continued to the day of his death which fell out on the 21 of March 1681. being 83 years [ink blot] 5 months and 9 dayes old. He was of a brown complexion, comely countenance Inclin'd to corpulancy, and had very little hair and used to wear a cap and a love of good men of all denominations. He was most Inclin'd to the presbiterian government and discipline, but when charles 2^d return'd he went to church alsoe for peace and order sake.

His wife Jane (my Mother whose name as much as his) I shall ever love and hon^r was a tall fair comly person exact in her morals, and as she was Religiously Educated & alsoe Religiously Inclin't and kept up a thursday meeting of her godly woman Neighbours, In which they spent in prayer, conference, and repetion of the foregoing Lords day serm[on], and singing, about 2 hours time which things I being a child and admitted into their company had the greater opportunity to know. Two things with relation to this I

yet remember, her singing the 4 psalm in the old metre for we
then knew no other, and he speaking with a greate deale of pleasure and pressing with a reat deale of Earnestness the meditation of
the 3 last verses of the 3 chap. of Malachy

[page 4]
Malachy upon them that were p^rsent. And I remember once she
severly chid me for my Backwardness in learning the Lords prayer,
and sd If I went to Hell I should there remember that she had
warn'd me of my danger and told and Instructed me in my duty.

She had a Long time of Languishing I think I have heard my
father say nere seven [ink blot] years und^r that flattering Lingering
distemper a consumption, which with other Afflictions she bare
with much christian patience and resignation, she dyed and was
buried in Ecton church-yard on the North-east side, about 4° November 1662 or 3.

We have a saying in the family, that My Father was twenty
years older than my Mother, my Mother 20 yrs older than my
brother Thomas, B^r Thomas was 20 years older than my brother
Josiah. and I think it near the [illegible cross out] matter. she was
neat huswifly and Industrious woman and her person most re-
sembled my Neece Sarah of any that I know among all our relations.

Thomas about the year 1665 persuaded my father to let his
land and leave off husbandry which in a year or two after he did,
and his own trade alsoe, and boarded with him for a while but —
his temper being passionate did not sute wth my fathers and so he
went to banbury. after and for some time before bro. Tho. kept a
school and sold tobacco, but when his business of writing Bills,
and bonds and Deeds &c was Increased he left off his schoole to
Samuel Roberts his Neighbour. and so his business still Increasing
he at length be–came a Noted scrivener, and having the advantage
of the Arch Deacon and Esq^rs Catesby two rich mens purses at
comand he raised

[page 5]
an Estate of about two Thousand pounds. He had by Elenor his wife one Daughter only, her name is Mary, she was married to Mr Richard Fisher of Welingborough in Northamptonshire who has sould all she had at Ecton, that was left by her father and mother. Thomas dyed at Ecton ^in com[m]ission for receiving the land tax for the King in that country.^ on 6 Jan^r. 1702. and his widdow dyed there about 10 years afterward. He was a black thin man of very mean appearance, but of great understanding and quick ap-p^rhension, very passionate, soon reconciled, & Just in his dealings, Highly for the church of Eng. yet wanted a cordial love for its Ministers and toward his end had almost turn'd dissenter.

Samuel, was put Aprentis to Mr Wilkinson a silk weaver in maid lane southwark. he dye din the time of his Aprentiship. of a dropsy. He is s^d to be very Ingenious, the most comly person in the family and religiously Inclin'd. He and John Loved on the oth-er Entirely In So much that when one had done a fault the othe would plead, and procure his pardon before he came in sight. He was burried in st. Mary overy · (alis) st saviours southwark church yeard about the year 1659 or so.

John served his time to m^r Glover a cloth Dyer at 3 crans in Thames street London. and being Importun'd to set up in the country by m^r Warren of Warmington weaver, and not hving his health in the city, he setled at Banbury in Oxfordshire, he lived a batchelor long and was a sutor to many young women whose love he seldom miss'd of gaining, but then some trifle or other turn'd his affections from them and I tho't he did not fairly leave them. at last he Married Mrs Ann Jeffs of Marson in warwickshire with whom he had about 250 £ by whom he had severall children whose names follow in order.

[page 6]
Thomas Born on 15 Sept 1683

Hannah
Ann · ·
Mary · ·
Jane · ·
Elenor ·

They were all born at Banbury and when their father and mother dyed they became the care of my bro. Thomas.

While John lived in the city he was as a father to me and helped me thro' my troubles with my Mr Pratt · to whom I served 5 years of my time. He was of a very pleasant conversation, could sute himselfe to any company, and did when he pleaded Insinuate himself into the good opinion of persons of all Qualities and conditions, in Marrying he missed it as to one maine designe he aymed at, which was the having a Wife that would Assist in his business, but she proved neither capable nor carful in that point and soe B^r Thomases prediction was in a great measure verified, who once in my hearing, reproving him for courting and for such little causes leaving, soe many whose Affections he has gained, Told him that it would return upno him, that he would be not with, and take up with the Worst at last and Indeed soe he did, according to his own consession when he thus Express'd himselfe. If my Wife was but like — other women, If she was but liek my sister Benjamin, (that is to say my wife) I should ever Adore her, but then he checkt himselfe and s^d: but, may be, It is best, it should be [crossout] as it is, for I should a been apt to set her in the first place. He was a dyer, lived in good repute at banbury many years. the cause of his death was a boyle or sweling which came by a hurt which he got in mounting his horse, It being in his privities (and thinking to keep it secret) he ^o^pened it with a Needle before it was ripe which caused it to Gangrene up into his body it killed him in 3 dayes time, He dyed I think in June 1689. Much lamented of rich and poor in Banbury in Banbury for he was a peace maker and a frind to the poor

His son Thomas is a dyer, lives at Lutterworth in Leicestershire, Han^a. and Mary are at London,

[page 7]
London in service there, the other three are Lacemakers and live, Ann at Hartwell with a gingerbread baker, Jane with David blunt at Ashton, and Nelly at Mr. Davis's a famer at Warden, Hannah lived at Mr Keat a banker's near Hungerford market in the strand, Westminster, at the unicorn. Tho. is married and has one son, the 3 tones above named I take to be in Northampton-shire.

Joseph was a carpenter, seved his time wth Mr Titcomb Just without Moregate London. that being one of the city Gates he helpt to build it, His time of Ap^{r}ntis being Expired Mr Cogshall a Suffolk Gent. took him down to Aldborough to build him an house which when he had finished he went and setled at Knatshalla town 6 miles distant from Alboro · in the same county where he married Sarah Sawyer, Daughter of Mr Saw᷈er s to · · · · · He had by her one son named Joseph, born after is fathers death. He was facetious in his comon conversation, his Judgm^{t} was for the Church of England. but his wife was otherwise Enclin'd. He dyed on St Andrews day, the 30 Nov. 1683. She married againe to Mr Blackmore by blybrow near Dunwich in Suffolk, and there her son Joseph dyed about 21 year of his Age.

Benjamin served his time to Mr Pratt 5 years, Mr Paine 2 years. Dyers of skeyn silk black. which he practised for about 7 years after. and then learned to dye skeyn silk into collours, that he followed for about Eleven years more, then turn'd Ragg dyer as tis called in London, that is dying wr't silk in the peece and when made into Garments, this he did for about seventeen years, but not having the desired success he left off and went to New England and Landed at Boston on 10 Oct. 1715

Before this Benjamin there were born two sons more, Twins, which as I sd (tis tho't) dyed unbatiz'd.

In the

[page 8]
In the year 1683 on fryday 23 Nov. He Married Mrs Hannah Welles, Daughter of Mr Samuel Welles — minister of Banbury in Oxfordshire, this Mr W. was wone of these 2000 that were turn'd out soon after King Charles 2^{d} restoration, on 24 Aug 1662 comonly called, Black Bartholomew day. Dr Mather is another of them, who in England are called Dessenters, together with those that follow them, Benj. had By his wife Hannah Ten children, Namly

Samuel born on	15 Oct. 1684
Benjamin · · · ·	6 Aug. 1686 dyed 22 Apr 87
Jane · · · · ·	14 feb. 1687
Hannah · · · ·	18 Nov. 1689 dyed 31 Dec. 1710
Thomas · · · ·	31 Aug. 1692 dyed 2 Mar:94
Elisabeth · · ·	27 Oct 1694
Mary · · ·	23 Apr. 1686 dyed 27 Aug 96
John · · · · ·	8 Apr. 1699
Joseph · · · ·	27 Jan^r. 1700
Josiah · · · ·	3 Jan^r. 1703 dyed 10 Jan^r.

Hannah the Mother of these dyed in princes street in st Ann's parish in Westminster on the 4° Nov· 1705 · and in her I lost the delight of – mine Eyes, the desire of my heart, and the comfort of my Life. she worte severall things for her own private use, some of them are in her son Samuels hands. Hannah My Daughter was of a weakly constituttion, as was her mother, and took after her as to writing, rediness of witt and curious working with her Needle, but

[page 9]
but was not soe happy in her Natural temper which was somwhat like her fathers. which he was apt to Impute to her sickly disposition when I had begun too much to set my Affections on her, as standing in her mother stead, and in good measure filling up her room, having a good understanding in the best things, of a discreet deportment toward others, and pruden^t houswifely neat and saving in all her managements. It pleased the holy God to take her (I hope) to himselfe on 31 Dec·1710 · bet. 11 and 12 at Night being the last day and the last hour of the old year. her brother Sam. has something that she wrote alsoe for her own private use.

Samuel who was born on wed. at 8 o clock in the evening in prescote street in Goodīn^s fields was baptiz'd by Mr James who used to preach near Nightingall Lane near Well Closs. who on that occasion did Exelently open and Apply that text in the 20 Ezek. 37 I will cause you to pass under the rod &c

Elizabeth was born Near the falcon staires in the parish of christs-church southwark on — saturday · and baptiz'd by m^r Nathaniel Vincent It was s^d of her by m^{rs} polly a Doctoress that —

betty was short lived she is of a good temper ^O dismal change
for Father to reherse, his Daughter Turned unto the Just reverse.^
and week spirit yet knows how to resent an Injury, she is of a
healthful constitution and is near the age of my Neece Mrs Mary
Holmes

It pleased God to take away all the rest of my children in their
Infancy, none except Ben. & Thomas lived twelve months if they
lived soe long which I am not certaine of.

Hannah, of whom my father used to say, when any asked how
many children he had, I have had seven

[page 10]
seven sons, and they have every one a sister. she had several good
offers, but as She was a hinderance in brother John's closing with
several good – offers, soe she her selfe refused severale and took
up with what proved the worst she was married to John Morris
son of Billing Morris of Ecton aforesaid who had with her 100P
He was a zealous son of the church and made her soe, he had
good and profitable business of his trade which was a rag dyer but
his fancy lead him to building – whereby he Involved himselfe,
and soon after dying he left his widdow 3 Daughters and six-
hundred pounds in Debt our of which she never got all her life
long · but dyed in debt to all and more than she dealth with {24
June 1712.

He dyed 17 June 1695 · and left 3 daughters whose names are
as follows but their age I doe not know, they are all single and live
in London she Dyed 24 June 1712 ·

Elenor   . Has a chaming tongue, is of a very obliging carriage free in her promises but far from endeavours to perform
them.

Jane   . is of few words, and many deeds, yet guilty of the
above named fault these two speak and write and read french near
as fluently as English, are redy witts and highly for the church of
England

Hannah   . is of very few words you – must draw them out,
or goe without them of a bashful countenance and a weak constitution, they are all 3 of very smal Appetites, I know some on

wom[en] that would eat more than they all, they did all to gether follow the dying silk garments and scouring since their mother's death which happend 24 June 1712. but now they all goe to Service.

[page 11]

Josiah was a dyer, servied his Aprentiship to his Brõ. John at banbury wher he married Ann child of Ecton the daughter of Robert Childe there. but things not succeeding there according to his mind, wth. the leave of his frinds and father he went to New England in the year 1683 · in order to which voyage he was come up to London at th^t time when the Noble Lord Russel was murder'd

He had by his wife Ann seven children ·

Elizabeth born ·	2	Mar.	1677	⎫
Samuel · dead ·	16	May	1681	⎬ these born banbury
Hannah · · · ·	25	May	1683	⎭
Josiah · dead ·	23	Aug	1685	
Ann · · · ·	5	Jan^r	1686	
Joseph } dead	6	feb.	1687	
Joseph 2^d	30	June	1689	

by his 2^d wife Mrs Abiah Foulger

John born · ·	7	Dec.	1690
Peter · · · ·	22	Nov.	1692
Mary · · · ·	26	Sept	1694
James · · · ·	4	feb.	1696
Sarah · · · ·	9	Jul	1699
Ebenezer } dead	20	Sept	1701
Thomas · · ·	7	Dec.	1703
Benjamin · ·	6	Jan^r.	1706
Lidia · · · ·	8	Aug	1708
Jane · · · ·	27	Mar 1712	

After he came to Boston in N. England, he made severall Essays, in several sorts of bussines, and at last fixed upon the trade

[page 12]
trade of Tallow chandler, and Sope Maker, in which it has pleased
God so to bless his diligence and Endeavours, that he has comfotably bro't up a Numerous family, providing for and disposing
off almost halfe of them in a credible maner and himself lives in
good repute among his frinds and Neighbours at the blue ball in
union street Boston the place where this briefe account was writen
on the 1 · 2 ·3 · of July 1717 by his brother

Benj. Franklin

BIBLIOGRAPHY

ORIGINAL RECORDS

Church of England
Abington St. Peter and St. Paul, Northamptonshire, Parish Registers.
Archdeaconry of Northampton Court, Original Wills and Register copy wills.
Brackley St. Peter, Northamptonshire, Parish Registers.
Bugbrooke St. Michael and All Angels, Northamptonshire, Parish Registers.
Castlethorpe Church of St. Simon and St. Jude, Buckinghamshire, Bishop's Transcripts.
Dallington St. Giles, Northamptonshire, Parish Registers.
Desborough St. Giles, Northamptonshire, Parish Registers.
Earls Barton All Saints, Northamptonshire, Parish Registers.
Ecton St. Mary Magdelene, Northamptonshire, Parish Registers.
Ewell St. Mary the Virgin, Surrey, Parish Registers
Fawsley St. Mary the Virgin, Northamptonshire, Parish Registers
Great Billing St. Andrews, Northamptonshire, Parish Registers.
Harbury All Saints, Warwickshire, Parish Registers.
Harlestone St. Andrew, Northamptonshire, Parish Registers.
Harpole All Saints, Northamptonshire, Parish Registers.
Holcot St. Mary and All Saints, Northamptonshire, Parish Registers.
Houghton Magna St. Mary, Northamptonshire, Parish Registers.
Irchester St. Katharine, Northamptonshire, Parish Registers.
King Sutton Saints Peter and Paul, Northamptonshire, Parish Registers
Ladbrooke All Saints, Warwickshire, Parish Registers.

Little Houghton St. Mary the Virgin, Northamptonshire, Parish Registers.

Lutterworth St. Mary, Leicestershire, Parish Registers.

Northampton All Saints, Northamptonshire, Parish Registers.
Church of England (cont.)

Northampton St. Giles, Northamptonshire, Parish Registers.

Old (formerly Wold) St. Andrews, Northamptonshire, Parish Registers.

Paulerspury St. James the Great, Northamptonshire, Parish Registers.

Peculiar Court, Banbury, Oxfordshire, Original Wills, Administration Bonds, and Inventories.

Rothersthorpe Saints Peter and Paul, Northamptonshire, Parish Registers.

Southwark St. Saviour, Surrey, Parish Registers.

Stoke-Bruerne St. Mary the Virgin, Northamptonshire, Parish Registers.

Titchmarsh St. Mary the Virgin, Northamptonshire, Parish Registers.

Upton St. Michael, Northamptonshire, Parish Registers

Wellingborough All Hallows, Northamptonshire, Parish Registers.

Westminster St. Clement Danes, Middlesex, Parish Registers.

Yardley Hastings St. Andrews, Northamptonshire, Parish Registers.

MANUSCRIPTS

Feoffment in Trust, Thomas Franklin of Ecton to Nathaniel Brimley of Olney, Taylor, and Robarte [Robert] Wellford of Earls Barton, Yeoman. 3 November 1635. Northamptonshire Archives E(S)/464.

Franklin, Benjamin "A short account of the family of Thomas Franklin of Ecton in Northamptonshire" 21 June 1717, Uncat MS Vault Franklin, Benjamin Franklin Collection. Beinecke Rare Book and Manuscript Library, Yale University, New Haven, Connecticut.

The Historical Society of Pennsylvania Collection of Benjamin Franklin Papers," Historical Society of Pennsylvania, Collection 215: Flat File 1.

Notes of P.I. King. Northamptonshire Archives, Franklin family c.1514 – c1790, Biographical notes.

PUBLISHED SOURCES

Bache, William. "Franklin Family" *New England Historical and Genealogical Register.* Boston, New England Historic Genealogical Society, 1847 – . 11 [1857]: 17 – 20.

The Boston Weekly News-Letter (Boston, Massachusetts).

Bunker, Nick. *Young Benjamin Franklin: The Birth of Ingenuity.* New York: Alfred A. Knopf, 2018.

Dallett, Francis James. "Doctor Franklin's In-Laws" *Pennsylvania Genealogical Magazine* 21 (1958): 297–302.

Duane, William, Esq. and William Bache, Esq. "Descendants of Dr. Franklin" *New England Historical and Genealogical Register.* Boston, New England Historic Genealogical Society, 1847 – . 8 [1854]:374.

Franklin, Benjamin. *Autobiography of Benjamin Franklin.* New York: John B. Alden, 1892).

Franklin Papers, Founders Online, National Archives, https://founders.archives.gov.

Goodwin, George. *Benjamin Franklin in London: The British Life of America's Founding Father.* London: Orion Books, 2017.

Holbrook, Jay Mack. *Massachusetts Vital Records: Boston, 1630–1849* (Oxford, Mass.: Holbrook Research Institute, 1985).

Huang, Nian-Sheng. "Franklin's Father Josiah: Life of a Colonial Boston Tallow Chandler, 1657–1745" *Proceedings of the American Philosophical Society*, Volume 90, Part 3. Philadelphia: APS, 2000.

Jordan, John W. "Franklin as a Genealogist" *The Pennsylvania Magazine of History and Biography.* Philadelphia: Historical Society of Pennsylvania. (1877 –) 23 [1899]: 1–22.

Labaree, Leonard W. ed. *The Papers of Benjamin Franklin Volume 1: January 6, 1706 through December 31, 1734.* New Haven, Conn.: Yale University Press, 1959.

McDonagh, Briony, and Stephen Daniels, "Enclosure stories: narratives from North-amptonshire" *Cultural Geographies* (London: Sage Publications, 1994–) 19 [2012]: 107–21.

New-England Weekly Journal (Boston, Massachusetts).

Pain, Mrs. J. trans., *Baptism and Burial Register of Banbury, Oxfordshire, Part Two: 1653–1723*, Volume 9 of *The Banbury Historical Society*, ed. J. S. W. Gibson. Banbury, Oxfordshire: Banbury Historical Society, 1968.

Sparks, Jared. *The Life of Benjamin Franklin, Containing the Autobiography, with Notes and a Continuation.* Boston: Tappan and Dennet, 1844.

Thomas, M. Halsey, ed., *The Diary of Samuel Sewall, 1674–1729.* New York: Farrar, Strauss, and Giroux, 1973.

Tourtellot, Arthur Bernon. *Benjamin Franklin: The Shaping of Genius, The Boston Years.* Garden City, N.Y. Doubleday and Company, Inc., 1977.

Towle George Makepeace. "Franklin, The Boston Boy" in Justin Winsor, *The Memorial History of Boston, Including Suffolk County, Massachusetts. 1630–1880.* Boston: James R. Osgood and Company, 1881.

Van Doren, Carl. *Benjamin Franklin.* New York: The Viking Press, 1938.

———, *Benjamin Franklin's Autobiographical Writings.* New York: Viking Press, 1945.

Venn, John, and J. A. Venn, comp. *Alumni Cantabrigienses.* London: Cambridge University Press, 1922.

Vital Records of Nantucket, Massachusetts, to the Year 1850. Boston: New England Historic Genealogical Society, 1925.

Winn, Arthur T., ed. *The Register of the Parish Church of Knodishall, Co. Suffolk, 1566–1705.* London: Bemrose & Sons, 1909.

Winsor, Justin. *The Memorial History of Boston, Including Suffolk County, Massachusetts. 1630–1880.* Boston: James R. Osgood and Company, 1881.

INDEX

Names in the index appear under standardized modern spellings (e.g., Franckline, Franckling, Francklyn, Francklyng, Frankline, Frankling, Franklyn, Franklyne, and Franklyng all appear under Franklin).

Michael J. Leclerc, CG[SM], a twenty-five-year professional in the field of family history, is a popular author, presenter and educator. He worked at New England Historic Genealogical Society, Mocavo, and Find My Past before founding Genealogy Professor. He has taught family history in many areas around the world.

He is author of numerous articles for scholarly journals and popular magazines. He has edited several books, including *Genealogical Writing in the 21st Century: A Guide to* Register *Style and More*, Second Edition, with Henry Hoff, and the fifth edition of the seminal guidebook *Genealogist's Handbook for New England Research*, and the "Crafting Family Histories" chapter in *Professional Genealogy: Preparation, Practice, and Standards*. He was a contributing editor for *American Ances*tors magazine, and a consulting editor for the *New England Historical and Genealogical Register*.

Michael served on the boards of the Association of Professional Genealogists and the Federation of Genealogical Societies. You can reach him at www.mjleclerc.com.

Made in the USA
Middletown, DE
21 June 2020

10310399R00152